# Teaching Sex

# Teaching Sex

### THE SHAPING OF ADOLESCENCE IN THE 20TH CENTURY

**Jeffrey P. Moran**

HARVARD
UNIVERSITY
PRESS

Cambridge, Massachusetts
London, England
2000

*Library of Congress Cataloging-in-Publication Data*
Moran, Jeffrey P.
  Teaching sex : the shaping of adolescence in the 20th century / Jeffrey P. Moran.
    p. cm.
  Includes bibliographical references and index.
  ISBN 978-0-6740-0982-0
    1. Sex instruction—United States—History. 2. Sex instruction for teenagers—
United States—History. 3. Sexual ethics for teenagers—United States—History.
4. Teenagers—Sexual behavior—United States—History. 5. Adolescence—
United States—History. I. Title.
HQ57.5.A3 M66 2000
613.9'071—dc21       99-054303

For Susan

# Contents

# Acknowledgments

I am grateful for financial support from the University of Kansas, the Harvard University Graduate Society, the Charles Warren Center for the Study of American History at Harvard University, and the Schlesinger Library at what used to be known as Radcliffe College.

My personal debts are more numerous. For their inspiring intellectual example and their help with the earliest incarnation of this book, I am thankful to Donald Fleming, Allan M. Brandt, Bernard Bailyn, and Patricia A. Graham and the members of her graduate research salon. David Klaassen, whose Social Welfare History Archive is one of the best-run repositories in the nation, provided additional guidance through various institutional materials. Helen Horowitz and Beth Bailey offered invaluable insight and support for the later revisions, and James T. Patterson generously weighed in with extremely useful suggestions in the final stages. My editor, Joyce Seltzer, and the rest of the staff at Harvard University Press prodded me at all times to make this a better book.

Over the past several years, I have been the recipient of many, many personal stories about sex education. I am grateful to all of the people who shared with me memories of their experiences, and I also want to thank Susan Wilson of the New Jersey Network for Family Life and Sex Education for generously agreeing to be interviewed.

Despite his stubborn loyalty to studying the Civil War era, Michael Vorenberg read more versions of this book than anyone else, and always provided a congenial mixture of criticism, support, and diversion. Elizabeth Neiva and James Ivy also provided intellectual and personal camaraderie.

Finally, I am grateful to the Moran family and to the Kang family for their tremendous patience. Two latecomers to the project, Hannah and Rebecca, lacked all patience but contributed immensely to the author's happiness. Finally, I owe my greatest debt to Susan Kang, whose high value as a proofreader and copyeditor is nevertheless dwarfed by her more personal contributions.

# Teaching Sex

# CHAPTER ONE

# The Invention of the Sexual Adolescent

> The most rigid chastity of fancy, heart and body is physi-
> ologically and psychologically as well as ethically impera-
> tive until maturity is complete on into the twenties, nor is
> it hard if continence is inward.
>
> G. Stanley Hall, *Adolescence* (1904)

At the dawn of the twentieth century, a sixty-year-old man invented adolescence. After decades of vocational uncertainty and then years of frenetic research in child study, philosophy, psychology, and the social sciences, G. Stanley Hall, a psychologist and president of Clark University, published in 1904 a two-volume work devoted to the special situation and needs of young people who had reached puberty but were still too young to marry. Only with the publication of *Adolescence,* Hall's masterpiece of research and creative interpretation, did Americans begin to speak of that new category of being, the Adolescent.

The new word signified deep changes. For decades—even centuries—before, Americans had considered young people to be more like inchoate, inferior adults than a separate class unto themselves. But by the late nineteenth century this older view was fading, gradually being eclipsed by a vision of youth as a unique period of life, with its own dynamic and its own demands. A great many Americans were growing vaguely aware of this shift, and young people were becoming increasingly conscious of their separateness as a group from adult culture, but overt recognition of youth's new position awaited Hall's investigations at the turn of the century. Adolescence is a modern invention.

While the American adolescent is a child of the twentieth century, Hall and his fellow popularizers of the concept invested adolescence with the moral values dear to the previous century. In particular, they built the structure of adolescence solidly upon a foundation of nineteenth-century sexual morality. Hall's plain demand for chastity in 1904, for example, seemed a fitting continuation of the warnings against "self-pollution" that pervaded mid-nineteenth-century America. This correspondence was hardly accidental, for Hall and the generation of men and women who developed the concept of adolescence were children of their times. They had grown to maturity under the public moral code that later generations would label— and libel—as "Victorianism," with its characteristic embrace of elevated sentiment and repressed sexuality.

Hall and his allies had also experienced firsthand the peculiar historical circumstances that led to the dominance of Victorianism among middle-class Americans. In the United States, the imperative for sexual self-control, which lay at the heart of Victorian morality, was rooted in a centuries-old tradition of Christian asceticism, but in the context of the unsettled American way of life early in the nineteenth century—the new excitements of democracy, an exploding economy, rapid urbanization, feminist reform—this imperative to curb one's desires grew more insistent, more dynamic, and more public. Far from a matter confined to the bedroom, sexuality and sexual control came to define the Victorian concern for the civilized self.

Although G. Stanley Hall had grown ambivalent about many aspects of this civilized sexual morality, at the beginning of the twentieth century he nevertheless tied the new concept of adolescence directly to the same tradition of sexual control that he had for years suffered from, exemplified, and, despite himself, perpetuated. Nor was Hall the only American at the time to link adolescence with sexuality, for many Americans had shared in one way or the other the experiences that led Hall to his conclusion. To understand the meaning of adolescence in the twentieth century is to come to terms with the Victorian sexual ideology of the nineteenth century and the social changes that gave this ideology such cultural force.

"I believe my whole affective life is as strong and deep, and perhaps more so, than that of most I know," wrote G. Stanley Hall as he neared eighty, "but I have never been able to entirely escape the early atmosphere of repression of sentiment."[1] Born in 1844 and reared by pious parents in rural Ashfield, Massachusetts, Hall early developed what his biographer calls an "ambivalence" between his own natural depth of feeling and his community's expectation that its citizens would suppress their emotions. As Hall's own youth and early manhood would demonstrate, nowhere was the expectation of repression stronger than in the sexual arena.

Hall's parents were farmers in Ashfield, and on their meager land Hall learned early the rudiments of sex and reproduction from observing the activities of sheep, pigs, cattle, and horses. Although that experience was undoubtedly instructive, Hall seems to have been much more struck by the unconscious and conscious sexual lessons his parents taught. When Hall was very young, he was taught to refer to his genitals only as "the dirty place," and for years he continued to believe that this was their "proper and adopted designation." Later on, his father delivered to Stanley and some other boys a brief moral about a youth who, as Hall recalled decades later, "abused himself and sinned with lewd women and as a result had a disease that ate his nose away until there were only two flat holes in his face for nostrils and who also became an idiot."[2]

The story unquestionably made an impression: for a long time afterward, every time young Stanley Hall had an erection or a nocturnal emission, he became "almost petrified" that he was growing feebleminded, and he carefully examined the bridge of his nose "to see if it was getting the least bit flat." From all that he heard and inferred from his elders and his fellow students, Hall concluded "that any one who swerved in the slightest from the norm of purity was liable to be smitten with some loathsome disease which I associated with leprosy and with the 'unpardonable sin' which my minister often dwelt on."[3]

Understandably, Hall dreaded the rather natural responses of his own body. In his early teens, he actually rigged an apparatus to prevent nocturnal erections, and further wrapped his genitals in bandages—tactics which, he recalled, "very likely only augmented the trouble." Later, fearing he was "abnormal," he consulted a physician in a neighboring town. "He examined me and took my dollar, and laughed at me," Hall noted, "but also told me what consequences would ensue if I became unchaste." Throughout his teens and on through his third decade, Hall suffered what he called "intense remorse and fear" each time he masturbated, and he prayed fervently for the strength to overcome this vice. Hall later discerned that this struggle was a primary factor in his "conversion" experience as a sophomore at Williams College, but he confessed that his new relationship with God "made the struggle for purity far more intense, though I fear but little more successful."[4]

Hall considered for years that his sexual impulses made him "exceptionally corrupt and not quite worthy to associate with girls," and he blamed his shame over these impulses for his acute shyness around women. Indeed, society's stern proscriptions against premarital sex prolonged Hall's feelings of unworthiness almost until the time he married in his early thirties. In later years, he mused about the "untold anguish of soul" he might have been spared had someone simply told him that nocturnal emissions and occasional erections were entirely common for young men.[5]

Even if one exaggerates Hall's later contributions to the concept of adolescence, his sexual experiences are of more than individual interest. These ideas about sexuality were not peculiar to him or his family or even his community, but rather were representative of broader trends in white, middle-class, American culture in the nineteenth century. The years around Hall's birth and childhood, in fact, witnessed an unprecedented rise of concern over sexual self-control. Although Michel Foucault has noted a "discursive explosion" about sex dating from around the end of the sixteenth century in Europe, in the United States it would be easier to locate an explosion of concern beginning in the 1830s and gaining in intensity over the course of the century.[6]

The increased anxiety about sex expressed itself partly through the proliferation of advice manuals. Works such as John Todd's 1837 *Student's Manual* were well within the tradition of Ben Franklin's "improving literature," but from the 1830s onward the amount of this literature mushroomed, and the tone of the advice grew edgier, more insistent on the dangers of failure and the need for strict conformity.[7] A small group of writers stood ready to provide their readers guidance in sexual matters and, by extension, in the mastery of the unruly self. Books are not the same as behavior, of course, and the spokesmen for Victorian morality often complained bitterly that their advice went unheeded, but even if Victorian respectability was only a "heroic ideal," an "ideology seeking to be established," it nevertheless provides a window onto the values of nineteenth-century America.[8] These writers reflected changing sexual mores at midcentury and also earnestly tried to shape those values to conform to their own peculiarities.

The unruly self of their concern was primarily a *male* self. Although our dominant image of Victorian sexuality has been formed by the era's severe condemnations of female sexual activity and desire, the sexual advisers typically addressed themselves to a male audience. As part of the general Victorian idealization of women as vessels of purity, moralists maintained that women suffered less than men of all ages from insistent sexual urges—indeed, "good" women were often considered to harbor no sexual feelings at all, and they were expected to raise husbands and children to their own elevated plane. Any woman who transgressed the narrow boundaries of purity found herself ostracized and severely punished, but these advisers claimed that women were quite unlikely to succumb to overwhelming sexual desire.

Not so with young men, who suffered particularly from imperious carnal urges. They needed all the help they could get to maintain mastery over their own bodies. Further, unlike young women, young men could not expect a smooth transition to adulthood. These writers expected that girls and women would be passed directly from their parents' house to their husband's, but they feared that boys growing to manhood were left to discover their own path to maturity. Thus, although their advice often applied to girls and women as well, the moral advisers of the mid-nineteenth century directed the bulk of their exhortations toward young men.

The young men who heeded this advice—as Hall was to do—embarked on a strenuous mission. Ministers, physicians, and occasional "unscrupulous quacks" brought moral perfectionism to the physical plane and demanded that readers gain complete self-mastery over their body and their mind. It would not be enough simply to avoid carnal acts; they must banish lust from their thoughts and even from their dreams. In this new literature, there was no reason a thirty-year-old man could not be as chaste as an infant, if only he would learn to educate his will and exercise that chief bourgeois virtue, self-control. Any falling away from this rigid self-government would be a perversion of the sexual instinct, bringing in its train dire consequences.

Built around the axis of self-control was a range of sexual prescriptions that partook of the biblical tradition of mortification of the flesh, but these intensified the self-denial beyond what earlier Americans would have recognized. Sexual intercourse, the advisers insisted, existed solely for procreation; to use it for mere pleasure was supremely selfish and betrayed the continued presence of the brute within the man. Outside of marriage, of course, full chastity was the only proper course of behavior. But even within marriage, partners were not to allow bestial lust to distort their relations.

For all Victorians, chastity extended not simply to the body but also to the mind: a lustful imagination was in many ways just as evil as carnal activity. In keeping with the need for mental purity, Victorians decried references to most bodily functions as "vulgar"—Hall was not the only child taught to refer to his genitals as "the dirty place." Activists in later generations—including a mature G. Stanley Hall—were to denounce this "conspiracy of silence" regarding sexuality, but Victorians felt that a prudent avoidance of such topics safeguarded them from the dangers of an inflamed imagination. Sexuality in this view was indeed a powerful force, but it was a subject to be cloaked in euphemism and silence, and its dynamic power existed to be contained.

Given this idealization of sexual reticence, it is ironic indeed that we understand the contours of Victorian sexual morality only because contemporary writers on the subject proclaimed the need for silence and control so insistently and conspicuously. These Victorian authors were adamant, however, that they broke their silence reluctantly and only to support more fully the other elements of the sexual and moral code.

The authors of advice manuals concerned themselves not solely with sex but with the entire constellation of values that made up Victorian respectability.[9] Social responsibility, personal discipline, moral rectitude—these were the hallmarks of the successful, respectable citizen. Sexuality was only the stubborn local dimension of a generally rigid self-government, for in no area of life did the Victorians condone selfishness and immediate gratification. Nevertheless, these authors were preoccupied with carnality, and their almost obsessive return to the theme of sexual control makes clear that meeting the challenge of sexual temptation was not only critical for social respectability but also central to the development of a person's very character.

Victorians did not conceive of moral development as a natural process. Recognizing only the rational will as sovereign, moral advisers were adamant that character was to be *created*. The idea of "finding yourself"—finding beneath the accretions of civilization a fixed self with its own integrity—is much more a product of the twentieth century and would have made little sense to Victorians, who found in "natural" impulses only a sordid animality. In the highly gendered world of Victorian ideology, character was primarily a male ideal. It connoted a sturdy independence in thought and deed; the man of character possessed a rational will, and with the certitude of this God-given faculty he could stand against the shifting winds of public opinion. And just as he stood firm against the public, so the man of character held his ground against his own baser desires.

Indeed, controlling the instinctual urges was itself the foundation of character. "You cannot give way to any appetite, without feeling instant and constant degradation," warned a New England minister, John Todd, in a manual printed and reprinted at midcentury, *The Young Man: Hints Addressed to the Young Men of the United States*. "Conscience can be deadened and murdered in no way so readily as by such indulgence."[10] The ambitious young man must not give in to selfish, "natural" desires. He must control not only his sexual drive but also his taste for strong drink and rich, spicy food. In most medical theories of the era, beginning with Benjamin Rush in the late eighteenth century and continuing through Sylvester Graham's interpretations in the 1830s, these three appetites had a reciprocal influence on one another. Highly spiced foods, too much meat, certain kinds of shellfish, and all forms of alcohol could inflame the system and stir up the embers of lust.[11] Indulging in such victuals was both sign and cause of weakening discipline. In addition to suggesting that these stimulants be avoided, the concept of self-regulation called for a young man not to be lazy and not to squander his time and energy on such useless activities as light reading and frivolous conversation. The young Victorian created character by mastering in all areas of life his too-human propensity for the easy path and immediate gratification.

Sexual regulation could be just another aspect of the general imperative to control one's impulses. But lust was more than just one appetite among equals; nobody warned that laziness or creamy sauces would inevitably lead to death. Sexuality became a metaphor for all of the appetites to be regulated, but it was supremely momentous.[12] Controlling his insistent carnality was the young man's greatest exercise of his sovereign will. After winning the battle with lust, the growing youth would find other temptations comparatively easy to master.

In the stadium of sexual temptation, the greatest foe was masturbation, and so writers of the time returned almost obsessively to the dangers of "self-abuse," as it was euphemistically known.[13] This seemed peculiarly a masculine vice: according to writers at the time, girls who fell prey to self-abuse were clearly aberrant, while so many boys wrestled with the temptation that the struggle was well-nigh universal among them. The pervasiveness of masturbation, however, was hardly an argument for its acceptance. Of all the animalistic urges the young man faced, masturbation threatened most powerfully to overrun the boundaries of civilized restraint: "I have had boys come to me, with complaints of ill health," wrote the antebellum health reformer Sylvester Graham, "who, on being closely questioned on this point, have confessed that they had indulged in this vice as often as three times in twenty-four hours; and sometimes thrice in a single night."[14] The moral writers' preoccupation with this constant temptation, which needed only privacy and ignorance to work its harm, lay in masturbation's symbolic representation of an entire flood of desires and indulgences; once a young man touched himself in that way, he threatened the entire structure of Victorian character. Self-discipline, social responsibility, character —masturbation symbolically toppled all of the pillars.

Happily, science combined with morality to condemn the private sensualist to lasting debility unto death. With some exceptions, experts in the nineteenth century adhered to a physiology in which the body was largely a fixed-energy system; vital strength invested in private sensuality was energy drained from the rest of the organism, and sometimes the loss was permanent. Thus, the masturbator first grew weak, less resistant to further indulgence. If he continued in the habit—and by the nature of the vice, he probably would—he risked far more than his moral standing. "Few of my own sex wholly escape this snare," maintained the phrenologist Orson S. Fowler, "while thousands on thousands die annually from this one cause!"[15]

Some doctors had derived from the eighteenth-century French physician Samuel August Tissot the idea that spermatic fluid was a concentrated form of the body's liquors: one ounce of sperm was thought to equal forty ounces of blood, so ejaculation was inherently a perilous business. But even those who rejected Tissot's hydraulic calculus retained the general notion that sexual expenditure was particularly draining.[16] In a trend that was to have far-reaching consequences, many Americans increasingly justified the ethical conventions of society with appeals not to God but to medical science or future success in the world.

Combatting the attractiveness of self-indulgence, moral advisers had faith in the young man's ability to avoid masturbation and kindred temptations, if only he knew the consequences. Advice manuals therefore contained scenes of Hogarthian damnation to warn the youth away from danger. One man whose mother had given him such a pamphlet when he was eleven vividly remembered the descriptions of "feeble mindedness, insanity, [and] early failing general health." "At this age I was not very critical and swallowed this garbage completely," recalled W. O. Frick, a physician, some sixty years later. "All during later adolescence I had intense guilt and became shy and somewhat withdrawn."[17] Frick was, in fact, a success story. Properly enlightened as to the results of sensuality, the young man rationally subjugated his passions under an iron will. By cultivating a sense of shame and morality, by exercising constantly and avoiding aphrodisiacal edibles, he found he could control his sexual urges and, by extension, all aspects of his self. In the crucible of this struggle he would forge a character that contained no trace of the baser human elements.

At the height of its effectiveness, moral willpower could prevent not only voluntary acts of debauchery but also actions that seemed to be involuntary. Nocturnal emissions seemed at first an unfortunate consequence of waking chastity, but Dr. Thomas Nichols, a "water-cure" specialist in the mid- to late nineteenth century, believed that the will, strengthened by conscience and religion, could curtail even this debilitating expenditure. The English physician William Acton was not alone in his belief that the individual could keep his dreams pure.[18] Again and again, Victorians trumpeted the efficacy of the rational, moral will.

If this willpower failed, however, "respectable" physicians were as ready as quacks to advocate more coercive methods of sexual suppression. Doctors did not offer a blanket endorsement of these mechanical aids, however. Despite his sympathy for their function, Dr. George Napheys felt that "spermatorrhoeal rings" used to prevent nocturnal emissions were both inconvenient *and* in lamentably short supply, while "cauterization" had perhaps been overemployed. Paralleling Stanley Hall's nocturnal experiments with a binding apparatus and bandages, Napheys noted with approbation a Dr. Wood's practice of applying strips of plaster along the back of the male member to prevent spermatorrhoea (or accidental spermatic discharge) and "self-pollution." In extreme cases, Napheys did not hesitate to recommend repeated blisterings and "infibulation," or suturing closed the female labia or male foreskin.[19] Such draconian measures, along with tying an offender's hands or performing a clitoridectomy, were better geared toward subjects, such as children and women, who were thought to have less willpower to begin with and, quite obviously, less power to resist being "cured," but moral and medical experts also recommended these treatments for the many adult males who took seriously the warnings about the dangers of indulgence.[20] Clearly, sexual control by one method or another was a critical value for many Victorians.

Physicians and ministers justified these drastic treatments and their overheated rhetoric with an appeal to the fixed-energy conception of human physiology, but the campaign for sexual control did not grow simply out of a new medical theory. Indeed, Tissot and Benjamin Rush had formulated the medical basis for the war on lust decades earlier without immediately inciting their fellows to join the crusade, and physicians had added little to this field of medicine in the intervening years. Rather, the ideology of sexual respectability that appeared quite notably around the 1830s arose in response to new cultural needs. More than an ideal imposed from above by physicians and other authorities, sexual respectability grew out of men and women's everyday needs, and its tenets in turn gave texture to their daily lives and desires and conceptions of themselves.

As a central expression of the evangelical revivals that began to sweep the nation in the 1820s, Victorian morality represented the quest for stability and certainty in the midst of an unsettled, industrializing, urbanizing America. The expanding capitalist economy, for example, demanded of its actors a certain amount of self-denial and delayed gratification. One could easily reduce this entire genre of advice literature to the terms of economic functionalism—the connections to Max Weber's depiction of the Protestant, capitalist spirit are obvious—except that the moral writers were often extremely anxious about capitalism's capacity to unleash selfishness and monomaniacal individualism—vices exemplified, in their minds, by the habits of masturbation and visiting with prostitutes.[21] Nevertheless, moral advisers still held out the promise that sexual respectability, temperance, and piety could lead to significant earthly rewards.

Moral character performed other functions in a nation that lacked a hereditary aristocracy and, by the 1830s, supported near-universal white male suffrage. Moral character was particularly important in the American democracy, Sylvester Graham maintained in an 1834 lecture, "where the aggregate of individual character and individual will, constitutes the foundation and efficiency of all our civil and political institutions."[22] In a nation with no hereditary elite, political virtue could grow only out of personal virtue. Perhaps paradoxically, personal virtue could also serve to recreate boundaries of status in an antiaristocratic nation. In the 1830s, families of merchants, shopkeepers, master artisans, and other aspiring men increasingly used their higher regard for religion, temperance, self-control, and sexual respectability to distinguish themselves from common laborers and the rising tide of Irish immigrants.[23]

For many middle-class women, sexual respectability not only helped to signify their family's status but also played a role in their strategy for domestic relations. Although many historians have treated middle-class, white women as the victims of Victorian respectability, elements of the system made a great deal of sense in their lives. For a woman in the nineteenth century, fear of sex was in part a rational response, for almost every act of intercourse could potentially result in pregnancy, and every pregnancy bore the risk of great suffering and even death.[24] This individual hostility toward sex became part of a broader "feminist" strategy to attack male sexual prerogative as a means to reform male behavior. Many female sexual reformers decried the male propensity for unleashed sexuality, as exemplified by what one historian, following the Victorian activist Lucinda Chandler, has called "the delirium of masturbatory orgies, uncontrolled marital 'carnalism,' and the 'furious' expression of 'selfish propensities.'"[25] In contrast to these bestial tendencies, respectable women could gain a certain amount of moral stature through their alleged freedom from carnal desire.[26] Sexual respectability also gave women a vocabulary to use in their struggle for the right to place limits on the husband's sexual demands. Victorian sexual respectability could be for women a tactic in personal and political negotiations.

As this interpretation suggests, the central target of this prescriptive literature was young men. The unsettled nature of American society in the early nineteenth century affected them perhaps most of all. With the transportation revolution that began around 1815, young men were increasingly abandoning agriculture for commercial and industrial occupations.[27] They fled not only their parents' traditional occupation but also the adult community's supervision and protection. Thus, the literature of Victorian morality was in many respects the expression of an older generation's uneasiness in contemplating the independence of male youth—indeed, the existence of the literature itself implied that the traditional mechanisms of cultural transmission had broken down.[28] Recognizing that young men were now less bound by traditional community restraints, advisers hoped their prescriptive literature would help youths internalize these inhibitions.[29] This argument might also explain why the moral writers directed their work more at young men than at young women, for girls were never given the liberty allowed to boys and hence seemed to have less need to internalize the moral code. By placing the proper books and pamphlets in the hands of their departing children, parents could perhaps assuage some of their own anxieties.

The arguments from women's concerns and parental fear, however, should not overshadow the primary object of concern in the Victorian advice literature. These sexual ideals had less to do with social control than with *self*-control, and young men, especially, demanded help in negotiating their own path through the twisting streets and dark alleys of an industrializing, urbanizing America.[30] The household economy and the system of apprenticeship in many trades were in decline throughout the century, and many white, middle-class young people who lived in the cities or left home for the cities were increasingly cut off from extended contact with their elders. Expected to leave for school or employment before their character was fully molded, these young American men had to "tread over quicksands that are to be found in the country," mourned John Todd, "and the breathing-holes of hell which fill the great city." Tempted by "panders, and seducers," perhaps in league with a woman who "exults in being a successful recruiting-officer of hell!" the independent boy also faced his own weaknesses, such as light and foolish reading and "reveries of imagination," which might call up lurid scenes of debasement.[31]

If the hazards of vice were not great enough, competitors and Herculean tasks obstructed the path to success. "Strong and mighty are the men who are to be swimmers with you in the stream of life," Todd continued, "— high the waves which you are to buffet,—swift the currents which are set against you, and fearful will be the results."[32] The author's tidal metaphors captured well the sense of helplessness that could come over an individual trying to make his way in the city, and his book offered hope that the reader, through habit, industry, and discipline, could himself become one of the strong swimmers. In a disrupted environment, the young man could control little other than his own self; perhaps the rigidity of his self-control was proportionate to the chaos that surrounded him.

Upwardly mobile young men in midcentury America purchased dozens of elevating books, attended scores of lectures at that urban haven, the Young Men's Christian Association (its first American branches sprang up in the 1850s), and in seeking advice on how to behave, they did not particularly care if the answers were medical or theological or, as most often, a great stew of both.[33] They wanted reassurance that they could somehow swim clear of the dangerous waves. Interlaced with John Todd's medical and moral advice were pertinent observations on the usefulness of conversation, so long as it was not idle, and other fortifications for the young man, perhaps fresh from the country, entering a sophisticated metropolis. Todd spent fifteen pages, for example, furnishing arguments for the reader to use if he should happen to meet an atheist while at school. Cut off from their parents and the community in which they grew up, many young men sought guidance where they could find it.

Sexual respectability therefore was an integral element of nineteenth-century middle-class life. It served as a stern guide to personal comportment, a necessary foundation for proper maturation, and a weapon in sexual negotiation. Indeed, the boundaries of civilized sexual morality gave shape even to those acts that men and women intended as transgressions of its borders. G. Stanley Hall's youthful terrors notwithstanding, perhaps the code's rigidity even added savor to its violation.[34] Although its ideological dominance did not necessarily compel Victorians to behave as they were supposed to at all times, this code of sexual morality nevertheless gave meaning to men and women's desires and daily acts. Such a powerful system of belief did not simply fade away as the nineteenth century shaded into the twentieth. On the contrary, as a code of behavior for young people, in particular, Victorian sexual respectability found renewed life at the dawn of the new era.

As the nineteenth century drew to a close, G. Stanley Hall had left his youthful contest with temptation far behind. His shame and shyness had largely dissolved in the face of his experiences in Germany's less puritanical atmosphere and his marriage, in 1879, to Cornelia Fisher. In the meantime, Hall had earned a doctorate at Harvard University and become an academic psychologist, specializing first in laboratory research and then, eventually, in the study of youth and education. It was in his role as a man of science, representative of a type that was rising to prominence late in the nineteenth century, that Hall began to investigate more intensively the feelings and experiences that had proved so central to his own development, and sought to reconcile them with Darwinian thought. Shortly after the turn of the century, Hall gathered the phenomena he and his students were studying into one unitary concept, inventing for the first time the discrete, observable stage of life they dubbed "adolescence." Just as sexuality was central to the Victorian moralists' hazy, undefined notion of "youth," so was it a critical component of the new, scientific concept of adolescence.

The category was new, but Sylvester Graham and John Todd would have recognized the content of Hall's definition. Although Hall hung the concept of adolescence on a novel evolutionary framework, he employed almost exclusively the traditional materials of Victorian sexual respectability. Channeling both his own idiosyncrasies and the general currents of thought around him into one enormously influential book, *Adolescence,* Hall placed chastity and self-denial directly at the center of his interpretation.[35] Indeed, adolescence was precisely that period of chastity between puberty, or sexual awakening, and marriage, when the young man or woman's sexual impulses could finally be expressed. Without the demand for sexual repression and sublimation, the modern concept of adolescence made no sense at all.

The invention of adolescence rested on three important material changes in the nineteenth century. First, as the end of the nineteenth century approached, young people were increasingly segregated and sorted by age, especially in the rapidly expanding public schools—by 1900, well over half of school-age Americans were enrolled in public or private schools at some point during the year.[36] Their separation from the adult world was thus sharper and more visible than before. Hall's work in child study and adolescent psychology both responded to and reinforced this trend toward segregation and age-grading. Second, due perhaps to nutritional changes, the average age at puberty declined over the course of the century, so young people were becoming sexually mature earlier in life. Finally, at the same time, the period of training and education for young men, especially, grew longer. So men and women increasingly delayed marriage until they were on a secure financial footing, even as they were physiologically prepared for matrimony earlier and earlier.[37] Toward the end of the nineteenth century, the median age at first marriage had risen to 26.1 years for men, 22 years for women; after the age at marriage dropped in the first years of the twentieth century, the nineteenth-century averages would not be approached again until the 1970s.[38] The contrast was more striking for the "better" sorts that Hall would have considered his social peers: the average age at marriage for graduates of Harvard and Yale Colleges was 29 to 31.[39] Many Americans at the turn of the century commented that this extended period of forbidden sexuality was a garden of temptation, an almost cruel prolongation of youthful Sturm und Drang.[40] Nevertheless, wrote Hall, "The ideals of chastity are perhaps the very highest that can be held up to youth during this ever lengthening probationary period."[41]

Chastity, for Hall, possessed evolutionary as well as moral significance. Hall dreamed of becoming the "Darwin of the mind," and as this would suggest, he was greatly taken with evolutionary theory. He interpreted the prolonged period of adolescent chastity in the United States not as a mere social convention but as a factor in the evolution of "civilized" races. Others agreed. "No one need be told how dependent all human social elevation is upon the prevalence of chastity," wrote William James, Hall's mentor at Harvard, at the turn of the century. "Hardly any factor measures more than this the difference between civilization and barbarism."[42]

The association between sexual control and social evolution at the turn of the century was not arbitrary. The Victorian ethnographers who were coming into prominence late in the century concentrated particularly on the sexual morality of "savage" cultures. These gentleman-anthropologists argued that polygamy, promiscuity, and incest were rife among the "lower races" as well as in the Anglo-Saxon's own racial history, but noted with relief that the progress of Anglo-Saxon civilization had educated its members in sexual control, elevating them above the immediate sensuality of the primitive races.[43] This sense of race consciousness and racial superiority grew sharper in the United States toward the end of the nineteenth century as hundreds of thousands of "new" immigrants arrived yearly from eastern and southern Europe, threatening the "old stock" Americans with their sheer numbers and their unfamiliar habits. Many "old stock" Americans commented with disdain on the distance between what they saw as the newcomers' degraded sexual habits and the native Anglo-Saxon's sexual purity. Thus, the moral code that originated as a highly personal response among middle-class whites to the disorder of American life in the early to mid-nineteenth century gradually came to be thought of as a group characteristic, even a racial trait. To young American men making their way in the world, the code of civilized sexuality still offered personal guidance, but it also functioned to signify the crucial distance between cultured Anglo-Saxons and the "primitive" races.

In Hall's formulation, adolescent chastity not only signified the social distance between "civilized" and "primitive" races, it *created* this distance through a complex biological process known as recapitulation. Like many educated observers in this first flush of Darwinism, Hall conflated cultural differences with biological differences: the different pattern of adolescence among the western European peoples, he argued, separated them from the savages biologically as well as socially. Hall and his many students postulated that the fetus first recapitulates its phylogeny—that is, the human fetus as it grows repeats all the stages of human ancestry, from the single-celled origins of life through a semiaquatic stage and an "apelike" stage, before emerging as an evolutionarily complete *Homo sapiens*. After birth, Hall argued, the growing child then recapitulates all the human stages of social or racial evolution: "The child comes from and harks back to a remoter past; the adolescent is neo-atavistic, and in him the later acquisitions of the race slowly become prepotent."[44] "Reason, true morality, religion, sympathy, love, and esthetic enjoyment" were some of the later acquisitions entirely absent in primitive races and in all children, but gradually appearing in the civilized adolescent.[45]

The differences between races developed out of the divergent paths taken by youths after puberty. In lesser races, noted Hall's colleague in psychology, Sanford Bell, "Pubescence marked the beginning of the distinctively sexual experience of both sexes."[46] The civilized youth, in contrast, also felt a surge of sexual feeling at puberty, but was gradually differentiated from his primitive brothers by "the system of sex inhibitions that are considered an essential part of the ethical habits of our young people."[47] In other words, a "savage" youth was considered fully mature, sexually active, at an age when the "civilized" adolescent was just beginning his most strenuous period of mental and spiritual growth.

Rather than indulging his sexual desires in the interval between puberty and marriage, the civilized adolescent devoted his energies to developing those qualities, such as reason and true morality, that marked his race's advancement over the lesser peoples. As civilization advanced, so did the probationary period increase to allow the individual time to develop the newer, higher evolutionary traits. This interval of chastity husbanded vitality for physical and mental growth and was the crucible that formed a disciplined character. Again, sexual control was the preeminent arena for the exercise of the will. In contrast to this male agon, Hall argued, the adolescent girl's chief developmental task was to avoid the kinds of mental and physical exertions that might deplete her reproductive capacity—he felt that too much education, for example, might have a sterilizing effect on a young woman.

After his own titanic struggles with sexual temptation, Hall never claimed that the storm and strife of male adolescence was easy. Hall romanticized the excitement and intensity of the struggle and waxed rapturous about the adolescent's potential to sublimate desire into religion or athletics or art, but he remained aware that the fight against temptation might involve much guilt and anguish as well. Indeed, the struggle might even go horribly wrong at some key moment. As the modern science of sexology publicized the existence of such sexual "perversions" as homosexuality, masochism, pederasty, and a Latinate list of variations on these themes, Hall and Sanford Bell argued that these deviations were themselves the consequences of civilized chastity.[48] As the "social inhibitions" tried to establish themselves during adolescence, the adolescent's thwarted heterosexual impulses sometimes were not sublimated into civilized characteristics but instead flowed into other sexual channels.[49] Despite his recognition of this danger, Hall refused to condemn repression: "This is the hard price that man must pay for full maturity."[50]

More broadly, repression was the price that the race had to pay to retain its superiority. Civilized sexual tension, the strain of "strong passions held in strong control," was as necessary for the race as for the individual, according to Hall.[51] He asserted that a sexually mature parent—one who had successfully sublimated during adolescence—would beget healthier offspring, who would perhaps repeat this cycle, until the race itself was composed of more intelligent, more moral, more advanced persons. The cumulative effect of this inheritance was the racial progress and racial differentiation that lay at the heart of Hall's recapitulation theory.

At the same time, just as an extended period of chastity could foster racial progress, premature sexuality could lead to racial decline. If Hall's adolescent did not advance past the stage of primitiveness before reproducing, he or she could not pass on the "later acquisitions of the race," and the child would be marked by atavism. Similarly, parents who had misspent their adolescence sexually risked passing on the consequences of vice to their children.[52] Citing Auguste Morel's "pessimistic vaticinations" that the European race may someday degenerate, Hall maintained that this decline "will be by the progressive failure of youth to develop normally and to maximal maturity and sanity."[53] In the charged racial atmosphere at the turn of the century, these warnings of Anglo-Saxon decline coursed with the energy of scientific "truth" and deep cultural anxiety.[54] Adolescents struggled for sexual control not just for their own sake but for the sake of society and their race.

Hall was not the first observer to claim that what we call adolescence exists as a separate stage of life, or even the first to claim the primacy of sexual urges during this period—Rousseau's *Emile* had already covered this territory—but *Adolescence* was the first sustained, systematic examination of the theme, and it arrived at a propitious moment of harmony between Hall's national position and the country's broader social needs.

Although Hall's theory of race and recapitulation was destined to have a very short life, the concept of adolescence quickly became so popular that many Americans accepted it as common sense, and it became part of the culture's mental furniture. Hall's reputation and extensive network of colleagues certainly played a role in obtaining a general hearing for the new concept. As a professor at Johns Hopkins and at Clark University, Hall had trained a significant proportion of all the nation's academic psychologists, and he exercised considerable sway over a number of disciplinary journals. Hall's history as a founder and leader of the "child study" movement at the end of the nineteenth century extended his influence still further over the nation's teachers and interested parents.

But the popularity of adolescence as a concept did not depend on one man. Rather, it owed its positive reception chiefly to its explanatory power, its usefulness in clarifying the meaning of confusing everyday phenomena so that they suddenly made sense. For one, young people as a group were becoming more visible: native-born parents, especially, were having fewer children and spacing them more closely in age, and youths were increasingly segregated by age into schools or supervised activities.[55] Earlier puberty and later marriage highlighted still further this awkward age between sexual maturity and legitimate sexual expression. In the 1890 census, 80 percent of men between the ages of twenty and twenty-four were still single, and over half of the women their age were as well; young men and women living in the largest cities were more likely yet to remain single well into their twenties.[56] Young people, in turn, began to be more conscious of their own separateness. Although a "youth culture" in some senses awaited the coming of the 1920s, youths at the turn of the century were already taking more of their social and sartorial cues from one another than from their

elders. As adolescents became more visible, so did their peculiar characteristics, such as gang activity, the rage for religious conversion, overwhelming
sentimentality, and, especially, sexual urges. Where these once seemed like
individual, if common, idiosyncrasies, they could now be explained as the
adolescent's "natural" impulses, subject to explanation and scientific investigation. As science continued its ascent to cultural preeminence, the aura
of scientific truth that surrounded adolescence helped ensure the new concept's acceptance.

The wide range of adolescence's explanatory power, however, should
not obscure its fundamental components and their implications. A great
many forces were at work in the creation of adolescence, but in the final
analysis, a combination of Hall's personal history, the Victorian moral inheritance, and racial fears at the turn of the century led to sexuality's taking
center stage in the drama of adolescence. With this heritage, adolescence
was from the beginning not simply an explanatory concept but a summons
to action.

By defining adolescence as a sexually tempestuous period and making
sexual control and sublimation the keystone of the maturation process,
Hall and his fellow investigators set themselves a mighty task. By their very
definition, adolescence demanded careful and sustained external control.
Proper sexual adjustment was critical to a successfully resolved adolescence, and yet it was constantly endangered, both by the adolescent's own
unruly impulses and by the American environment's corrupting energies.
Although Hall waxed eloquent about the glories of the youthful sexual instinct, even he ultimately came down more on the side of suppression and
sublimation than freedom. Few Americans went even as far as he toward
embracing adolescent sexuality, but many agreed with Hall on one central
point: young men and women could not be left to face this crucial struggle
against temptation on their own. The question to be answered in the first
two decades of the twentieth century was, Who would help them?

The perceived power of the adolescent's sexual drive was itself sufficient
to demand external aid in mastering it, but this impulse seemed to investigators like Hall even less manageable in the context of American life at the
turn of the century. As many contemporaries saw the problem, urbanization was a major culprit. From the beginning of the Civil War to the turn of

the century, America's urban population had increased almost fivefold, from 6.25 million to just over 30 million, with 8 million people living in metropolises with 500,000 or more inhabitants; in contrast, the rural population, while larger in absolute numbers, had not even doubled during the same period, increasing from 25 million to 45 million.[57] G. Stanley Hall was utterly typical in fearing that the "contagion of vice" was most virulent in the burgeoning cities of the United States.[58] "At its best," he wrote, "metropolitan life is hard on childhood and especially so on pubescents, and children who can not pass these years in the country are robbed of a right of childhood that should be inalienable."[59] Although Hall grounded his animosity toward urban life in recapitulation theory—the urban youth's precocious sexual experiences disrupted the gradual unfolding of the stages of growth—he partook of the common nostalgia of a people born in the country and transplanted to the city. As more and more Americans moved to the city, they increasingly feared that the allure of urban excitement would pull adolescents from the proper path to maturity.

Even without being familiar with all the tenets of the new "adolescence" as Hall defined it, many parents at the turn of the century had good reason to fear the effects of their children's sexual awakening. Disease, exploitation, and unwanted pregnancies were common dangers, and soon reformers would make society much more aware of the health threats that premarital sex could pose. As always, adolescent sexuality also aroused deeper parental fears of separation. Whatever its other associations, a child's sexual activity connotes at some level a new independence, a rechanneling of intense emotion away from the parents and onto another object. Always a tension in family life, such sexual independence became at the turn of the century a more critical blow against many families, especially in the cities, where fertility rates for the native born were falling and family size had been contracting through the late nineteenth century. Rather than producing a large crop of children, parents had fewer children and made a larger investment of resources in each one. Adolescent independence, or simply sexual experimentation, could have a greater impact in a family of four than in a family of ten. Many parents, especially among the educated middle class, were increasingly receptive to the idea that their adolescent children needed help regulating their desires.

To control youthful sexuality, the nineteenth century offered a handful of methods that students of adolescence judged, in the end, insufficient. Hall, for example, placed the storm and strife of adolescent sexuality at the service of the religious impulse, hoping that a religious conversion experience would eventually grow out of the adolescent's sexual struggle and in turn make that struggle easier to bear.[60] Conversion, however, was no longer the common experience that it had been in Hall's youth, and laments about the general decline of religious sentiment grew increasingly loud after the turn of the century. Similarly, the ability of the community to police its young seemed in decline because of the perceived anonymity of modern city life. Finally, the family still had a role to play in fostering self-control among its children, but academic experts, public schools, and youth agencies increasingly sought to assert authority over the growing youth.

Meeting the needs of the modern adolescent required a modern method. Medicine, eugenics, psychology, education—all of these modern fields promised to help the adolescent meet the inevitable struggle with sexuality. Their successes and failures form a major part of the story of adolescence in the twentieth century. For Hall and the hundreds of men and women allied with his project, doing nothing was never an option. Having created adolescence, they were bound to manage it.

# CHAPTER TWO

# Regulating Adolescent Appetites

> There was a time when to teach the three R's with exact-
> ness and skill was to do the full work of a public school,
> for the home, the church, and the wholesome atmosphere
> of community life could be trusted to complete the circle
> of a child's education. But those days were long ago.
>
> Clifford Barnes, "Moral Training thru the
> Agency of the Public School" (1907)

It was the adolescent's fate to be "discovered" at the same time that many Americans were becoming aware of a wider crisis in sexual morality. On the eighth of February, 1905, Dr. Prince A. Morrow arrived at the New York Academy of Medicine for the first meeting of what he hoped would become a society dedicated to the war against venereal diseases.[1] After months of canvassing his colleagues for their support, the bearded, dignified New York dermatologist had high expectations. A professor of genitourinary diseases at New York University, Morrow was convinced that physicians had a solemn duty to commence a crusade not only against these diseases but also against the widespread moral breakdown that allowed them to flourish. Although Morrow had been born into a prominent Kentucky family in 1846, he had lived and practiced medicine in New York City since 1874—long enough to have gathered incontrovertible evidence of urban social deviance. Prostitution, promiscuity, and venereal diseases, Morrow concluded, were far more common than anyone suspected. The degraded condition of urban living therefore compelled all of society's authorities to act.

Morrow himself had begun the crusade against disease and sexual immorality in 1904—the same year in which G. Stanley Hall published

*Adolescence*—with the publication of his own landmark study, *Social Diseases and Marriage.*[2] He hoped that the physicians at the Academy of Medicine would carry the crusade beyond what he alone had been able to accomplish.

Although Morrow did not on this day dwell on the place of youth in the current social crisis, his speech to the Academy of Medicine embodied themes that would become dominant in the management of adolescent sexuality. Most important, Morrow focused on the ways in which individual sexual behavior was inextricably linked with public issues. For the rest of the century, adolescent sexuality would rarely seem to stand alone; instead, the men and women who studied the subject would consistently tie adolescence to its role as a cause of, or solution to, broader social crises. In his call to attack these social problems, Morrow did not appeal to the traditional authorities in American culture—the family, the church, and the community—but rather proclaimed that social dysfunction was now the province of professionally trained experts. Public health physicians, the psychologists G. Stanley Hall had been training at Clark University, and professional educators would all claim authority over sexual behavior and social morality. Eventually, they would proclaim that the growing child was as much a creature of the school and the state as of the home and the church.

Finally, in his speech Morrow began to suggest that in his program for social reform, education would stand preeminent. By the end of the first decade of the twentieth century, in fact, activists allied with Morrow would conclude that explosive adolescent sexuality and society's sexual crisis actually shared the same solution: sex education by professional experts. To manage the adolescent's insistent sexual energies, and to reverse the moral decline they saw around them, authorities would have to break the habit of "respectable" silence about sex and teach members of the younger generation something about the use and misuse of their body.

The vision was compelling, but even on the day of Morrow's speech at the Academy of Medicine there were hints that bringing adolescent sexuality and social morality under expert control was not going to be easy. When Morrow first entered the lecture hall, he found a mere seventeen persons scattered about the room, and most of these were attending more out of loyalty to their friend than concern for public health. "The array of empty

benches was so dispiriting," Morrow recalled, "that the meeting was adjourned to an adjacent smaller room."[3] Although Prince Morrow was almost sixty and, by all accounts, "a tower of rectitude and respectability," his
fellow physicians were reluctant to follow him into the shady territory of
the venereal diseases: syphilis and gonorrhea only recently had become
topics of discussion within the medical community itself, and in society at
large newspapers would not print the words and well-bred persons would
not speak them.[4] A "conspiracy of silence" about sexuality prevented "respectable" persons from discussing not only the venereal diseases but also a
vast array of other topics related directly or tangentially to sex.[5] Around
children, respectable adults enforced the conspiracy of silence even more
rigorously—childhood innocence was not to be sullied with suggestive talk.
Reticence reigned.

Despite the obstacles, Morrow did not waver in his faith. By the end of
the academy meeting, the charismatic physician had convinced the small
gathering that here was a cause worthy of their status as healers and moral
arbiters. Over the next two decades, they and their allies would smash the
conspiracy of silence, and along the way they would discard the older vision
of the innocent child in favor of an image that more closely resembled G.
Stanley Hall's sexual adolescent. In treating the problems of adolescence
and sexual immorality, reformers would agree with Morrow that the modern methods of education and scientific expertise were more useful than a
sentimental regard for childhood innocence.

The movement for sex education, however, was in many ways a strange
reaction against the Victorian past. At the same time as the new experts
stood solidly on their prerogatives as modern, scientific professionals, they
wavered in their attacks on the conspiracy of silence, for reticence was not
the sole possession of the opponents. Sex educators, too, shared a deep discomfort with the youthful sexuality they were pledged to regulate. This discomfort imparted a peculiar shape to their proposals, so that the management of adolescent sexuality eventually resembled a hybrid of traditional
and modern concerns, of prudery and progressive thought.

A dawning sense of social crisis inaugurated the twentieth century. Events
in Chicago exemplified the growing fear that sexual morality was on the

decline. With an endearing mania for scientific precision, investigators in Chicago estimated that the city's 5,000 prostitutes in 1910 had participated in 5,540,700 "assignations." The results of such exchanges, noted the members of Chicago's Vice Commission, were not only annual profits in the tens of millions of dollars for the city's procurers and tavern owners, but also an epidemic of venereal diseases, untold misery for the prostitutes themselves, and lasting damage to Chicago's moral foundation. As other American cities investigated their own moral conditions the numbers would change, but they always told a similar story of commercialized vice, disease, and social decay. Building on this growing sense of a national moral crisis, medical experts joined with moralists and professional educators in what came to be known as a movement for "social hygiene," or the eradication of venereal disease and prostitution.

Few elements of the sexual crisis were new. Physicians had known for centuries that many of their patients suffered to various degrees from some sort of sexually transmitted disease, just as doctors had also before maintained that men and women contracted venereal diseases almost exclusively through prostitution. But even in the later nineteenth century, few public authorities were overly concerned by the connection between venereal diseases and the "oldest profession." In an era that valued male and female chastity as a sign of respectability and Christian character, the medical problems that arose from prostitution and promiscuity merited little more than inaction or grudging individual treatment.[6] Indeed, in some quarters a positive bias existed against curing the diseases at all, for venereal disease's association with prostitution reinforced the notion that syphilis and gonorrhea were the legitimate wages of sin. Some suspected that a fear of disease was, in fact, the only force preventing more gentlemen from visiting prostitutes in the first place. Further, middle-class and rural Americans had long believed in the wickedness of the nation's cities; outside of an occasional paroxysm of moral reform, most "respectable" Americans were resigned to letting the urban rabble continue to misbehave. Pessimism about medical and moral reform ruled the day.

Prince Morrow's genius was to form these scattered insights about medical and moral failings into a coherent vision of social crisis and social reform. Changes in medicine first gave Morrow and his allies cause for optimism, for the turn of the century brought a wave of scientific discoveries that gave medicine unprecedented power over venereal diseases. More sophisticated diagnostic procedures in the late nineteenth century revealed, for example, that gonorrhea and syphilis were separate entities.[7] In 1905 researchers identified the spirochete microorganism that causes syphilis; in 1906 the Wassermann test for diagnosing syphilis became public knowledge; and in 1910 Paul Ehrlich proclaimed the development of salvarsan, a chemical "magic bullet" that would seek out the *Spirochete pallida* and destroy it. Such advances did much to dispel the medical pessimism that had attended venereal disease in the nineteenth century, but medical advances alone did not account for the dawning recognition of a sexual crisis in society.

Rather, the public crusade against venereal disease and prostitution derived its strength from a new analysis of the problem, an analysis that treated venereal disease as more than a sign of individual turpitude. Morrow and his allies first based their case on a foundation of new facts about the prevalence and destructiveness of social vice. When the Chicago Vice Commission, for example, concluded in 1911 that 1 in every 200 Chicago women was a professional prostitute, respectable members of the middle class could no longer claim that prostitution was only a minor annoyance or confined to a small group of misbehaving urban dwellers. With prostitution so widespread, Morrow concluded, no one should be surprised that venereal diseases had reached epidemic levels. At the same time, advances in medicine allowed physicians greater insight into the dangers of the venereal diseases. Gonorrhea could persist throughout a man's lifetime, causing discomfort, impotence, and sterility, and physicians began to discern syphilitic origins for a great many cases of insanity, physical debility, and even death.

Important in themselves, these facts about prostitution and venereal disease also resonated with broader social fears at the turn of the century. Prince Morrow's writings demonstrated two central ways in which the new thinking fostered a broader sense of crisis. First, Morrow did not deny that prostitutes and their customers were personally responsible for contracting syphilis or gonorrhea, but he pushed the issue of guilt to the side to concentrate on the prevalence of *innocent victims* of venereal disease. Second,

Morrow and his allies connected their concerns to the anxiety that many members of the native-born, white middle class were feeling as their country grew more urban and ethnically diverse. Under this pressure, many Americans came to perceive venereal disease and prostitution as metaphors for social decline, as the stigmata of a decadent modern world.

Well aware that many Americans considered syphilis and gonorrhea the proper price that prostitutes and their customers paid for intercourse, Morrow emphasized that the wages of sin were not paid by the sinner alone. Of the many women who came to the New York Hospital to be treated for syphilis, 70 percent were by Morrow's estimate not prostitutes but "respectable married women who had been infected by their husbands."[8] Together syphilis and gonorrhea were responsible for the "invalidism, surgical mutilation and death of many wives," whose doctors often left them in ignorance as to the cause of their suffering.[9] Further, the ravages of venereal disease were not confined to one generation: "One of these infections produces a sterilizing effect upon the procreative capacity of both men and women," Morrow warned the readers of *Good Housekeeping Magazine* in 1912, "the other poisons the sources of life and so vitiates the processes of nutrition that the product of conception is killed outright or blighted in its normal development."[10] Afflicted infants were stillborn, born blind, or grew up as "physical and mental weaklings stamped with organic defects."[11] With this knowledge came a changed conception of venereal diseases' moral efficacy. "We cannot impute to divine agency," wrote Morrow, "a disease which, like syphilis, ruthlessly smites the innocent wife and her offspring."[12] Although Morrow's rhetorical focus on the innocent victim also strongly implied that other persons with syphilis and gonorrhea were indeed morally responsible for their illnesses, the image of the afflicted wife and child evoked great sympathy.

Morrow's interest in protecting from venereal disease the "innocent wife and her offspring" was only one particular instance of the much broader concern at the turn of the century with defending women, the family, and, in many reformers' eyes, the race.[13] These three were closely connected, for women, in the conventional view, set the moral tone of the family and society, and their noblest function was motherhood. As mother to the coming generation, the woman was a conservator of the nation; upon her reproductive success rested the fate of the United States. G. Stanley Hall's odes to the "deathless germ plasm" were only the most lyrical expression of this post-Darwinian affection for the power of heredity and each generation's responsibility for the future.[14]

Social hygienists and other middle- and upper-class reformers at the turn of the century feared that changes in the family were actually threatening the survival of society as they knew it. In support of Theodore Roosevelt's warning that the Anglo-Saxons were in danger of committing "race suicide," acute observers hinted darkly that an evolutionary crisis was at hand. "To begin with," noted George E. Dawson, the better-educated, native-born Americans "are not marrying as commonly as they did a generation ago."[15] Around 1870, Dawson estimated, "The average annual number of marriages per 10,000 of the population of the United States was ninety-eight." In the North Atlantic states, which led in such trends, 1900 saw a mere eighty-two marriages per 10,000. Further, Dawson noted, these marriages were less stable than ever before. "Each successive five-year period since 1867 has witnessed a marked increase in the number of divorces." Together, these trends supported the demographic shift that caused the most anxiety for advocates of Anglo-Saxon superiority: native-born white Americans were simply reproducing less and less. At the same time, social Darwinists complained that the state and charities were "coddling" the lower strata in society and not allowing the forces of natural selection to "weed out the race," with the result that those at the bottom were reproducing in greater numbers even as the "upper, better stratum" was dying off.[16] Adding most to the alarm over this "decaying parenthood" was the simultaneous explosion of immigration from southern and eastern Europe.[17] To "eugenicists" interested in the project of breeding a better class of human, it seemed that the upper stratum was in danger of being swamped by the "inferior" races.[18]

Like eugenics, temperance, and other reform movements, anxiety over sexual behavior in the first decades of the twentieth century was fueled by middle-class fear of a changing moral and social order. The "epidemic" of venereal disease and prostitution became a particularly useful symbol of these fears, for it signified the breakdown of a sexual code that had been central to Victorian respectability.[19] Uneasiness over the new immigrants was thus bound up with concern for sexual morality, sometimes explicitly.

In blaming the "white slave" trade, or traffic in prostitutes, on eastern European immigrants, for example, antiprostitution reformers betrayed a clear ethnic bias.

But what really alarmed reformers was mounting evidence that the Victorian sexual code might be in decline even among middle-class Americans. In the reformers' view, the poor had perhaps always behaved badly, but when white, middle-class young people began to visit dance halls and prostitutes, that was cause for alarm. Chicago's red-light districts beckoned men and boys from "some of the best homes in the suburbs," complained Herbert Gates, a volunteer social worker. "It was a common experience to find from two to three thousand men and boys in that district in a single hour, and they were by no means all of them from the lower class."[20] A similar concern about the spread of venereal disease and licentiousness to the "better classes" in society lay behind the popularity of Eugène Brieux's drama *Damaged Goods*, whose run on Broadway and at Chicago's Blackstone Theater in 1913 was subsidized by antiprostitution and social hygiene societies.[21] In both cities, theatergoers crowded in to hear Brieux's high-minded doctor roundly criticize the sexual morals of his well-to-do Parisian patients. Prince Morrow had recognized from the beginning of his crusade that syphilis and gonorrhea showed no respect for class lines, and similar dismay over the middle class' moral descent animated his followers and allies.[22]

Victorian sexual morality had been central to the middle-class's self-definition, but now it seemed as if middle-class men were themselves descending to the moral level of immigrants. Not only were men and women from unfamiliar countries crowding into the cities, bringing their foreign manners and their lack of deference to traditional cultural leaders, but native-born white Americans were themselves flocking toward urban centers, leaving behind in their rural past (and perhaps then only in myth) the ties of social stability and communal modes of moral enforcement.

The magnitude of prostitution, venereal disease, and immorality suggested despair, but that emotion was foreign to a new generation of activists inspired by the Progressive reform impulse. Just as reformers like Morrow created a novel interpretation of the sexual crisis, they also suggested radically new solutions. The social crisis had convinced them that older cultural authorities were too weak to meet the new century's demands, and so they argued that their rising status as professional experts qualified them to implement properly "modern" solutions. Building on an existing tradition of moral reform, physicians and educators appealed to medicine, the state, and the schools to halt both individual and social decay.

When Prince Morrow first launched his crusade, he found a number of reformers already toiling in the fields of moral activism. In 1895 a New York minister and reformer, Aaron Macy Powell, had brought together a number of "moral education societies" into the American Purity Alliance, which then combined with the National Vigilance Committee in 1912.[23] Many of the reformers in these organizations had first come together in opposition to legalized prostitution in the 1870s and then had thrown themselves into a sweeping movement for social "purity," including temperance, woman's suffrage, and restraints on lust.[24]

These purity reformers initially mistrusted Morrow, for American physicians had a long tradition of attempting to heal venereal diseases while merely winking at the prostitution and promiscuity that helped to spread them. Morrow, however, was at pains to emphasize the points of agreement between his colleagues and their potential allies in the purity movement. "The prophylaxis of venereal diseases and the prevention of prostitution are indissolubly linked," wrote the doctor in *Social Diseases and Marriage*. "We cannot dissociate the effect from the cause."[25] "Every physician worthy of the honored name," seconded Charles Henderson, a social hygienist on the faculty at the University of Chicago, "will insist that the best and the only sure and final prevention of these diseases is not a chemical bactericide, or mercury, or iodine, but a noble purpose, a clean character."[26] This consonance between morality and health would provide a foundation for agreement and common action.

Due in large part to Morrow's strenuous schedule of speaking and publishing, associations dedicated to eradicating prostitution and venereal disease sprang up in large cities throughout the nation. They were generally modeled on Morrow's original Society for Sanitary and Moral Prophylaxis —the association formed in 1905 by the "half-hearted" gathering at the New York Academy of Medicine. As with the original society, physicians usually provided the initial drive and continuing strength in these allied associations, but they tried to enlist the aid of prominent reformers, clergy, and educators. Social hygiene society letterheads were studded with the names of such Progressive-era luminaries as Jane Addams, Charles W. Eliot, and David Starr Jordan. By 1910 so many organizations had appeared that the Boston philanthropist Delcevare King, himself converted to the cause by the power of the doctor's writings, urged Morrow to create a national organization to coordinate the local societies.[27] Further, by then Prince Morrow had joined the advisory council of the Women's Christian Temperance Union's Purity Department, and the initial suspicion between hygienists and purity groups was fast being replaced by close cooperation.

One purity crusader remembered finally meeting Morrow in the red dining room of Grace Hoadley Dodge's Manhattan mansion: it was there, recalled the Reverend Anna Garlin Spencer, "that we all met together and found out that we were an interlocking directorate, that we were on all the things, and, as Grace Dodge in her practical way said, 'If we are on everything, why don't we all come together and be on one thing?' And so we did."[28] Shortly after Morrow's death in 1913, his American Federation for Sex Hygiene merged with the American Vigilance Association to become the American Social Hygiene Association (ASHA), which was to remain for decades at the center of American efforts to eradicate venereal disease and prostitution.[29] Not one of the original eighteen physicians at the Academy of Medicine could have envisioned such success.

Despite their ties with the older purity movement, these expansive, optimistic organizations could not depend on the methods of the past. As the reforming professionals cast about for solutions to the sexual crisis, they criticized the older ordering institutions of society—the church, the family, and the community—suggesting that these enforcers of public order were no longer equal to the task of safeguarding morality in a modern, urban society. "The need of our work would be far less," noted G. Stanley Hall in an address to a New York social hygiene society, "if religion had not lapsed to a subordinate place in the life of the average youth." George A. Coe, a prominent liberal theologian at Northwestern University, echoed Hall in his conviction that social upheaval in the cities was exposing children to unprecedented temptations at the same time as the churches could no longer present clear religious lessons through the schools, and families and Sunday schools appeared incapable of picking up the slack.[30]

Indeed, just as the forces of modernity seemed to be weakening religious ties among certain segments of the population, the pressures of modern city life seemed to threaten the family's ability to pass on a fund of moral knowledge. Besides the prevalence of sexual vice, the exploding divorce rate in the cities seemed clear evidence that the urban family was in disarray. As one of Coe's allies maintained nostalgically, the urban "home" was no longer a spacious, economically integrated farmhouse (if it had ever been) but was now "too often only a four-roomed flat in which the children hardly ever see their father."[31] Thus, urban children lacked both the ennobling rural contact with nature and the enlightening influence of working alongside their parents at the plow or churn.

Some progressive reformers suggested that the new society was simply leaving parents behind—especially sexually—because the average parent did not possess the proper scientific information about sexual hygiene and other critical aspects of modern living, and suffered, in general, from overly traditional and ineffectual attitudes.[32] "Parenthood," asserted Dr. Helen C. Putnam, an early leader in the social hygiene cause, in 1909, "rarely confers the ability to train twentieth-century citizens." She observed that "a very large part of recent legislative and social endeavor concerning ignorance and idleness, vice, intemperance, and child labor" had been summoned into existence precisely because of "parental incapacity."[33] If parents had done their part in raising hygienic and morally strong children, the "social evil" could never have taken root. The parents' problem was not merely their scientific ignorance but also their sexual attitudes. According to reformers, parents were handicapped by generations of prudery.[34] Even those few parents who admitted the existence of social vice still clung to what one educator called the "fatuous hope" that *their* children could escape without particular instruction about the dangers around them.[35]

Finally, the parents' ineffectiveness was related to the loss of communal social control in the city. In contrast to rural areas, a city was so populous that a man could patronize a prostitute without fear of retribution, secure in his anonymity, and a woman living on her own could "fall" into an immoral life or consciously choose that path with none to stop her. Neither the strictures of the church nor the internal moral voice of the parents nor the censure of the community seemed equal to the forces of modern living.

Reformers suggested that society must now rely on the modern methods developed by university-trained experts. As part of this "modern" program, reformers in ASHA and its predecessors pursued an expansive program of medical and legal reform. More important, Morrow and many of his followers placed their highest hopes on the transformative power of education. Today, this turn toward education seems a natural part of social reform, but the birth of sex education out of the congress between the new study of adolescence and the social hygiene movement was by no means an inevitable event. Rather, the turn toward youth and the schools embodied a number of historically contingent factors, including the rise of expertise as a force in American culture, Prince Morrow's ideological disdain for coercion, and the ascendant Progressive faith in education.

Sex education was not, initially, at the forefront of reform efforts. As a movement dominated by physicians and concerned overtly with the physical consequences of syphilis and gonorrhea, social hygiene naturally included medical measures for protecting the public health. In supporting hospital treatment for venereal disease cases and calling for syphilis testing as a precondition for a marriage license, social hygienists' prime concern was to sterilize the sources of contagion promptly, thus preventing the carriers from infecting others. Medical social hygienists joined groups such as the Illinois Vigilance Association in supporting legal measures to repress prostitution. Out of local efforts to eliminate "white slavery" grew national legislation, such as the 1910 Mann Act outlawing the transportation of women across state lines for "immoral purposes." Reformers also demanded laws against red-light districts where prostitution was tacitly tolerated, such as the levee in Chicago, and urged the suppression of entertainments related to the traffic in women, such as dance halls, steamboat and beach excursions, indecent posters, "demoralizing plays," and obscene literature.[36]

Medical and legal measures, however, were limited and largely reactive. Reformers soon placed their greatest hopes in the power of education, broadly conceived as enlightenment of the general public through publicity, lectures, pamphlets, and the schools. This Progressive faith in publicity and education expressed itself widely in muckraking exposés, electoral reform efforts, and a variety of public health movements, including new attempts to make the public aware of cancer and mental illness. Thus, sex education from the beginning was defined by instrumentalist goals; reformers supported sex education for the behavioral and social changes it promised to deliver.

Social hygienists began to educate the public directly about the dangers of venereal diseases and prostitution. ASHA and related organizations published dozens of pamphlets, and a network of physicians opened union halls and YMCAs for public lectures about venereal disease that were as memorable as they were novel. Illustrating their talks with "lurid stereopticon slides," social hygienists stressed the physical horrors of syphilis with such vigor that it was common for listeners to faint where they sat. Attendants stood by to carry away the unconscious, who must have been deeply impressed by this new approach to public health.[37]

Publicity and education could help people attain the ideal of carnal restraint, in Morrow's influential and perhaps overly optimistic opinion, because sexual vice was the product of ignorance rather than innate viciousness. Social hygienists did not completely discard the Victorian conviction that sexual immorality could be the product of an evil soul, but they tended to stress more the environmental causes of vice. They agreed with purity crusaders that prostitution, for example, was based on a fallacious belief in male "sexual necessity," or the folk wisdom that young men suffered from the periodic buildup of spermatic pressure in their testes, and their continued health depended on releasing this pressure. This scientific nonsense, insisted reformers, induced young men to seek release from prostitutes and other women.[38] Reformers complained that young women, too, believed in male sexual necessity and thus tolerated a different standard of morals for men. Equally damaging to sexual health was the widespread ignorance about connections between venereal disease and prostitution, for what else but ignorance would allow young men to expose themselves to the prostitute's contagion? Young men "should be warned of the pitfalls and dangers which beset the pathways of dissipation," wrote Morrow; "they should be instructed in the knowledge that venereal diseases are the almost invariable concomitant of licentious living."[39] Believing in the power of rational understanding and a wholesome fear of disease, social hygienists felt that an individual who comprehended the true functions of the sexual organs and the dangers of venereal disease would no longer be in thrall to lust. When audience members occasionally fainted at the sight of the educators' slides, they reinforced the social hygienists' belief that the public lectures were effective.

Although this sex education for adults certainly made an impact, social hygienists soon suspected that the lectures did little to foster the moral regeneration of society. By the time Americans had grown to adulthood, reformers concluded, they had already been corrupted by at least a decade of licentious images and experiences; they were simply too far gone for the social hygiene message to make an impact. Morrow himself gloomily reported that many German men, "their pockets full of edifying literature," continued to tromp eagerly up the front steps of the brothels.[40]

To effect a true change of heart, reformers agreed that they needed to direct their energies toward a younger audience than was reached by the newspapers, city committees, and public lectures for adults.[41] "You cannot teach a drunkard abstinence after he has become a drunkard," explained a physician during a debate over social hygiene education, "you must teach him before he has become an inveterate drunkard. If you want young men to be chaste, you must teach them about sex matters before they ever [have] any such connections."[42] "In all things for the reform of the world and for betterment," agreed a midwestern public health official, "we must commence with the child. There seems [sic] to be no good results attending reform work with adults."[43] Rather than exhorting adults, who had already been corrupted, social hygienists hoped to educate the malleable youth toward a change of heart. Education would help individuals police themselves, if reformers could only reach their audience in good time.

Reaching a younger audience meant turning to the public schools. This was a novel idea for public education: in 1907 Dr. Helen Putnam had investigated schools in some twenty cities and uncovered little evidence of sex education in any form, and other educators were close to unanimous in their unstatistical conviction that experiments with sex education were until that point nonexistent.[44] Nevertheless, American education in many ways stood ready for the new task. Concern over sexual vice coincided with an unprecedented expansion in the public schools' influence and their sense of mission. More young people than ever before were passing through the educational system, and an increasingly professional teaching force was becoming conscious that it had a broader social role to play. The movement for sex education in the public schools supported the new conception of the school's cultural authority, and it comported well with the professional pedagogues' desire to train students' bodies and hearts as well as their minds.

In the decades before and after the turn of the century, the public high schools were changing in ways that would make them a logical site for sex instruction. Most obvious was the explosion in attendance and its consequences. In 1871, 80,000 pupils attended public high schools; in 1913, more than 1 million students were enrolled, and after the First World War, this number would increase exponentially.[45] Immigrants and children of immigrants bulked large in this expanding population, and as one historian has noted, the newcomers' unfamiliarity with American customs pressured the schools into teaching "practical" subjects, such as "manners, cleanliness, dress, the simple business of getting along together in the schoolroom."[46]

By the 1890s, such practical pressures were finding formal expression in speeches to the National Education Association (NEA) and articles in education periodicals.[47] Disparate groups of insurgents began to call for replacing the older program of classical education with education as preparation for "complete living" and education as moral instruction. Recognizing pressure from public health movements as well as the needs of the students themselves, educators focused much of their concern for "complete living" on the practical matters of hygiene and health. In the 1880s, for example, the temperance movement prevailed on every state to pass a law mandating that schools teach about the pernicious effects of alcohol.[48] Similarly, many educators would make comparisons between the need for sex education and the schools' existing commitment to teaching about proper cleanliness, diet, and health.[49] Sex education was part of the general trend toward a pragmatic vision of pedagogy.

Teachers at this time were also better prepared for their expanded role. In accordance with their enlarged responsibilities, teachers were receiving more professional training, including courses on pedagogical methods and the psychology of the child. Moral educators and progressive reformers were confident that well-organized schools and professional teachers could compensate for what they saw as the decline in church, family, and community.[50]

The question of sex instruction furthered certain tendencies toward educational expansiveness. As part of their drive toward professionalism, teachers were already claiming that they possessed esoteric, "expert" knowledge that prepared them to take over many functions performed by parents and other child-rearing agents.[51] Sex education was the most intimate expression of the schoolteacher's tendency to extend her influence into areas once reserved for the home. Of course, teachers could be heirs to the same legacy of prudery and sexual misinformation that handicapped parents, but their professional education held out the promise that they could be reformed. Helen Putnam recognized the practical basis for using public schools, and schoolteachers, to prepare twentieth-century citizens: "We have courses for training teachers, not parents."[52]

By focusing on education, social hygienists hoped to escape some of the dangers associated with moral crusades. The campaigns Morrow had witnessed against prostitution tended to be short-lived and frenzied.[53] By contrast, education was a persistent and quiet route to reform. Prostitution and venereal disease might not disappear in the current generation, but the rising generation, educated in the proper spirit about sex, might avoid these dangers to a greater degree, and might in turn teach a stronger morality to their own children. While moral crusades that worked through the churches or volunteers tended to burn out after a short time, social hygienists hoped to make sex instruction regular and self-sustaining by gradually handing the teaching over to the public schools. Leaders also hoped that grounding sex education in the schools would help them avoid the danger of *too* much publicity for the delicate subject, for social hygienists always fretted that they were calling too much attention to the seamier side of life—indeed, in 1916 a prominent sex educator said he was much pleased that "public interest in sexual questions has waned decidedly in the last few years." "It is," he noted, "a most fortunate indication of approaching sanity."[54] Sex education also allowed this wing of the social hygiene movement to avoid more repressive legal measures.[55] "Liberty enlightened by education," Morrow maintained, "is a stronger force in influencing human conduct than restrictions imposed by law."[56]

Moving sex education into the schools brought problems of its own, however. Although sex education in the public schools might avoid the twin dangers of moral frenzy and coercion, the shift from educating adults about sex to educating adolescents directly violated the conspiracy of silence. Most "respectable" people already believed that a conspiracy of silence about sexual matters was necessary to protect adults from immorality; they were unlikely to break that silence when educating "innocent" youths. Sex education's defining dilemma therefore consisted of the tension between teaching young people proper information about sex before their minds were thoroughly debauched and avoiding the possibility that this education would itself arouse precocious interest in sexual matters. Between the need for timeliness and the dangers of suggestiveness lay an exceedingly narrow path.

The conspiracy of silence rested on a traditional interpretation of youth. "How many of you have ever stopped to think that in the heart of every child there is 'a chamber of imagery?' the walls of which are ever being decorated," Anthony Comstock asked a receptive audience of teachers, psychologists, and parents gathered for the 1909 Clark University Conference on Child Welfare. "How many of you realize that in this commissary department of the heart there is constantly being stored up good or evil influences; that the Spirit of Evil is ever active in crowding through eye and ear materials which he can use to the destruction of the soul?"[57] As the nation's foremost crusader against obscenity—the federal law against sending obscenity through the public mail, the Comstock Law, had been named for him forty years earlier—Comstock considered himself an expert on the ways in which a child could be corrupted by sexual influences. And though he responded to sexual corruption with rather more vigor than his contemporaries, Comstock's vision of the "innocent child" he was protecting was fully typical of the time. In Comstock's view, the "Spirit of Evil" was invariably sexual, and it entered a child only from the outside. Growing youths were not naturally sexual but were empty "chambers" awaiting decoration for good or evil.

The corollary of Comstock's position—indeed, the task to which he had devoted his life after leaving his job as a dry-goods clerk in 1872—was that any public suggestion of sexuality must be ruthlessly suppressed, for its influence on the innocent was immediate and disastrous: "Imagination is defiled and perverted; thoughts are corrupted; the conscience is seared, the heart is hardened, and the soul damned."[58] The "chamber of imagery" stored scenes of both good and evil, but a single "vile" picture seemed to have the power to crowd good images off the walls entirely. Like many middle-class Victorians, Comstock sought to protect the innocent youth and the moral tone of society through a judicious silence about such subjects as intercourse, venereal disease, and the reproductive system.

Such an interpretation had made the nation's schools understandably reluctant to teach about sex. Attempts to instruct students about sex in the schools in the nineteenth century were so few that they only underscored the general absence of sex education, and sex educators in the new century were meeting stern opposition from Americans who agreed with Comstock.[59] "The subject of sex and sexual functions," one educator had concluded in 1908, "has long been associated with prevarication, secrecy, and other mental attitudes . . . prejudicial to the proper moral development of the child. It would be impossible to find any other subject regarding which children are so uniformly lied to."[60]

In response, sex educators and other reformers needed to undermine the older vision of innocent youth. The sex educators began to argue that the official silence about sex did little to preserve young people in their purity. The alarming prevalence of prostitution and venereal disease was the simplest and clearest proof that silence did not protect innocence. Although some traditionalists argued that such evidence meant society needed *more* silence about sex, not less, reformers broke with this argument to assert that "innocence" as popularly understood was itself impossible.

In a fundamental shift away from the Victorian idealization of youthful purity, sexual reformers began to refine and publicize G. Stanley Hall's concept of the sexual adolescent. Hall, himself a social hygienist, was already having an enormous impact on teachers and psychologists with his occasionally recondite theories about adolescent development, and the sex educators further emphasized Hall's interpretation of the role sexual impulses played in child development.[61] Following Hall, a substantial number of educated persons, especially those involved with education, broke away from the overly sentimental ideal of purity as the "natural" state of youth.

Sex education orthodoxy on the nature of the sexual instinct was mostly built by three men united in mission and, to some extent, background. Max

Exner was a public health physician affiliated primarily with the Young Men's Christian Association (YMCA), and Maurice A. Bigelow of Columbia's Teachers College and Thomas W. Galloway of Illinois's Millikin University were both biology professors. All three were born in the decade after the Civil War, and each had worked toward advanced scientific degrees by the turn of the century. They experienced the same social changes that led G. Stanley Hall to "discover" adolescence, and as they studied medicine and biology and worked directly with young people, they came to agree with Hall that the sexual instinct governed the process of maturing. Further, they agreed with Hall that the definition of adolescent sexuality demanded that they intervene to control, shape, and channel the growing youth's impulses.

As men of science, Galloway, Bigelow, and Exner considered the sexual instinct in the light of evolution and natural history. Rather than condemning the sexual instinct on religious grounds, Exner explained it as only the most powerful of many natural impulses, such as greed, hunger, and curiosity. "No one of the inborn moral urges has any inherent moral quality," he explained, apparently without sensing a contradiction. "They are neither good nor bad in themselves. They are only biological facts."[62] Despite this naturalistic orientation, the sex educators held that human sexuality differed from animal sexuality in two crucial, related aspects that made conscious social control necessary. First, human sexuality was uniquely a function of consciousness rather than instinct; second, human sexuality was peculiarly susceptible to environmental influences.

Whereas the sexual urge in animals was periodic, merely equivalent to the need for species reproduction, the impulse in humans lacked this natural regulating mechanism. "In contrast to the animal, which lives in the present," Exner wrote, "the superior form of human consciousness enables man to intensify the strength of his present appetites and desires by memory of past indulgences and anticipation of future indulgences. Thus," he concluded, "man's appetites become more powerful than nature needs to serve her biological ends."[63] Consciousness had made humans, alone among the animals, oversexed.

Echoing Hall, the three sex educators claimed that this excess sexual energy was critical to the human species' development of civilization. By deferring, sublimating, or substituting for physical sexual impulses—taking what Exner called the "long-circuit" between hypertrophied desire and satisfaction—the human race had fostered conjugal love, social solidarity, aesthetics, and spirituality.[64] A mental passion laid the base of humanity's highest achievements—a young man, for example, longed for a maiden's love, and to bring her to love him he turned to poetry. Thus did human consciousness and thwarted, excessive sexuality create the world of literature and other necessities of culture.

Just as heightened human sexuality could nurture high civilization, however, it could also enslave the individual. Indeed, lacking the animal's natural regulation of appetites, humans faced a strenuous and possibly losing battle against what Bigelow portrayed as the "driving, instinctive impulses or desires which are intensified by massed memory associations and by numerous environmental stimuli or temptations."[65] Thus empowered by the human's own superior consciousness, the sexual instinct could break free of social inhibitions and come to dominate the subject's mental and emotional life. Far from setting free the "natural" human, this rule by instinct or impulse was for modern rationalists such as Exner and Bigelow—no less than for their Christian forebears—the *essence* of unfreedom. Masturbation, prostitution, promiscuity, these were not the fruits of freedom but evidence that millions were in bondage to their own impulses. Perpetual arousal threatened to usurp reason and will as the governing forces in human existence.

Against this threat of instinctual domination, sex educators aimed to bring susceptible adolescents to the point at which they could exercise "intelligent choice."[66] The path to intelligent choice, however, consisted not of free will but of external direction, or social control. "We deliberately seek," explained Exner, "to build up from early childhood the attitudes, tastes, desires, ideals, and habits which make for sound character."[67] Although Bigelow, in particular, sympathized with the difficulty of adjusting the individual sex instinct to society's demands for renunciation, the sex educators felt that only external direction leading to internalization would allow the individual ultimately to become master of his impulses and not their servant.[68]

Sex educators rested their hopes on the insight that the human sexual instinct, unlike the animal's natural urges, was profoundly modifiable. Indeed, because human sexuality was so much a product of consciousness, it was believed to be peculiarly amenable to environmental influence.[69] Like most Progressive reformers who shared this environmentalist attitude, sex educators were optimistic that enlightened leaders and public sentiment could create a human environment that would help rather than hinder moral development. The sexual impulse was itself amoral, but proper education and pure surroundings could direct it toward the highest human ends.

Despite their general optimism, sex educators fretted that malleability also left youth at the mercy of modernity's most destructive forces. Not only were young people in the cities increasingly independent of the old social controls on their behavior, they were at the same time dwelling in an environment that seemed calculated to undermine what residual moral impulses they still possessed. Although reformers did perceive a biological basis to sexual awakening, they frequently placed the blame for precocious sexuality on the "social dangers of modern society," as Galloway, put it, and "in the artificial strength of the downward pull through the commercialization of lust and vice."[70] Like Anthony Comstock, sex educators hoped to protect the chamber of imagery from pollution, but they were less confident than he that the child's "chamber" could be kept pristine. Sex educators did not ask *whether* the child would obtain information about sex but from whom.

Preliminary indications of sexual knowledge were not encouraging. To the sex educators, the growing youth seemed propelled by internal and external forces for curiosity, but when he turned to parents, ministers, and teachers for information, he met only silence or the embarrassed evasions of the "stork story." This secrecy itself kindled a great curiosity in young people, who then sought sex information from their "more enlightened companions."[71] In a widely reported study for the YMCA in 1915, Exner surveyed 948 college men about the sources of their sex knowledge. To the physician's distress, fully 85 percent of these men reported receiving "their first permanent sex impressions, which must necessarily exert a powerful influence upon the life," from "boy companions (mostly older), and . . . only 4 per cent. received them from their parents." In total, noted Exner,

"91.5 per cent. of these college men had received their first permanent impressions about sex from unwholesome sources."[72] Clearly, not everybody was involved in the conspiracy of silence.

Exner and other investigators dealt the sentimental view of childhood another blow when they discovered that children were receiving these first impressions much earlier than anybody had expected. Among Exner's college men, 87.6 percent reported receiving their first striking impressions about sex "before the thirteenth year, that is, before the beginning of puberty," Exner noted. "The average age at which the first permanent impressions were received was 9.6 years."[73] Similarly, Thomas Galloway found that among the young men and women of Millikin University's Christian associations, 58 percent of the boys had received lasting sexual impressions by their tenth year, and half of the girls by their eleventh.[74] Children were learning about sex even before puberty awakened their sexual interest, and well before reason and good habits were sufficiently developed to guide them past sexual errors.

The information youths learned from what Galloway called "their more sophisticated companions" tended to endorse rather than prevent sexual misconduct.[75] In particular, investigators found that older youths passed on the folk belief of "male sexual necessity." This belief seemed prevalent throughout the land, and responsible authorities had done nothing to dispel it. Even though it made society's sexual problems worse, not better, informal sex education seemed unavoidable.

Even when young people were isolated from their more sophisticated companions, they could not avoid the city's corruption. Although they denied that sexual impulses entered the child only from the outside, sex educators did not absolve the urban environment of responsibility for misleading youth. The commercialized forces of sex, in particular—prostitutes, dance hall operators, distributors of obscene literature—all tried to make a profit by inciting the youth's innate sexual impulses to a higher pitch. Confined as they were to red-light districts, these businesses had become in effect a densely packed advertisement for vice.

In the absence of responsible adult guidance through this confusing landscape, young people were cobbling together a sex education for themselves that Galloway called "partial, inaccurate, and freighted with vulgar

and degrading suggestions."[76] Society's reticence did not preserve the innocence of youth but sent young people to "haphazard sources," as Exner
suggested. From these sources, the adolescent would obtain information
that only "tended to distort the whole question, to poison the mind and
imagination, to sensualize the whole atmosphere of the life, to lead to destructive sex habits, and to cause untold mental misery."[77]

Observing such evidence, Dr. Prince Morrow concluded that although
youths did possess sexual impulses, the twin evils of venereal disease and
prostitution grew out of ignorance and not innate viciousness. His followers agreed that young men began visiting prostitutes not because the young
men were deeply immoral but because they had grown up "in ignorance of
the relationship between immorality and disease."[78] Reformers accepted
this information about youthful ignorance and misinformation as proof of
parental delinquency, but such results also pointed to the existence of a
growing youth subculture, as schools and other institutions increasingly
segregated young people by age and removed them from the everyday life
experience of their elders.[79] A dim awareness of this "generation gap"
added to sex educators' anxiety: they worried that the conspiracy of silence
had silenced only the responsible, mature authorities, while the forces of
misinformation pressed freely on the coming generation. The social crisis
demanded that educated Americans dispense with the chamber of imagery
and recognize the sexual nature of adolescence.

In fact, as sex educators and their allies publicly proclaimed the youth's
sexual nature, they also called for a more general appreciation of the sexual
impulse, and decried what G. Stanley Hall called the "morbid modesty so
common in this country in all that pertains to sex."[80] These reformers
played a central role in the rebellion against Victorianism that has long
been associated with small groups of literary realists and scattered bohemians in the decades before World War I. Unlike the more "liberated" sexual
rebels in Greenwich Village, however, social hygienists attacked Victorian
prudery not for repressing sexual desires but for inciting them. The distinction was critical for shaping the early years of sex education.

Hall's use of the phrase "morbid modesty" was not accidental. By a neat
rhetorical twist, early supporters of sex education managed to equate the
"prudery" of the conspiracy of silence with its apparent antithesis, "pruri-

ence." Just as prurience degraded the sexual act to mere sensual gratification, so did prudery confine sexuality to the gutter. Prudery, as a sex educator noted, "regards sex as unclean and perhaps loathsome, and the sex
relationship as a purely physical one." He continued, "It is this attitude
which is in part responsible for the prevalence of prostitution, for this is
exactly the phase of the sex life which prostitution represents . . . It represents a complete failure to appreciate the spiritual side of sex."[81] Victorian
prudes, according to these activists, shared with prostitutes and porno-
graphers a vulgar view of sex. Even the purity activists had given the impression that sex was always "something shameful and even sinful," so social hygienists found it natural that young men and women would accordingly
treat their sexual endowment with contempt.[82]

Sex educators further feared that an overweening prudery was beginning
to threaten the reproduction of the race itself. In the wake of Theodore
Roosevelt's popularization of the idea of "race suicide," such a criticism
resonated deeply. "Even expectant motherhood is commonly concealed as
long as possible," complained Maurice A. Bigelow in 1916, "and all reference to the developing new life is usually accompanied with blushes and
tones suggestive of some great shame."[83] In his position at Columbia's
Teachers College, Bigelow gleaned that many thoughtful young women believed that "ideal marriage is platonic friendship and that it is a sad fact of
life that husband and wife must lay aside their high ideals in order to
become parents."[84] At the same time, one of Bigelow's allies, Miriam C.
Gould, found that nearly 20 percent of the young women she taught were
more repulsed by the revelation that physical sexual desire existed at all
than by learning about venereal diseases or prostitution.[85] Indeed, one
opponent of birth control and abortion during this era discerned the cause
of the declining birthrate in "the baneful sentiment which is gradually
developing among young people that bearing children belongs to low life,
and is degrading, which now and then becomes evident in aspersions cast
upon those with large families, implying that their life is vulgar and sensual."[86]

In responding to sexual ignorance and excessive prudery, sex educators
did not turn toward a recognizably modern sexual "liberalism"; on the contrary, they embraced a sexuality that had been emptied of its erotic con-

tent.[87] Unlike the prudes, who condemned any suggestion of sexuality as evil, sex educators agreed with Bigelow that vulgarity and impurity existed "only when the functions of sex have been voluntarily and knowingly misused and thereby debased . . . when sexual instincts are uncontrolled."[88] When properly directed toward reproduction, in contrast, the sexual impulse was "lifted to a place of dignity and purity." Thus Bigelow could attack reticence and the "old ascetic point of view" about sex, while at the same time he favored censoring the bawdy passages in Shakespeare, Boccaccio, and the Old Testament.

Sex educators, then, sought neither to crush the sexual impulse nor to strike off its civilized shackles. Rather, they intended to rehabilitate reproductive sexuality. "If you have gotten it into your head that there is anything 'nasty' or 'horrid' about sex itself, you must get rid of that idea forever," counseled Dr. Mabel S. Ulrich, a sex educator. "Sex is the means by which, in all except the lowest forms of life, Nature sees to it that there shall be enough babies of every kind in the world . . . It is simply a scheme for making and bringing together those two tiny scraps of life we call germ-cells, from which each new life starts. In other words, sex is a natural law, just as growing up is, and so it isn't 'nasty' or 'horrid' but is simply right."[89] Similarly, at the 1910 Child's Welfare Conference, Prince Morrow defended sex by making it synonymous with reproduction: "There can be no greater satire upon creative wisdom than to assume that the creative function which most nearly assimilates man with his Maker, and to which the life of the race is entrusted, is in any way shameful."[90] Indeed, the early social hygienists' lurid denunciations of sexual vice were equalled only by their effusive praise for reproduction.

This approach had its merits for the sex educators. If reformers were uneasy about dispersing what Morrow called "the fog of ascetism [sic] and prudery"—and they most certainly were—they could reassure themselves that sex was, after all, a "natural law," a subject "most worthy of scientific study."[91] Its "nastiness" existed only in the minds of prudes and libertines, who concentrated on the selfish misuse of sex because they could not grasp the elevated, scientific view of reproduction. Social hygienists, in contrast, operated under the purifying sanctions of medicine and science. They could therefore smash the prudish idols of the past while maintaining their conception of themselves as high-minded, respectable conservatives. They discussed not pleasure but procreation.

At the same time as it justified the reformers' rebellion, the rehabilitation of reproductive sexuality tended to perpetuate many of the attitudes they decried. When she denied that sex was "nasty" or "horrid," Mabel Ulrich protested too much. Indeed, in her determination to speak well of sex, she spoke of it virtually not at all and implied that an otherwise unpleasant act was redeemed only by its reproductive results. In reacting against prurient prudery, the educators took no account of the very real experience of sexual pleasure, whether associated with or independent of attempts to procreate. Their weak gesture toward the positive aspects of sexuality did little to dispel the movement's general focus on disease and sexual danger.

Clearly, Anthony Comstock's chamber of imagery did not entirely disappear along with the conspiracy of silence. No less than adherents of the Comstockian view, sex educators feared that their teachings might arouse precocious sexuality, and this apprehension shaped their entire program. In particular, the educators' fear of prematurely debauching their adolescent students led them to emphasize their scientific status. As a new class of professional physicians and pedagogues, sex educators claimed that science, above all else, would allow them to teach about sex without besmirching the adolescent's chamber of imagery.

A "scientific" sex education possessed three qualities that allowed it to skirt the dangers of suggestiveness. First, science was precise. Following G. Stanley Hall's popularization of the idea of "stages" in adolescent development, sex educators claimed that the professional teacher was trained to discern the stages of youthful sexuality and could accordingly give each child enough information—and no more—for each period of life. ASHA's secretary, William F. Snow, even called for the development of a "Binet Scale" or some similar IQ standard to measure how much sex knowledge a child needed at each age.[92] Second, science was too pure to be suggestive. "I do not know of a single scientific fact that will harm the child," maintained Ralph E. Blount, a biology teacher in Chicago, in a characteristic defense of science's purifying powers. "The scientific way of looking at sex cannot possibly harm a child."[93] As part of the sex educators' attempt to redeem

reproductive sexuality from its disgraced associations with prudery and venereal disease, they promoted a biological teaching that simply removed
the erotic elements from sex by remaining, as Morrow put it, "altogether
impersonal."[94]

Third, "scientific" sex education was fundamentally too boring to be
suggestive. In an unprecedented pedagogical maneuver, educators for the
first time aimed for lessons that would suppress rather than incite greater
interest in the material at hand. "Sex instruction must differ in one important respect from other scientific instruction," noted a group of prominent
sex educators, "in that it must not seek to create interest and awaken curiosity in the subject with which it deals . . . The less children and youth think
of sex, and the later they mature sexually, the better both physiologically
and ethically."[95] As a guiding principle, "science" was both recognizably
modern and reassuringly traditional.

Although science was always the central rationale for sex education, the
form and content of sex education underwent a transformation in the
movement's first decade. Or rather, the *ideology* of sex education underwent a transformation, for as a practical matter sex education programs in
this century have continued to perpetuate elements of the first experiments
in sex instruction—sometimes in bits and pieces, sometimes wholesale.

In the first years of the movement, the social hygienists who led the fight
for sex education answered the question of what to teach fairly easily.
Prince Morrow and his followers were primarily physicians, and they had
been galvanized to action by revelations about the venereal diseases. Conse-
quently, their early lectures to public gatherings and school assemblies conveyed a definite impression of the venereal clinic.[96] Much sexual ignorance
had blossomed under the conspiracy of silence, so early lecturers felt they
had to draw explicitly the connection between sexual vice and its medical
consequences. Further, medical lecturers tried to dispel the fallacy of male
sexual necessity, which they saw lying behind prostitution, the double standard of morality, and countless other sexual errors. They emphasized that
continence was perfectly compatible with good health. As physicians, they
were confident that the moral life was a hygienic life.

In general, physicians relied on their listeners to respond rationally to this new knowledge, but social hygienists were also not averse to creating what one called a "wholesome fear of the known results" of promiscuity.[97] For example, at the Fifteenth International Congress on Hygiene and Demography, in 1913, Morrow's American Society for Sanitary and Moral Prophylaxis set up an exhibit consisting of "wax models, drawings, charts, and photographs" and a constant schedule of illustrated lectures on the effects of venereal diseases. By far the most popular exhibit of the congress, the "sex hygiene" display quickly came to be known as "the hall of horrors."[98] A hint of fear could only make the facts about sexual behavior more impressive.

The early impulse to carry sex education into the public schools found its grandest expression in what came to be known as the "Chicago experiment" of 1913.[99] As the home of Hull House, the University of Chicago, and a variety of women's clubs already active in municipal and social improvement, Chicago had long been a leader in social reform, and its social hygiene society was among the most vigorous in the nation. No city seemed to need the social hygiene movement quite as much. Crusaders had attacked vice in Chicago for years, but when the Vice Commission of Chicago claimed that nearly 1 in every 200 Chicago women was a professional prostitute, in a trade that delivered up tens of millions of dollars to procurers and tavern owners and corrupt authorities, the city leaders were finally compelled to move.[100] Their search for solutions eventually led them to the public schools.

Social hygienists, urban reformers, and a number of "progressive" educators demanded that the schools play a role in fighting vice, and they found a particularly receptive audience in Ella Flagg Young, the superintendent of the Chicago schools. At first glance, Superintendent Young seemed an unlikely sex crusader: sixty-eight years old in 1913, she appeared—in her wire-frame spectacles and high, starched collar—to be "austere and even cold," the model of a prim nineteenth-century schoolteacher. Young was always at the forefront of reform, however, from education to suffrage to teacher unionization. She fitted well into that firmament of Chicago female reformers that included Jane Addams of Hull House and the numerous social investigators associated with the University of Chicago. Although Young had not previously shown a great deal of interest in sexual matters, she had built her career on the progressive conviction that the public schools existed to pass on to each generation the knowledge and skills necessary for modern living. Indeed, far from being fixed in the past, Young herself grew more flexible and liberal over time. She did not, however, forget her sheltered upbringing in Buffalo, New York, nor lose faith in her parents' Presbyterian morality. Childless and sexually inexperienced, Young could nevertheless discern the threat that urban Chicago posed to young people. "In all the years of service in schools," wrote her contemporary biographer, "she recognized the dangers to children of the excitements of modern city life which she saw in the light of her own more primitive, quiet, sympathetic world of home."[101]

In this spirit, Young insisted shortly after her elevation to the superintendency in 1909 that the school board appoint a Committee on Sex Hygiene as the first step toward instituting a full sex education program. The committee was no minor operation. Its leader was Dean Walter Sumner, of the Episcopal church and the Chicago Vice Commission. Sumner approached the delicate task of sex education cautiously: at his committee's recommendation, the school board first offered trial lectures in sex hygiene to groups of *parents* before it considered conveying sex information to their children. Sumner's experience with those lectures, however, reinforced the conviction he shared with other reformers that efforts must begin with the child, for the classes averaged only sixty parents each and appeared utterly incommensurate with the ambitious goals reformers had in mind. In response to this failure, Young and Sumner prevailed on Jacob Loeb, a conservative real estate developer and trustee of the board of education's school management committee, to propose that the Chicago public high schools inaugurate a sex hygiene course.[102]

Young justified sex education in the language of progressive education. "The child is told in school that if he doesn't keep his skin clean, his system will fill up with poison, that if he abuses his stomach, he'll suffer with indigestion, if he gathers the contagion of tuberculosis, he'll die of consumption, but never a word of sex organs and the terrible cost of abuses." Further, Young expected that a course on sex hygiene would prove "highly beneficial, and not alone in its effects on the health of the pupils but in its ethical effects."[103]

At the end of June 1913, Young proposed a course of three lectures to be
given by outside physicians at each of Chicago's twenty-one high schools.
The first talk would outline some fundamental biological and physiological
facts—a necessary first step when physiology textbooks of the day displayed
human torsos but trailed off discreetly somewhere below the waist. In the
following lectures, the physician would explain "personal sexual hygiene"
and "problems of sex instincts" before concluding with "a few of the
hygienic and social facts regarding venereal disease." Young recognized,
further, that only a small percentage of eligible young people stayed in the
educational system long enough to attend high school, so she also recommended that specialists in "personal purity" give one talk (a less detailed
one) to students in middle school and in the upper elementary grades.[104] In
keeping with the developing common wisdom of the sex education movement, male physicians would speak to the boys, female physicians to the
girls, and parents, if they desired, could pull their children out of the lectures.

As students filed back to high school that fall, the "personal purity" talks
went forward successfully. By Thanksgiving, at least 20,000 pupils had attended the lectures on physiology, moral hygiene, and venereal disease. As
planned, a male physician addressed the boys on the fundamentals of male
anatomy before pushing ahead to explode common sexual fallacies that un-
derlay the double standard of morality and the popularity of prostitution,
such as the doctrine of sexual necessity, and the idea that a young man's sexual abilities and organs would atrophy if he did not somehow exercise
them.[105] The lecturer stressed a single standard and the fundamental health-
fulness of continence, cleanliness, and clean thoughts. Finally, the visiting
physician forcefully outlined the social and physical devastation that "inevitably" accompanied prostitution or virtually any promiscuity. A female
physician lectured in rather less detail to groups of high school girls.

Young Chicagoans received the talks with only minor complaints. A pair
of physicians who went into several schools circulated a questionnaire
among students after the talks. In one school, they found that more than 90
percent of the girls favored introducing the topic regularly into the curriculum, though the girls preferred it be taught by a familiar teacher, for they
were too shy to ask their questions of a stranger. Students also expressed

"an almost universal demand for more plain facts," but they were not satisfied with merely biological teaching. "There was also a strong demand," noted one physician, "for advice regarding the attitude of one sex toward another." And though parents were perhaps less enthusiastic about further innovations, fewer than 8 percent of children were withdrawn from the lectures.[106]

Despite these encouraging signs, the Chicago experiment in sex education did not last past the 1913–14 school year. Although the social hygiene movement and fears of urban life had certainly prepared the ground for sex education, the controversial program had passed almost solely on Ella Flagg Young's personal prestige, and this was a finite resource. From the first, a board member had advised Young that if she continued to advocate sex hygiene, she would arouse dormant board opposition to *all* of her proposals. After the "personal purity" proposal was instituted, conservative board members grew openly hostile.[107] They found support particularly among the city's Catholic leaders and parents. "Smut smutches," commented one representative editorialist, and he denied that "smut" was any less dangerous in the classroom than in "the cheap theatre, in the department store . . . or on the street."[108] In November the U.S. attorney ruled that circulars containing excerpts from the physicians' talks were obscene and therefore prohibited by the Comstock Law from being sent through the mail.[109]

Much emboldened by the sex hygiene dispute, Young's opponents on the board of education attempted to remove her directly that December when she adopted a spelling textbook printed with nonunion labor. Tellingly, Chicago Typographical Union No. 16 did not confine its criticism of the superintendent to her choice of textbooks but also submitted resolutions against the teaching of "sex hygiene" as an "unwarranted interference with the rights and prerogatives of the parents." Young again rebuffed the "hecklers," as she called her enemies on the board, but these battles took their toll on the educator. Facing continued opposition to the teaching of sex hygiene, as well as a general reaction against her "progressive" methods, Young was unable to prevent the curriculum from sliding into disuse after its first year. The Chicago experiment, which had aroused such high feelings on both sides, was soon only a fading memory.

Ella Flagg Young's Chicago experiment became an object lesson of sorts for how *not* to implement a sex education program. The most obvious error lay in the program's high visibility. "To appoint physicians to give such instruction and ask the board of education for a special appropriation to pay them, and then announce in the public press what it is proposed to do, is the most effective way I conceive of making such instruction impossible," proclaimed a sex education supporter to the National Education Association.[110] In the face of persistent public opposition, or at least the absence of strong public support, the "emergency" method of sex instruction, as sex educators dubbed the Chicago approach, called too much attention to itself. To avoid a repeat of Ella Young's very public struggle, educators would increasingly try to "sneak" the subject in first and ask permission later, if at all.[111]

Publicity, however, was not the only problem with the Chicago program. By the time Ella Flagg Young had proposed to bring physicians in for "purity talks" in 1913, educators in the social hygiene movement were already turning away from the medical-centered approach of the early years and toward a new style of teaching. These educators indicted emergency teaching, as exemplified by the Chicago experiment, with many of the arguments they had already used against prurience and prudery. Like those discredited approaches, the system of outside instruction did not satisfy and thereby dampen youths' sexual curiosity. Rather, the purity talks piqued students' interest, for the pageantry of special lectures and visiting physicians signified to pupils that this was an exceptional subject.

In addition to the mechanics of the emergency program, the content of the early courses violated emerging sex education precepts. Rather than rehabilitating reproductive sexuality, the "pathological" approach favored by physicians continued to focus on the degraded aspects of sex. "The physician," noted Exner, "if he has not caught the larger appreciation of the problem, is pretty sure to deal with it too largely in terms of the venereal clinic."[112] More alarming, a professor of psychology at the University of Pittsburgh was to confirm the liberals' suspicion that this concentration on "genital education" and sexual vice could directly threaten sexual harmony. In 1916 Miriam C. Gould studied the effect that revelations of venereal disease and sexual vice had on fifty adolescent females, half of them college students. Of those surveyed, "11 developed a pronounced repulsion for men," Gould noted. "They now avoid association with them as much as possible, although they are not so extreme in their declarations as 6 who say they have totally lost faith in the moral cleanness of man."[113] In addition to discovering "neurasthenia, melancholia, pessimism, and sex antagonism directly traceable to this knowledge," Gould found that eight of her interviewees had already refused to marry or intended to refuse because of their fear of infection. Teaching the "plain facts" of venereal diseases, as physicians did, furnished the chamber of imagery with destructive portraits and threatened to defeat the reformers' goal of reproductive harmony. Mass celibacy would certainly eliminate venereal disease, but this was not quite what the sex educators had in mind.

In contrast to the blunt educational tools wielded by Young and other early supporters, the second shift of sex educators sought to employ more delicate instruments of instruction. The new orthodoxy on sex education was already developing before Chicago's experience highlighted the need for a different approach. At the Fifteenth International Congress on Hygiene and Demography, held in Washington, D.C., in 1912, the American Federation for Sex Hygiene (which became ASHA the following year) created a special committee to report on new methods in sex education.[114] The committee comprised not physicians but educators: Harvard's former president, the ubiquitous Charles W. Eliot; a dean of pedagogy, Thomas M. Balliet; and an instructor from Columbia University Teachers College, Maurice A. Bigelow.[115] Only the committee's leader, Morrow himself, was not an educator, and Morrow had long managed to straddle the intellectual divide between medicine and education. The next several years would see the group's recommendations codified and amplified in such works as Bigelow's influential textbook, *Sex Education*, and in numerous experiments undertaken by school districts and individual teachers.[116] Fully attuned to the most recent educational trends, these reformers proposed to avoid the pitfalls of medical pathology with a more sophisticated approach to sex instruction.

The committee agreed that the "new" sex education would enter the schools not through special lectures but primarily through regular courses on biology and nature study. These courses were only slightly older than sex

education itself. Prior to the twentieth century, secondary students had typically learned about biology through separate courses on botany, zoology,
and physiology; pupils divided their time between memorizing Latin terms
for plant and animal parts and dissecting smaller animals. Around the turn
of the century, however, many educators began to advocate replacing these
"mental discipline" approaches, with their emphasis on static morphology
and memorization, with a "general biology" course that would, in the words
of C. W. Hargitt in 1905, deal with living plants and animals together "as being, acting, interacting; sensitive, irritable, responsive and adaptive to a degree seldom realized by those untrained to observe."[117] Student demand
played a significant part in the change: "Pupils were uninterested in dead
material," recalled one biologist. "Biology, therefore, should become truly a
study of living things."[118] The new biology courses focused on the general
functions and behaviors of live organisms in nature, and though instructors
in the older disciplines decried the new approach as "merely a smattering of
botany and zoology, imperfectly synthesized," the courses' emphasis on
practical knowledge and an appreciation of nature helped general biology
become the dominant mode of biological instruction in the first two decades of the twentieth century.[119] Sex education not only fitted well with the
impulse toward practicality, but also its examination of reproduction could
serve to unite the still-separate units on botany and zoology.

   Although a Binet scale for sexual knowledge had not yet been invented,
the special committee's report divided an ideal course of instruction into
several age levels, designed to bring the youth gradually from ignorance to a
chaste state of sexual maturity.[120] From ages one to six, the child was under
the mother's care, and her responsibility was simply to protect him from
"immature" or "injudicious" nurses, as well as to answer the child's questions about birth. From six to twelve, the child's tutelage would be shared
by parents and the school, their roles mostly calling for them to answer the
child's random questions with a minimum of detail, and to prevent the formation of "injurious sexual habits."

   As the child approached twelve years of age, however, the parents' contribution faded into the background, and the teacher began to instruct the
youth in plant reproduction and reproduction in animals "below" the
mammals—"the birds and the bees" has a historical basis. With this scien-

tific foundation, the student of twelve to sixteen years took up the study of reproduction in the mammals. Sometimes teachers would eventually explain human reproduction, but just as often the students would be left on their own to determine the connection between, say, reproduction in gophers and their own human endowments. Teachers were supposed to cover some simple facts of human heredity and the dangers of "abnormal sexual habits," such as masturbation, resulting from precocity and improper personal hygiene. Although the sex educators did not entirely follow Victorian physicians in associating masturbation with insanity and death, they nevertheless foresaw that the "solitary vice" would lead to "excess or to prostitution," and would at any rate arrest a youth's mental and physical development.[121] To convey these warnings strikingly, educators drew a connection between masturbation's "draining" effect on the testicles, and the similar consequences of castration, discussing, for example, how eunuchs in "some Oriental countries" were "likely to become cowardly, tricky and indolent." A poster series put out by the U.S. Public Health Service under the title "Keeping Fit" made a similar point by contrasting the physical development of brawny stallions and diminutive geldings. "The gelding," read the caption, "has no testicles (balls)."[122] For boys and girls at this stage, the instructor would link the doctrine of evolution inextricably with sex ethics and the "sacredness of the home." Finally, the teacher would offer the late adolescent—those older than sixteen—some concrete information on the dangers of the venereal diseases, as well as fuller instruction in heredity and its role in sexual morality and immorality. Examination of "dysgenic" families, such as the "Kallikaks" and "Jukes" whom scientists had lately been publicizing as examples of inbreeding and impecuniousness, would be the sobering final lessons for an adolescent preparing to leave school and settle down in marriage.[123] Members of the special committee were confident that the program was on the proper side of the boundary between comprehensiveness and suggestibility, and for good reason. Propriety was their fundamental rationale.

Although the new course was a substantial departure from the policy of silence and the program of "smut talks" that preceded it, sex educators continued to discuss its advantages mainly in Comstock's own language. Indeed, many supporters praised the new program for how *seldom* it referred to sex and how effective it was in *quashing* curiosity. The mechanics of the course offered the simplest expression of the educators' continued uneasiness with sex. Rather than an isolated series of lectures by an outside physician, which educators feared would give the subject "undue prominence in the childish mind," sex education was now to be embedded within a regular course of biology, with no special markings to signify that anything about the topic was exceptional.[124] Under the regular, trusted teacher, lessons about sex would flow logically and inconspicuously from the scientific study of plants and animals. Nor would the program give sex "undue prominence" in the adult mind. The understated approach not only directed the students' interest away from purely sexual matters, but it also prevented prejudiced parents and school committees from realizing that the disreputable topic was being taught at all.[125] Thus the sex educators hoped to avoid individual preoccupation as well as highly publicized disasters—and in the year after the committee's report, the Chicago experiment was to fully vindicate these fears.

Classroom teaching further helped to solve the problem of individual reading on sex topics. Although sex educators themselves published a small library's worth of books and pamphlets on hygiene, eugenics, and the social evil, they nevertheless worried that reading about sex was too "secretive," that it lent an air of covert vulgarity to the topic and concentrated the child's mind too much on dangerous material.[126] Even a moral publication could inflame the youth's imagination if he were allowed to read and reread its pages as often as he liked. This danger dissipated, however, when a trained teacher governed the intervals between books, and then supervised the reading personally.[127] To ensure safe reading, even biology textbooks by comparative "liberals" such as Maurice Bigelow did not touch on the issue of human reproduction, leaving more explicit lessons to the teacher.[128]

The educators also expressed their discomfort with sexuality through the language of stages. The special committee's report counseled that educators must be careful at each stage to give enough information, but no more than enough, "to preserve health, develop right thinking, and control conduct."[129] The sex educators' goal was to satisfy and thereby *divert* sexual curiosity; instruction that was overly explicit or overly advanced was at least as likely as a prudish silence to arouse the child's harmful interest. The

care sex educators took to "inoculate" the child against his newfound impulses without arousing a precocious interest in sex illustrated that they
had not discarded the chamber of imagery but had refined the concept into
a chamber that changed dimensions over the course of adolescence.[130]

Both the old and the new sex education offered hygienic information
that was mostly Victorian ethics dressed in scientific raiment. In particular,
the courses perpetuated older ideas about the contrasting sexuality of
men and women. Contrary to many interpretations of the Progressive
Era, sex educators were more preoccupied with controlling male sexuality
than with harnessing the urges of women. Sex educators derived their focus
on male lust from the antiprostitution movement and from G. Stanley
Hall's own overriding concern for male sexual development. Whereas previous antiprostitution crusaders had usually concentrated on saving the
"fallen women" who occupied the brothels and street corners, the modern
social hygienists took aim squarely at the man's involvement in the traffic.
"Friends, this is your problem," Harriet E. Vittum, president of the
Women's City Club, told the all-male Chicago City Club, "it is a man's
problem." The reason was obvious: "Wherever all over the world men have
created a market for goods," Vittum explained, "that market has been supplied." Prince Morrow himself wrote a pamphlet entitled *The Boy Problem*,
and associates described after his death the heart of Morrow's approach:
"The only way to cure the sexual evils thoroughly, the only way to dig them
up by the roots, [according to Morrow] was to prescribe the same standard
of morality for man as for woman . . . Men must be as chaste as women."[131]

Sex educators felt that boys had to travel a much greater distance than
girls toward the single standard of sexual morality. In a worldview inherited
from Anglo-American Victorianism, reformers considered young men sexually active, young women sexually passive.[132] The young man's sexual instincts, maintained Maurice Bigelow, were "characteristically active, ag-
gressive, spontaneous, and automatic."[133] Deeply sympathetic to the young
man's plight, Bigelow argued that moralists should not underestimate his
struggle, since "maintaining perfect sexual control in his pre-marital years
is for the average healthy young man a problem compared with which all
others, including the alcoholic temptation, are of little significance." So ingrained was this theme of self-control that Max Exner could, in the midst of

the First World War, compare the struggle for purity to warfare. For the soldier, wrote Exner, fortifying himself against sexual temptation

> is the supreme fight of his life. It will test his manhood, his courage, his heroism more severely than the plunge into the carnage of modern battle at its worst. Thousands of men who have made that plunge without flinching and with utter abandon have been woefully defeated in the severer battle with self. That soldier of the allied forces who was the first over the walls of Peking at the time of the Boxer uprising, afterwards committed suicide on a park bench, utterly defeated in the fight for manhood.[134]

The young man who succeeded in reining in his spontaneous instincts reaped the benefits of unbendable, "manly" character, but to reach that point he needed the sex educators' professional help.

Whereas young men seemed to face a pressing danger from within, young women seemed to risk corruption only from without. "The first definite sexual temptation," Bigelow explained, "is likely to come to a young woman from outside herself."[135] Without the "localized passions that naturally and automatically develop in young men," Bigelow argued, women did not have a problem with premarital continence. (And for those few who did, Bigelow's "Progressive" allies were developing an elaborate female-controlled system of juvenile justice to coerce as well as reform "wayward girls.")[136] But reformers felt that the vast majority of young women needed only a sex education that consisted of some brief menstrual advice, along with more sustained instruction in fear—that is, in the danger of arousing male lust, the stigma of sexual immorality, and the prevalence of venereal diseases among their future husbands. One historian has concluded that the sex educators' goal was to make young women "sexually unresponsive, even frigid, in intimate situations that might lead to violations of sexual norms."[137] Fear of premarital pregnancy was not a part of the curriculum, either because at this time such a pregnancy would have forced a young woman into marriage or because the educators' rehabilitation of reproductive sexuality did not allow them to claim *any* pregnancy was unwanted.

Despite their lack of sexual impulses, or perhaps because of it, young women had a central role to play in sexual reform. Reformers wanted young women to insist on "purity" in their male companions, for feminine expectations of right living would be a powerful force in leading men to the single standard. Ideally, the female's higher standard would be met by respect from the boys, who were to exercise what one educator called "a radical self-restraint in every relation to girls."[138]

As intriguing as their different approaches to boys and girls were, though, too much can be made of the sex educators' gender assumptions. Rather than departing radically from received wisdom, sex educators basically perpetuated an older distinction between male and female sexuality, and if they offered women a backhanded compliment by denying that men and women had the same instinctual drives, at least they asserted the principle that men and women were both to be held to a single standard of behavior. Whatever the differences in their instinctual attitudes, both boys and girls were to learn to regard sexual processes with disinterested—even uninterested—respect.

Social hygienists and sex educators pursued, all in all, an ambitious program: to bring society to recognize that a sexual crisis was lurking, to break the cherished silence about sexuality, to change society's view of adolescence, to wrest the sexual and moral education of the young away from traditional authorities, and to reform sexual relations. They did not succeed with their entire program, of course, and many would no doubt have denied that they had such an extensive program in mind. The reformers' practical impact was not obvious: even at the height of the social hygiene movement's prewar activity, in 1914, the United States commissioner of education found that efforts in sex education were more rhetorical than tangible. "The teaching of sex hygiene, a topic so much discussed recently in conventions," noted the commissioner, "is mentioned in only 2 of the 200 reports [from school systems in cities with population over 25,000] available for study."[139]

Nevertheless, sex educators and their fellow reformers in the first two decades of the century wrought a great change in the ways in which scholars and professionals viewed society. By drawing a direct connection between adolescent sexuality and the social crisis, they energized G. Stanley Hall's definition of adolescence and created a wider public concern over youth. This connection between adolescence and social decline would remain in many people's minds for decades to come. Critically, these experts in medicine and education also managed to convince many Americans that professional training made them the proper authorities to manage the adolescent's sexual development. Sex education was one major expression of the new experts' claim that they possessed the right to pass on society's moral code to the next generation.

Morrow, Bigelow, Exner, and the others claimed this right because they felt their modern methods allowed them to walk a middle path between an anachronistic Victorianism and the threat of widespread sexual license. But they soon learned that their middle path lacked clear boundaries. Even as they reassured themselves that scientific understanding and modern educational methods could manage adolescent sexuality without simultaneously encouraging promiscuity, reformers found their own vocabulary and reasoning being used by the opposition—by traditionalists who did not renounce older ideas of youthful innocence and the centrality of home and church, and by sexual "liberals" who embraced the new freedom of sexual discussion without the sex educators' corresponding sense of responsibility and restraint. As the sex educators discovered, placing modern methods at the service of traditional morality created a program that was prone to shocks from all sides.

Because their new program focused less on the prurient and the pathological, sex educators hoped to avoid the kind of opposition that Ella Flagg Young had faced in Chicago, but they were to be disappointed. Naturally, traditionalist opponents shared the educators' goal of enforcing chastity in thought and deed, but their paths toward this aim overlapped only infrequently. Although these opponents drew from the same pool of ideas as the fundamentally conservative sex educators, they concluded that sex education would be a direct violation of society's moral underpinnings.

When even supporters of sex education picked their way around the chamber of imagery with such care, we should not be surprised that the course's opponents also made the youth's "chamber" a central image. "The imagination of the child is flighty, the will weak," explained a Jesuit educator, Richard Tierney, in an oft-delivered jeremiad against sex education.

"The detailed teaching of sex hygiene makes a strong impression on the imagination."[140] Like Anthony Comstock, traditionalists who opposed sex education found the youth's mind to be peculiarly susceptible to the sexual "Spirit of Evil," so they treated precocity and "sensuous images" as far more dangerous than mere ignorance.[141]

Although Tierney sounded much like the sex educators themselves when he concluded that "safety lies in diverting the attention from sex details," he did not believe that the new sex educators could accomplish this diversion.[142] However careful such teaching was, the details were still more likely to pollute the student's mind. Traditionalists saw further danger lurking in the sheer clumsiness of sex teaching. In the delicate matter of sex, they argued, every child developed at a different rate, and no teacher was capable of instructing each student at his or her exact level of need. Even with developmental stages carefully plotted out, the teaching would inevitably be too advanced for some students, too slow for others. One scholar even enlisted Freudian thought on individual development to argue against teaching sex hygiene to students en masse, "as though it were analogous to algebra or history."[143] Thus, opponents turned the progressive educators' rhetoric about the individuality of every child against this progressive educational reform.

Opposed to a "scientific" education for chastity, traditionalists sought moral safety in what Tierney called "the two great natural protections . . . modesty (reserve, if you will) and shame."[144] Although children were easily corrupted from without, they were nevertheless naturally moral and modest; the educator's only real task was to build carefully on those instincts, and not to dispel with harsh facts what one sex education opponent called the "sweet shame which is the child's natural right and possession."[145] The best sex education, according to opponents, was an education purged of sex.

Sex education's traditionalist detractors expanded their critique of the reformers to include their effect on society at large. Traditionalists worried that breaking the silence about sex would necessarily open what Agnes Repplier, in the staid *Atlantic Monthly*, called "the flood-gates of speech" about carnal matters.[146] Modesty and shame protected the "tone" of society no less than they protected the child, in Tierney's view; therefore, he argued, "public and frequent discussion of sex details will destroy both [protections]."[147] Like a "bad girl" who no longer found obstacles to spreading her immoral influence once sex became part of the curriculum, observed Repplier, "teachers, lecturers, novelists, story-writers, militants, dramatists, social workers, and magazine editors" all had begun to "chatter freely" about sex after the social hygienists had weakened the barriers of modesty.[148] "Knowledge is the cry," Repplier complained. "Crude, undigested knowledge, without limit and without reserve."[149] She and Tierney were at least consistent in hoping to deny adult society the same knowledge and openness they feared to give its children.

Although the traditionalists' concern for public "tone" echoed the social hygienists' own critique of a morally disintegrating American society, traditionalists clearly dissented from the proposal to use the school system to buttress these crumbling walls. Contrary to the sex educators' opinions, traditionalists vigorously denied that religion, the family, and the community needed to be replaced as institutions of social order. Instead, many opponents broadened their criticism of sex education to condemn the general tendency of state institutions to encroach on traditional prerogatives of the family and community.

From the traditionalists' perspective, sex educators compounded their offense of corrupting the child by attempting to interfere with parental prerogatives. The "rights of parents" to teach or not to teach their children as they saw fit was one of the traditionalists' most potent arguments, for it spoke to fears that were larger than the struggle over sex education. "If any person attempted to 'instruct' my innocent children in subjects that modesty tells us to ignore," threatened one intemperate Boston mother, "I would horsewhip the 'educator' and thus give him or her a needed lesson in respecting the rights of parents to bring up their little ones in innocence of the terrible evils of life."[150] Traditionalists were disturbed in general by what a Minnesota educator called "the downward tendency of the home for throwing off its duties and the equally downward tendency of outside agencies to take from the home its privileges."[151] By "outside agencies" the educator intended precisely those creations in which progressive social reformers took such pride: social settlements, the courts, social work, the schools. Nothing seemed to exemplify the "downward tendency" of these agencies better than the schools' taking over such an intimate function as the teaching of sex behavior.

Opponents suggested that sex education signified a broader evil, as well. The Catholic press, in particular, interpreted sex education as representative of the modern tendency away from the spiritual interpretation of life and toward the mechanistic or naturalistic theories espoused by the Darwinists. By the time of the Chicago experiment, the *Chicago Citizen,* a Catholic newspaper, had spent years complaining of the pernicious influence of Darwinism, decrying in particular the sociologists' habit of relying on Darwinian notions in their prescriptions for government and human conduct. Their "crude and extravagant notions," an editorialist maintained, would "degrade man to the level of an irresponsible piece of cosmic machinery." Eugenics and sex education seemed particular offenders in this degradation. Rather than reduce children to the level of their biological and mental impulses, pleaded the *Citizen,* "Suffer them to regard themselves as something higher than mere animals." Such a regard was not only ennobling but was also the only solid foundation for morality. "Good morals," concluded the *Citizen* in its clearest statement of the Catholic position, "is the efflorescence of religion."[152]

The public schools, because of the separation of church and state, could teach only a "low naturalism," which had minimal ethical effect. "What evidence, and what assurance are we to have that the new pedagogy is not going to be the last word in breaking down every vestige of supernatural restraint?" queried the *New World,* another Catholic newspaper, "For what motive or sanction can the teacher of sex hygiene give for his teachings? What can he teach, other than hygiene is as good as the ten commandments, and that disinfectants are an excellent substitute for the moral code?"[153] Thus, Catholic opponents disaggregated the sex educators' easy equation of health knowledge and virtue. In the Catholic position, as laid out by Cardinal Silvio Antoniano in 1583, only moral education, suffused with a faith in the supernatural, could teach morality; lacking connection with such faith, "intellectualist or naturalist" sex education could not avoid disaster.[154] Even if the sex educators' motives were entirely pure, critics charged, their methods led ineluctably to degradation and further vice. In their respect for the chamber of imagery and the overriding need for chastity, opponents of sex education could sound, at times, very much like its supporters. But traditionalists were ultimately unwilling to go along with the educators' new view of the child and their expansive conception of education and the state's modern role in society.

Rejected by traditionalists, sex educators came to be unwillingly associated with sexual "liberals" who demanded more openness in the public discussion of sex and even proposed a greater freedom in sexual relations proper. Although much diversity existed among them, sexual liberals decried, in general, traditional strictures against divorce and birth control, and cautioned against the Victorian habit of condemning all sexual pleasure and openness.

Sexual liberalism drew strength from the social hygiene movement's attack on sexual reticence. As the high walls of Victorian respectability began to erode, they were scaled and left behind by vaguely feminist "free lovers" such as Emma Goldman, realist writers such as Theodore Dreiser, and such urban experimenters as the pre–World War I Greenwich Village bohemians. Before the war, Sigmund Freud's sexually suffused work was beginning to influence small circles of physicians and intellectuals, and many other people were becoming familiar with the equally frank publications of Austrian sexologist Richard von Krafft-Ebing and the more popular English polymath Havelock Ellis.

Activists and regular citizens everywhere were exploring the consequences of what they perceived as the bankruptcy of older interpretations of sexual morality. In 1912, the same year as the special committee's landmark report, Margaret Sanger launched her crusade for birth control, which threatened as nothing else to disaggregate the sex act from reproduction. In states throughout the nation, men and women were going to court in unprecedented numbers to secure divorces, or, where the laws set up impediments, such as the stipulation that one party must be named as at "fault," men and women were petitioning the legislatures for redress. The rumblings of dissent from the code of civilized sexual morality were unmistakable. Sex educators shared with these "rebels" a sense that the older code of absolute morality, reinforced by a powerful and respected religious establishment, no longer held sway over most Americans.

Although the rebels against Victorianism might have perceived the sex educators as allies, the educators were equally likely to condemn the "rebels" as representatives of a broader decay in society's moral structure. Thus, despite their alliance with liberals in opposition to Victorianism, sex educators ultimately longed for the moral certainty that inspired their traditionalist opponents. Where rebels saw in the crumbling of absolute morality the opportunity to create a new moral code, sex educators saw only a wall that needed patching. Well aware of New York's bohemians as a professor at Teachers College in New York City, Maurice Bigelow asserted in 1916, "The one great fact is that our national code of morality is a monogamic one, approved as ideal even by many of those who fail to live strictly in harmony with its dictates." Sex education was not to create new sexual ideals, but rather to make young people into what Bigelow called "strict adherents of the *established* code of sexual morality." The mere prevalence of vice, according to the young instructor, was hardly an argument in its favor.[155]

Despite their confidence in modern methods of social control, the sex educators' new moral approach would ultimately prove less stable than they had hoped. Educators could conceive of new means for enforcing moral behavior, but they lacked fundamental justification for the morality they wished to pass on to the next generation. In the absence of religious arguments for monogamy and chastity, Bigelow had to fall back, alternately, on a theory of cultural hierarchy, in which the "monogamic ideal" was the best code because it prevailed in "the world's best life," or on an argument from agreement—that sex was moral only within marriage because the "chief citizens of every civilized country" agreed that it was so.[156] So long as most "respectable" Americans did not question the monogamous code, sex educators could teach adolescents about chastity with no sense of disconnection between their curriculum and the dominant adult morality. But sexual liberals in substantial numbers were already beginning to dissent from this agreement, and Bigelow himself came to long covertly for a code of "super-morality" beyond conventional morality.[157] As social changes in the 1920s would soon demonstrate, the sex educators had built their impressive structure upon a shifting foundation.

# CHAPTER THREE

# The Revolt of Youth

> ALEC: Does Rosalind behave herself?
> CECELIA: Not particularly well. Oh, she's average—
> smokes sometimes, drinks punch, frequently kissed—
> Oh, yes—common knowledge—one of the effects of the
> war, you know.
>
> F. Scott Fitzgerald, *This Side of Paradise* (1920)

In his brief sketch of debutante Rosalind Connage—the model of a "flapper" who smoked, drank, and kissed without apologies—F. Scott Fitzgerald sought to capture the atmosphere of moral release that seemed to arrive with the disruptions of World War I. In Fitzgerald's view, the war unleashed a new freedom in social and sexual behavior that young women like Rosalind were only too eager to explore. Although Fitzgerald overestimated the novelty of many of these changes— moral codes and sexual behavior had been shifting significantly even before the war, and reformers had already spent much energy lamenting the dire state of American morals—some truth remains in the popular image of the war years and the Jazz Age that followed as allowing a bold departure from Victorian strictures. The social transformations that took place during the war and its aftermath would ultimately lead sex educators to discard many elements of their Victorian inheritance in the name of retaining what they considered essential to civilized sexual morality.

In spite of their prewar efforts to fight the erosion of American morals, many social hygiene activists perceived that World War I accelerated the decline. Fully conscious of the reactionary pressures and social dislocation that entry into the war would unleash, Woodrow Wilson portrayed the

European conflict as a holy war in which America's high purpose would dissolve the common domestic dangers of wartime. Indeed, with the backing of such prominent American reformers as John Dewey, Wilson argued that U.S. participation in the war would be as good for the American character as it was for the European balance of power. Despite Wilson and his allies' high hopes, however, the conflict's moral effects would prove decidedly mixed.

The war began well for reformers. The government—with the progressive former mayor of Cleveland, Newton Baker, filling the position of secretary of war—offered to make the American army itself into a laboratory for moral reform. Experience had taught Baker that prostitution and alcohol vendors sprang up like weeds around any army encampment, bringing with them drunkenness, belligerence, and, most threatening to military efficiency, debilitating venereal disease. In the past, governments had accepted these diversions as the inevitable consequences of military mobilization, but the social hygiene movement and progressive reformers in general had been agitating for a decade for recognition that these vices were preventable. Spurred on by Raymond Fosdick, a young attorney from the American Social Hygiene Association, Secretary Baker created the Commission on Training Camp Activities (CTCA) just a few days after the nation's official entry into the war. Schooled in the prewar movements for social hygiene and sex education, the men in charge of the CTCA promised that they could control the soldiers' environment and education to provide America with what they called "the cleanest army in the world."[1]

The reformers' first impulse was to view the young army recruits as they had been accustomed to regard young, unmarried men before the war. The sex education movement had brought reformers to recognize that young men, in particular, harbored strong sexual impulses, but leaders in the movement had also maintained that a scientific approach to the problem made mass chastity an attainable goal. In their initial, optimistic view, young men in the army could remain chaste; they differed from their prewar civilian counterparts only in number, not in kind.

Although the CTCA's program would soon depart from sex education orthodoxy as laid out by Prince Morrow and others on the 1912 Special Committee on Matters and Methods in Sex Education, leaders retained many elements from the earlier programs to manage adolescent sexuality. They sought first to control the young man's environment, to protect the young recruit from external incitements to vice. With unprecedented thoroughness, the army and civilian authorities cooperated in jailing suspected prostitutes and suppressing such notorious red light districts as New Orleans' Storyville. To further prevent the forces of vice from preying on uprooted, bored, and generally susceptible young men, the CTCA combined these coercive measures with positive recreational activities, such as soldier sing-alongs, to occupy the trainees' time and imagination.

Finally, lecturers in the Social Hygiene Instruction Division of the CTCA delivered sex education lectures to hundreds of thousands of soldiers who, despite the social hygiene movement's earlier efforts, seemed to lack the most rudimentary knowledge about sex. Like their prewar civilian counterparts, these lecturers spent time outlining the basic functions of the genitals, and clearing up such common misconceptions as the belief in male sexual necessity.

In the beginning the CTCA's program appeared to be the fulfillment of the prewar social hygienists' vision for reform. But the direction that sex education soon took in the training camps made it clear that the young soldier was not the same as the young civilian, and that the army's needs were quite different from domestic society's. In the CTCA, according to one lecturer, "The fear of disease forms the backbone of practically every preventative medicine educational campaign."[2] Where the 1912 *Report of the Special Committee on the Matters and Methods of Sex Education* had scorned "smut talks" in favor of focusing on the "uplifting possibilities" of sexuality, army lecturers concentrated almost exclusively on the dangers of venereal disease and prostitutes. The CTCA instructors even dusted off the social hygienists' collection of venereal disease photographs and did not shrink from displaying the most grotesque consequences of syphilis and gonorrhea. The army's instructors prided themselves on avoiding ineffective moralizing in favor of blunt, "scientific" arguments for continence.[3]

In this most ambitious sex education program, the context of an army at war overrode the civilian sex educators' orthodoxies about the nature of youth and the methods of sex instruction. Most important in reviving the pedagogy of fear was the army's concern with manpower lost to venereal infections. Prince Morrow had estimated that during the American occupation of the Philippines, venereal diseases had robbed the army of millions of work hours, and syphilitic complications had killed four times as many soldiers as any other disease.[4] In a world war of unprecedented scale, preventing a repeat of such disasters was more important than the delicacy of the recruits' sensibilities. Further, in the training camp environment those sensibilities seemed rather less delicate. The audience of recruits was not only slightly older than an average high school assembly but it was also all male—instructors did not have to worry about corrupting the more "innocent" young women. In addition, the results of mental tests that recruits took at their induction seemed to suggest that an enormous percentage of the young soldiers—particularly African Americans and recent immigrants—were "feeble-minded" or "borderline morons."[5] CTCA lecturers concluded that such minds were best molded with blunt instruments rather than with delicate prodding.

The imperative for military efficiency soon eroded even further the reformers' hopes for chastity and led to the army's decisive departure from social hygiene's program of moral reform. The medical department of the Allied Expeditionary Force recognized that American soldiers might not retain their self-control once they traded the well-regulated environment of the training camp for the libertine precincts of France. Indeed, the French premier, Georges Clemenceau, justified these fears when he sent a letter gallantly offering American soldiers access to French prostitutes, whose profession was flourishing under the continental system of regulation. ("For God's sake . . . don't show this [letter] to the President," the secretary of war supposedly remarked, "or he'll stop the war.")[6] Accordingly, General John Pershing and the medical department in 1918 ordered that each division establish a chemical prophylaxis station where soldiers could obtain postcoital treatment against syphilis, gonorrhea, and chancroid. Chemical prophylaxis at the time involved the laborious process of scrubbing the genitals, injecting a chemical solution into the urethra, and then wrapping the genitals for a while in calomel ointment and waxed paper. Performed competently and within a few hours of intercourse, the treatment was quite effective. At the armistice the army issued individual "prophylactic packets" to many of the soldiers going on unsupervised leave, to ensure that they would be prepared for all eventualities.[7] Thus, the war offered a great many young men both an explicit sex education and the opportunity for premarital or extramarital exploration, seemingly with the U.S. government's approval.

More critical for sex education were the opportunities that the war created on the domestic front. Although certain elements of the army's program, such as its support for chemical prophylaxis, could not be transferred to a civilian program, an increased awareness of sexual irregularity and venereal disease during the war would lead to more governmental and public support for sex education in the schools. To the great concern of military and social hygiene authorities, the soldier's wartime freedom seemed to find its domestic counterpart among the civilian men and, especially, women who poured into military and industrial communities.

"The girl problem has assumed a totally different aspect with the coming of the war," explained Henrietta S. Additon, an assistant director of the CTCA, in 1918. Additon expressed her agency's deep concern about "the concentration of a large number of young men in comparatively few places, the tendency of women to flock to the camp towns, the danger of the rapid spread of venereal disease, [and] the unsettled social conditions in these towns."[8] In addition to the camp towns newly teeming with young girls "attracted by the khaki," industrial cities found themselves awash in young transient workers: Bridgeport, Connecticut, added 50,000 inhabitants in a single year of the war; Akron, Ohio, added 60,000 residents over the course of the conflict.[9] Many of these new residents were newly independent women—one million additional women began to work for wages during the war, and their income and their move away from home brought unprecedented freedom from parental control. According to Additon, a combination of independence, low wages, and the "peculiar charm and glamour which surrounds the man in uniform" caused many of these women to lose "their foothold upon the ladder of respectability."[10] "One such girl," reported Additon, "said that she had never sold herself to a civilian but she felt she was doing her bit when she had been with eight soldiers in a night." When military and civilian authorities caught unattached women soliciting or sometimes merely walking alone near a military camp, they typically threw them into jail, had them examined for venereal diseases, and often sent them back to their home community, but the wartime wave of sexual immorality also prompted many civilian authorities to ponder the possible uses of sex education for enforcing morality.

The greatest impetus for domestic sex education came from a set of shocking medical statistics gathered for the war effort. After physicians in the medical department of the army studied the induction records of recruits, they made the astonishing charge that venereal disease was not so much a problem of military life as of civilian life. The surgeon general estimated that five of every six infected soldiers had contracted their disease *before* entering the service.[11] Later, the Kansas Board of Health would report in 1919 that fifty cases of venereal disease in the state were in children under fifteen—and the board estimated that the actual incidence was perhaps ten times higher.[12] Even if the CTCA prevented every soldier from becoming infected during his time in the service, the army and society would still face a formidable venereal disease problem.

The surgeon general's alarming figures compelled many reformers to take a harder look at civilian efforts in venereal disease prevention. Citing the prevalence of venereal disease and immorality in the army in 1917, Norman Coleman of Reed College accused American society of failing to prepare its young men for the test of their character. "Many a youth goes up to an army camp from a home where the simple facts of sex health were not told him," Coleman noted, "from schools where all the bodily functions and their relation to health and disease were explained except the function that at his age he most needs to understand." "The soldiers of today," Coleman concluded, "were in our schools yesterday. The soldiers of tomorrow are in our schools today. They have a right to the scientific facts and the fortifying moral suggestions and counsel that will give them a fighting chance to reach the battle front unshamed and untainted by vice."[13] Coleman's was one voice in a chorus of alarm at domestic conditions.

Pressure from activists like Coleman eventually led to government action. Norman Coleman's state senator, George Chamberlain of Oregon, and Representative Julius Kahn of California proposed a massive domestic social hygiene program to parallel the army's own efforts.[14] Congress passed the Chamberlain-Kahn Act in July 1918, creating the Venereal Disease Division of the United States Public Health Service and the U.S. Interdepartmental Social Hygiene Board to coordinate governmental efforts. As with the CTCA, these new entities were staffed by social hygiene activists. The problems of venereal disease lay at the heart of this growing support for sex education, but sex educators hoped to turn the general sentiment for sexual awareness to their own, less medically oriented purposes. Never before had sexual reformers had so much influence.

At least half of the act's $4 million appropriation was earmarked for state boards of health and for local law-enforcement agencies, which incurred heavy costs in detaining prostitutes, but Chamberlain-Kahn's effect on these organizations paled beside its great impact on the sex education campaign.[15] An underfunded campaign before the war, sex education now had money for new courses, instructors, and materials. Further, this new government support had its counterpart in a wave of public support for sex education.

The act's primary effect was on the nation's college students. The Chamberlain-Kahn Act disbursed over half a million dollars in 1919 and 1920 to create or buttress hygiene departments at more than forty normal schools (colleges for training teachers), colleges, and universities. Under Chamberlain-Kahn funding, more than 50,000 college students ultimately learned about the venereal diseases through hygiene courses in either the regular curriculum or summer programs, such as the Columbia Teachers College summer sex hygiene course taught by Maurice Bigelow and ASHA's Colonel William Snow.[16]

Although college students did not suffer from high rates of venereal disease, they seemed a likely population to commence with. In part, their age simply made teaching them about sex less controversial, but more important, college students seemed likely to form the front line of support for sex education in the future. The Interdepartmental Social Hygiene Board hoped that college men and women would spread the social hygiene gospel beyond their limited numbers. Educating students at the normal schools had a particular advantage, noted the board's executive secretary, Thomas A. Storey: "They become the teachers of teachers and the moulders and fashioners of educational hygiene in the schools of the land." College students in general were ideal targets for this message. "They are the source of support for wise policies of public health in the municipality and in the commonwealth," Storey noted. "The college graduate of tomorrow will give and demand a better public hygiene and he will give and demand a better standard of private hygiene."[17]

In the meantime, the Chamberlain-Kahn Act did help sex education take tentative steps into the nation's public schools. A particularly advanced program was started in Senator Chamberlain's home state.[18] Under the Oregon Social Hygiene Society's prodding, and with a grant from the Interdepartmental Social Hygiene Board, a handful of grade schools in the state began weekly half-hour biology courses on plant and animal life for fourth-graders. Students acquired a scientific vocabulary for plant and animal reproduction in the next two grades, and then they were introduced to human physiology and hygiene in the seventh and eighth grades under the same trusted teacher, though the teacher's approach to human reproduction at this stage varied from school to school, and sometimes the teacher did not touch on this subject at all. The program concluded with Oregon Social Hygiene Society lecturers, who traveled to the various high schools to deliver sexually segregated lectures on "sociobiology"—that is, heredity, reproduction, "catastrophes of adolescence" (probably masturbation), and the need to avoid venereal diseases.

To convey such lessons, sex educators participated in the creation and standardization of new educational materials for both civilians and soldiers. The U.S. Public Health Service created a series of pamphlets presenting the "true facts of sex" that focused primarily on venereal diseases, but that also conveyed the leading sex educators' concerns. Army educators created poster exhibitions utilizing the most advanced techniques of the advertiser's craft, and the CTCA pioneered the use of film for the social hygiene crusade. In one celebrated training-camp presentation, a film, *Keeping Fit to Fight,* portrayed the drama of soldiers resisting or succumbing to the temptations of prostitution and the (dramaturgically inevitable) contraction of venereal disease, and pointed to the educational potential of the movie screen.[19] With its references to chemical prophylaxis excised, *Keeping Fit to Fight* was even shown to the civilian public after the war. New materials and the dissemination of older ideas helped to keep the social hygiene campaign before the public eye.

In addition to inducing the creation of new programs and materials, the war fostered respectability for sex education and social hygiene. As social hygienists entered government service with army commissions, and Congress appropriated hundreds of thousands of dollars to groups like ASHA, some of the "taint" attached to a concern with sexual matters seemed to dissipate. Responding to this new prestige and to wartime needs, such groups as the Young Men's Christian Association, the Young Women's Christian Association, and even the National Congress of Parents and Teachers allied themselves with the sex education campaign, and ASHA's membership during the war rose to more than 11,000 people.[20]

Such support fulfilled a deep craving for recognition on the part of the sexual reformers that went back even further than their courting of Charles W. Eliot for the presidency of ASHA. Aside from their personal desires for acceptance, reformers recognized that they needed respectability and money if they were to go beyond the role of cultural critic to obtain actual influence over social policy in the areas of sexuality and disease control. Without prestige, they could be lumped in with any variety of marginal "free love" or birth control advocate.

Perhaps the most important legacy of the war for sex education was the creation of a federal bureaucracy committed to sex education in the public schools. The new Venereal Disease Division of the U.S. Public Health Service had subsections devoted to educational policy. This institutionalization meant that support for sex education in the schools was no longer solely dependent on isolated, local efforts or the caprice of elected officials, though these would continue to be significant factors in the spread of sex education. In the years to follow, the Division of Venereal Disease cooperated closely with sex educators in funding experiments and sex education programs, and the division sponsored surveys on the extent of sex education that would prove very useful to the movement. Such support ensured that at least some form of sex education would receive a respectful hearing.

At the war's end, sex education seemed to have a strong future. Concern over syphilis and gonorrhea had fostered unprecedented respectability and stable governmental support for sex education, as well as a heightened public awareness of the need for some form of sex instruction. High school teachers and principals, for example, besieged the U.S. Public Health Service with requests for sex education pamphlets—the service received 5,165 requests in May 1919 alone.²¹ Some educators complained about the wartime preoccupation with venereal disease, but even liberals such as Bigelow had never denied the necessity of preventing venereal disease; rather, they had promised that prevention would follow naturally from their program of teaching biology and morality. Moreover, sex education leaders believed, with some justice, that this change of emphasis was merely a temporary wartime shift.

With the armistice signed, reformers further expected that many of the social and sexual freedoms of wartime could be contained. If the war had been a "moral holiday," they felt, it had been so primarily for the men who had served in the military, and particularly for the fraction that had shipped overseas and seen "Gay Paree." Reformers felt that these men must now return to normal civilian morality, and they were confident that the small number of female civilians who had also taken advantage of wartime freedoms would soon learn that their holiday was over. In the months after the armistice, reformers reassured themselves that the war's erosion of morals meant only a temporary shifting of society's moral foundation.

They soon concluded, however, that the erosion instead portended a landslide. "This generation," bluntly observed a judge in New York, "is sex mad." In 1920 a "Mr. Grundy" in the *Atlantic Monthly* cataloged the younger generation's offenses against modesty: "the perfect freedom of intercourse between the sexes, the unchaperoned motor-flights at night, the intimacies of modern dancing, the scantiness of modern dress, and the frankness of conversation between young men and girls. There are even whispers," he concluded, "concerning the sharing of the smuggled bottle during the early prohibition days, and the indulgent attitude of some of the most popular girls toward the evident intoxication of their partners." In all its manifestations, the problem was national: as Florence Guy Woolston observed in the *New Republic*, "No matter what the locality: a Boston suburb, a small town, New York, Chicago or San Francisco, there is no doubt that boys and girls have a freedom and a frankness which their elders never experienced."²² In the general revolt against Victorianism, young people seemed to be everywhere on the front lines, and to the great consternation of many, young women seemed to be leading the charge.

The "revolution in manners and morals" was as much a product of perception as of actual behavioral change, for the media in the 1920s not only recorded the "revolution" but also helped create it. Advertisers interested in targeting consumers through sexual themes, motion pictures concentrating on passionate romance, and, above all, the newspapers and magazines publishing hundreds of articles about the "revolt of youth" led most Americans to believe they were living through a major transformation. The media's preoccupation with youthful misbehavior was critical for disseminating new images, new "styles," throughout the country—indeed, young people interested in misbehaving "properly" depended as much on the media to inform them of what their peers were doing as the media depended on young people for their stories.[23] "Public criticism," lamented a contributor to the *Literary Digest,* "has seemed to have the effect of jokes about Henry Ford's cars—the more the talk the greater the advertising."[24] This is not to deny that college youth and a great many other Americans were indeed behaving in novel ways, but in the decade that first really discovered "fads" and contrived "media events," the lines dividing any social trend from its publicity became exceptionally blurred. The "revolt" of the 1920s and the reporting of it were mutually reinforcing.

In the first years after the war, observers focused on the most visible aspects of the new youth culture—female dress and dancing. One college president in Texas, for example, condemned the new styles of female dress with perhaps an excessive attention to detail: President Bishop of Southwestern University noted that he had seen "on every 'full-dress' social occasion, examples of the style of women's dress which leave the arms, shoulders, back, and part of the bosom uncovered, and also expose, in certain postures or in unguarded movements, an inch or more of the naked limbs between the end of the short skirt and the rolled-down stocking."[25]

In its postwar offensive against such impropriety, the Young Woman's Christian Association (YMCA) supplied a photograph that detailed the differences between "proper" and "improper" attire for young women. The improper flapper on the right of the photograph wore rouge and lipstick; her blouse exposed most of her arms and at least a fraction of clavicle, and her hemline had risen almost to meet the bottoms of her knees. To complete the portrayal, the flapper's posture was poor, and she stood with her hands on her hips in a saucy attitude. In contrast, the proper maiden on the left allowed only her hands and her face to peek out from her garments, and her posture was rigid—perhaps morally upright. Although the viewer was to understand that she was the more virtuous of the two women, her tight expression also suggested that virtue, whatever its other rewards, was simply not much fun.

The new dances caused equal alarm among moralists—particularly as young women tended to dance while wearing their "improper" dresses. The more intimate, sexual style of dancing was not completely new—working-class dance halls had been filled with "rough dancing" and "turkey trotting" before the war—but "respectable" youths until recently had primarily danced waltzes and other steps that were too swift and complex to permit much physical intimacy between dancers. Now the "fox trot," "shimmy," and other postwar steps offered even well-bred youngsters ripe possibilities for pleasurable contact. One college newspaper editor found it "tremendously suggestive" for the dancers "to jig and hop around like a chicken on a red-hot stove, at the same time shaking the body until it quivers like a disturbed glass of jell-o." Dancing to the new "jazz" music, noted another writer, was merely a "syncopated embrace."

These open displays of sexuality, disturbing in themselves, were often the outward expressions of an even more alarming private sexuality. In an attempt to experiment sexually without risking the physical or social consequences of intercourse, postwar youth often indulged in "petting," or sexual foreplay that stopped short of actual intercourse. For social hygienists, this change represented ironic progress: young men in the 1920s visited prostitutes far less often than before the war, but "respectable" young women seemed to be picking up the slack from the decline in prostitution. Decades later, Alfred Kinsey would confirm what contemporaries had suspected: he discovered that the female rate of premarital petting to orgasm had been rising steadily for each generation born after 1900, and young women in each subsequent generation were becoming sexually active earlier in their adolescence.[26] As Florence Woolston observed in 1922, the postwar youths "pursue pleasure with an ardor that leaves the more recently emerged Puritans of an older generation astonished and aghast." Dorothy Parker summed up the new standard of morality with characteristic venom. "If all the young ladies who attended the Yale promenade dance were laid end to end," she quipped, "no one would be the least surprised."[27]

Such jokes were not calculated to ease Americans' fears for youth. While the journalist Frederick Lewis Allen famously proclaimed a "revolution in manners and morals," others referred to the new situation less happily as a "devolution" and possibly a "devilution."[28] President Bishop of Southwestern University confessed that his "heart turns cold with apprehension concerning the womanhood and the motherhood of the coming generations," and his counterpart at the University of Florida agreed that "rolled hose and short skirts are born of the Devil and his angels, and are carrying the present and future generations to social chaos and destruction."[29] College presidents and ministers tended not to be invited to student dances, and so usually refrained from commenting on them, but a great many young people attended, and some concluded themselves that the new dances' effects were baneful. "The dance in its process of its degradation has passed from slight impropriety to indecency, and now threatens to become brazenly shameless," claimed the editor of the Hobart College *Herald*. "American morals have undoubtedly degenerated with the dance."

Greater dangers yet seemed to lurk on the horizon. Although college students had set the trend, one author noted with alarm "the tendency toward laxity among boys and girls of high-school age, where, in the belief of many observers, the greatest danger, or the only real danger, lies." As the *Boston Sunday Advertiser* proclaimed in a bold headline, "The girl of fourteen is the problem of to-day." The nation, warned the president of Fordham University, "is in danger of a harvest of social demoralization."

As they contemplated the new situation, sex educators seemed unaware of the extent to which they were responsible for creating a foundation of sexual frankness and media freedom for the 1920s "revolt." As early as 1916, sex educator Maurice Bigelow had noted, "The sex-education movement has already brought the problems of sex out of the old-time secrecy, and no other topics of the times are so freely read and discussed."[30] The government's wartime barrage against prostitution and venereal disease had sent defenders of a "genteel silence" about sex into full retreat. Even the most mainstream of magazines were publishing frank articles about the danger of venereal disease, and the army's own propaganda was not overly

fastidious in railing publicly against the "dirty whore." Reformers had unwittingly helped destroy the informal code that had long existed in the literary world as to which works and words were fit to print and which were obscene.[31]

In breaking this "conspiracy of silence," reformers had meant only to
make it easier for respectable authorities to distribute information about
sex, but their efforts created unintended consequences. Just as the antiprostitution agitation before the war had allowed hundreds of authors to
churn out tawdry but tantalizing exposés of the "white slave" trade, so the
explicit social hygiene crusade during the war had opened opportunities for
less "proper" writers and artists to pursue sexual themes. Such a loosening
of standards in the 1920s allowed a new generation of publishers to disseminate works by James Joyce, D. H. Lawrence, and other "serious" writers,
and the new openness also invited in such eager capitalists as the self-
inventing strongman-publisher Bernarr MacFadden, whose publications
ranged from risqué muscle magazines like *Physical Culture* to lurid serials
like *True Stories* and lowbrow tabloids like the *New York Evening Graphic*.[32]
Reformers had been right to fear the new openness.

"Much of the popular interest in sexual problems seems to be a craving
for the abnormal," Bigelow had earlier observed. "Everywhere it is the sexual abnormality, perversity, and even bestial vulgarity that seems to attract
the most attention."[33] With the end of the war these themes became more
prevalent while, at the same time, publishers grew reluctant to print any
more articles about venereal disease. The openness that social hygienists
had labored so hard to create seemed to help them less than it did the pur-
veyors of what one sex educator labeled "sensationalistic trash."[34] As the
mainstream press, too, joined the disreputable and semirespectable magazines in their turn against Victorian propriety, the reformers' continued
calls for gentility and mild forms of censorship seemed more and more like
asking for a little modesty in the middle of a burlesque show.

Whether the reporters were writing in *True Stories* or the *New Republic*,
they agreed that the most unsettling (and titillating) trend unleashed by the
First World War was the desire for sexual freedom among young women—
or, rather, among young middle-class women. Many of the "new" styles in

clothing, dance, and sexual relations were already common in working-class and immigrant communities, but they seemed to qualify as trends worth noticing only when they began to percolate upward to the middle and upper classes.[35] Whatever her background, the "respectable" young woman of the 1920s seemed noticeably different from her older sister. "To the girl of to-day," explained an editor at the University of Pennsylvania's student newspaper, "petting parties, cigaret-smoking, and in many cases drinking, are accepted as ordinary parts of existence. The girl who will not permit a kiss from any fellow who pleases her these days is practically non-existent."[36]

After demanding for decades that men give up their double standard of sexual behavior and move toward the higher female standard of chastity, sex educators and purity crusaders were dismayed to observe that exactly the opposite was occurring. "All that elaborate theory of feminine chastity, that worship of virginity, goes by the board, and women are given a reversed theory—that they are just the same as men, if not more so," scoffed Charlotte Perkins Gilman, the redoubtable feminist philosopher, in a symposium on contemporary morals sponsored by the *Nation* toward the end of the 1920s. "Our 'double standard' is undoubled and ironed flat—to the level of masculine desire."[37] While sex educators had previously found the innate purity of girls to be their most reliable ally against sexual misconduct —indeed, they had occasionally feared that feminine purity would hyper-trophy into a sterile prudery—now observers found young women every-where eager to cast off this moral burden, to shock, to misbehave just like the boys.

So unexpected was this shift in sexual behavior that cultural commenta-tors did not, at first, possess a vocabulary adequate to describe it: the U.S. Public Health Service's 1920 *Keeping Fit* pamphlet warned men against the dangers of "[a]ll prostitutes, whether they are professionals who sell them-selves for money, or girls who only occasionally have sex relations with men."[38] This writer thus clumsily made explicit the confusion many adults were experiencing, for behavior that was becoming conventional for many college women in the 1920s, such as wearing lipstick and makeup, "bob-bing" their hair, smoking, baring their ankles and knees, and indulging in "petting" or other forms of premarital sexual activity, had hitherto been the distinguishing characteristics of the "ladies of the night." To observers who clung to the old meaning of these symbols, the new single standard of morality seemed to hover at a very low level indeed.

Although Gilman suspected that the new sexual code was another strategy for male exploitation of women, she underestimated the conscious, deliberate action in this movement both by a new breed of feminist activists and by innumerable female allies in the factories, offices, colleges, and high schools.[39] No doubt a great many men reaped the benefits of the American woman's greater sexual freedom, and the "emancipation" of women was unquestionably limited by our standards, but the ambiguous results of this behavioral upheaval should not obscure the power of women's demands. Certainly Charlotte Perkins Gilman's fellow contributors to the *Nation* symposium recognized that women's demands were the driving force of change. Beatrice Hinkle, a progressive Jungian psychiatrist, held that recent changes in sexual morality were being produced almost solely by women, "in full view of all with no apologies and little hesitation." "It can be said," Hinkle continued, "that in the general disintegration of old standards, women are the active agents in the field of sexual morality and men the passive, almost bewildered accessories to the overthrow of their long and firmly organized control of women's sexual conduct."[40]

As members of the first significant generation of educated career women, Hinkle and other prominent participants in the *Nation* symposium argued that the feminine revolt grew inevitably from American women's dawning economic independence. "As long as women were dependent upon men for the support of themselves and their children," Hinkle maintained, "there could be no development of a real morality, for the love and feelings of the woman were so intermingled with her economic necessities that the higher love impulse was largely undifferentiated from the impulse of self-preservation." Their work in factories, department stores, and professions ranging from social work to journalism, the psychiatrist noted optimistically, was allowing women to disentangle their dependence on masculine support from their sexual and romantic expectations. Women were demanding greater fulfillment—even sexual fulfillment—within marriage, access to birth control to make this possible, easier divorce when marriage went sour, and "the right," as Hinkle proclaimed and Gilman complained, "to act as their impulses dictate with much the same freedom that men have enjoyed for so long."[41]

Perhaps unwilling to credit young women with responsibility for their own "liberation," commentators cast about for other causes of the revolt. "It is everything," concluded a "Mrs. Grundy" in the *Atlantic Monthly:*

> Give the motor-car its due share of responsibility. Give the movie more blame, please, than it has hitherto received. Give the war some—but not too much; for all this antedates the war. Give the radical intellectuals a little, for their tendency to howl down everything that has ever, anywhere, been of good repute. Give a lot of it to the luxury of the *nouveaux riches . . .* Give "Prohibition" a little . . . And give all you can heap up to the general abandonment of religion . . . When, as a social group, we threw over religion, we threw over— probably without meaning to—most of our everyday moral sanctions.[42]

Other authorities added to this list the failure of parents to guard their offspring. "Unless fond and foolish mothers are awakened," argued a president of one southern college, "the engulfing wave of sensuality will continue to take its fearful toll from their fireside."[43]

No matter which side of the dispute a writer took, he or she usually pronounced Sigmund Freud the champion of this new morality of instinct. "You can tell a girl that she is appealing crudely to the physical nature of men," explained Mrs. Grundy in the *Atlantic,* "she may admit it, and at the same time justify herself with something out of Freud or Theodore Dreiser."[44] Owing to a careless reading of Freud, his numerous popularizers, and his putative allies, many people concluded that the dour Viennese psychoanalyst had adduced scientific evidence that all sexual repression was harmful. Indeed, Freud's theories about the sexual drive, complained social hygienists, seemed to have replaced male sexual necessity as a physiological concept with a psychological sexual necessity that applied to both men and women.[45]

Freud's opinions about the necessity of repression notwithstanding, supporters and detractors all thought the psychoanalyst believed that the individual's natural instincts were a surer guide to life than were the dictates of a coercive society.[46] The eagerness of many Americans to embrace such "naturalism" as a guide to behavior was evident in whites' embracing of black jazz and the Harlem Renaissance, in the anthropological vogue that followed the publication in 1928 of Margaret Mead's *Coming of Age in Samoa,* and in the general glorification of "primitive" art and unrepressed cultures.[47] "We turn," scoffed one college president, "to the dark forest and the dusky, untutored savage, loathsome of habit, for our modern music, dances, and, in some measure, dress."[48] Although sex educators, unsurprisingly, joined in the conservative condemnation of primitivism and impulsiveness, they were not free from the taint of naturalism. Their own prewar rehabilitation of reproductive sexuality—their attempt to convey the divinity and purity of the sexual impulse—might have unwittingly contributed to this new faith in benign instinct.

Many prominent intellectuals captured the magnitude, if not the true meaning, of the change, when they interpreted these developments as a wholesale reaction against Anglo-American Victorian culture, against what Ezra Pound bitterly dismissed as "an old bitch gone in the teeth."[49] "Revolt has become characteristic of our age," observed two prominent American radicals, V. F. Calverton and Samuel D. Schmalhausen. "The intellectuals are in revolt against an entire civilization. The revolt against the old sex attitudes, with their silences and their stupidities, is a vital part of this entire revolt against a decaying culture."[50] The "bohemians" and sexual liberals of prewar Greenwich Village had shown the way: the "sexual revolution" was to affect not just college youth or individual men and women, but American culture itself.

Sexuality was a vital question because it embodied in concentrated form the conflict between past and present. The dispute, according to commentators on all sides of the issue, was fundamentally one of whether individuals would be governed by custom and convention, or whether they should heed the demands of instinct and personal choice. The tension between social responsibility and antinomian desire had for centuries structured the way people thought about sexuality, but now that many intellectuals were challenging all the conventions of Victorian morality, the resolution of this conflict between society and sexual desire carried a heavier burden of meaning. In a 1927 article ostensibly concerned with the spread of venereal disease, Assistant Surgeon General Thomas Parran could not help commenting more broadly on "the relaxation of the moral code which has occurred during recent years." "This seems to be," Parran observed, "a part of a widespread revolt on the part of the individual against all forms of restraint, of a desire for personal freedom unhampered by the shackles of law or social custom."[51]

From the front lines of the battle over behavior, the dean of women at the University of Vermont agreed with Parran that postwar youth clung tightly to "the intense individualism, the clamorous demand for a selfish, unrepressed personal freedom, the right of the individual to seek and demand gratification of his or her personal will, regardless of tradition and oblivious to many ethical standards which we, perhaps conservatively, consider foundation stones of civilization."[52] At the same time, a favorably inclined Beatrice Hinkle told the *Nation* forum that the sexual revolution was a hopeful sign that "natural, long-restrained desire is being substituted for collective moral rules, and individuals are largely becoming a law unto themselves."[53] Enemies and supporters agreed that sexual freedom was the modernists' weapon of choice against conformity, convention, religion— against the bulwarks of Victorian society.

"Responsible" authorities did not allow the war against decency to proceed unchecked. The twin evils of suggestive dancing and dress first furnished what one writer called "the stuff of passionate conversation" everywhere.[54] Soon they also furnished the stuff of legislation, focused particularly on female deportment. Even as the Catholic archbishop of the Ohio diocese issued condemnations of the "toddle," the "shimmy," and "bare female shoulders," New York state appointed a "censor of dances," and numerous other states entertained legislation that prescribed the precise latitudes of a woman's skirt and décolletage. "Were these to become laws," reported the New York *American* in 1921, "the dress with its four-inch-high skirt which would be moral in Virginia would be immodest in Utah, while both the Utah and Virginia skirts would be wicked enough in Ohio to make their wearers subject to fine or imprisonment. Undoubtedly, other State laws would add to this confusion, and therefore a standardization acceptable to all is something that might ultimately be welcomed by women."[55] Others had arrived independently at the need for standardization. Also in 1921, a Dress-Reform Committee of prominent Philadelphia citizens sent 1,160 local clergy a questionnaire about what they felt constituted "immodest dress" for women. Learning from the replies that the clergy "were absolutely at odds themselves," the committee, it was reported, "adopted the device of striking an average of the answers and building a dress upon these averages."[56] The committee must have been confounded, rather than gratified, when it learned that the next year's Parisian fashions were even more "demure" than the clergymen's "moral gown."

In proposing such superficial solutions, detractors risked ignoring the deeper changes taking place in American society. The declining economic usefulness of a large family and the greater recourse to birth control among couples had led middle-class families to become smaller by the turn of the century. Birth control and the reduction in numbers of children allowed a greater intimacy to develop within the family, and partners began to expect marriage to offer them more than economic security and offspring. By the 1920s many middle-class, white Americans were coming to believe in the value of "companionate marriage," or a relationship that stressed personal satisfaction, social adjustment, and sexual fulfillment.[57] The revolution in manners and morals signified not moral anarchy or mere licentiousness but rather a new set of social conventions formed by the pressures of an advanced industrial society.

Among adults, this broader transformation expressed itself, for example, in the soaring popularity of marriage manuals in the 1920s and in a rising divorce rate. While superficially contradictory, these trends both grew out of the same new ideas about family and marriage. Marriage manuals promised to help husbands and wives adjust to each other for the greatest possible social and sexual satisfaction, and divorce became a highly desired option when the union failed to meet these raised expectations.[58] Divorce became what one historian calls a "safety valve" for a culture that demanded stronger, more rewarding marriages.

These changes in adult behavior had their corollary among the young people of the 1920s. "Petting" and the other premarital indulgences of the "flaming youth" were not so much the results of moral abandon as they were means of accommodating late marriage and sexual proscription to the culture's dawning emphasis on personal congeniality and sexual fulfillment.[59] Young people had always had trouble reconciling their early sexual maturity with society's taboo on premarital sex, and the wave of late-adolescent "neurasthenia," or nervous exhaustion, toward the end of the nineteenth century reflected an intensified conflict between these two forces as white, middle-class Americans increasingly delayed marriage until their mid- to late twenties.[60]

The taboo on sex seemed at once more repressive and less valid to the white, college-bound youth of the 1920s. Themselves products of smaller, emotionally intense late-Victorian families, they governed their behavior more on the basis of personal interaction and peer acceptance than on abstract morality.[61] This change in personality structure was buttressed not only by developments in family form but also by the broader shift in American culture from an economy based on production and delayed gratification to one based on consumption and immediate satisfaction.[62] The same root of demographic change had nourished new patterns in adult marriage and youthful behavior.

The new social norms for middle-class youth allowed a certain amount of sexual gratification and experimentation before marriage without fundamentally challenging that institution. Despite some radicals' desires to see monogamous matrimony abolished, greater premarital sexual freedom aimed at preparing—practicing, even—for a successful, satisfying marriage. Premarital sexual activity was not the same as unbridled carnality. Although the youth culture accepted a greater degree of personal indulgence, it nevertheless hedged in sexual behavior with a wide range of prescriptions, including who was and was not acceptable as a date, what counted as a "date," and for girls, especially, what separated "romantic" and therefore "legitimate" sexual exploration from intercourse and simple promiscuity.[63] "There were no decisions to make," recalled Marion L. Weil, who was a teenager in the late 1920s, "—it was a great big deal and nice girls didn't— simple as that."[64] According to the new sexual norms, the changes that so many observers saw as harbingers of anarchy were, rather, codified adjustments to the realities of twentieth-century life.

Even when they accepted that American youth were not bent on recreating Sodom and Gomorrah, experts concerned about adolescent development were reluctant to accept a social code that granted young people the right to premarital sexual experimentation. The common basis of adult behavior and youthful misbehavior therefore presented sex educators and other social reformers with a problem. How could they reconcile what they considered to be society's new and generally laudable emphasis on sexual fulfillment with their continuing refusal to endorse premarital pleasure seeking? Before the war, sex educators had based their moral lessons for adolescents largely on the argument that chastity was best because everyone agreed that it was so, and in the days when ministers and moralists warned seriously against sexual overindulgence even within marriage, adults could condemn adolescent sexuality with consistency. But now middle-class adult sexual norms seemed to be diverging more strongly from the behavior expected of adolescents and young unmarried people. If reformers wanted to continue defending premarital chastity for young people without seeming hypocritical, they would have to develop a new vocabulary and a new rationale.

Although the direction their search took would seem almost obvious in retrospect, the reformers' actual inquiry was a blind, halting process whose outcome was never clear to the participants. Only after years of false starts and heated debates would they discover their new justification, ironically, in the very language of indulgence and fulfillment that had bedeviled them in the first place. Rather than denounce premarital sexual activity in the same old language, professional sex educators would attempt to incorporate popular postwar sentiments about individual fulfillment, mental health, and "positive" sexuality into their programs. At the most basic level, educators would come to allow adolescents the same desires for sexual fulfillment and companionship that married adults were now expressing, but they would also argue that premarital chastity was the only path to these prizes. The resulting hybrid of indulgence and prohibition turned out to be imaginative but internally inconsistent.

Sex education had to travel a considerable distance to reach this new interpretation. In the prewar period, even as reformers had rehabilitated reproductive sexuality, they had not discarded their Victorian animosity toward indulgence and personal gratification. Rather, they had crafted their arguments for premarital abstinence out of the language of science, responsibility, respect for God's creation, and, of course, a wholesome fear of the known results of sexual indulgence. Even in the context of marriage, the most liberal sex educators had had little to say about fulfillment and individual happiness beyond admonishing listeners to heed their eugenical duty to produce healthy offspring. Although Maurice Bigelow and Thomas Galloway before the First World War had occasionally discussed the "fulfillment of personality," the theme was, at best, a heavily muted note in the sex education symphony.

The prewar insistence on self-denial and moral responsibility—not to mention botany and mammalian reproduction—had come to seem increasingly old-fashioned in the 1920s. To many sexual liberals, ideas that had once been radical now seemed almost quaint. Mary Ware Dennett, Margaret Sanger's ally and sometimes rival in the birth-control movement, dismissed as prudish the kind of sex education literature that ASHA and similar groups had been publishing for years. "In almost none of the books for young people that I have thus far read," she complained, "has there been the frank, unashamed declaration that the climax of sex emotion is an unsurpassed joy."[65] Distressed with the timidity and conservatism of the sex information materials she saw, Dennett in her own privately published sex education pamphlet, *The Sex Side of Life,* actually described for young people human intercourse and the orgasm, and mentioned the existence of birth control, for which she found herself indicted in 1928 under the Comstock Law against obscenity.[66] Dennett explained these matters not because she wanted to shock but because she felt that society's increasing stress on marital fulfillment made it imperative that young people be taught about sexual relations without so much obfuscatory talk of flowers and the lower mammals.[67] Concerned for their own respectability, mainstream sex educators had never entered Dennett's treacherous territory of birth control and sexual pleasure.[68]

The rapidity with which young people after the war were thought to rush into sexual misconduct, however, prompted experts to reevaluate their approach to moral enforcement. At an international social hygiene conference in 1920, Thomas D. Eliot, an assistant professor of sociology at Northwestern University and a field secretary for the American Social Hygiene Association, expressed uneasiness for the future of moral standards.[69] As

Eliot explained, not only were the ideological supports for chastity eroding under pressure from psychoanalytic ideas and female independence, but also the practical justifications for chastity were at risk of becoming obsolete. The birth control movement and the "Mutterschutz" movement (to abolish the stigma of "illegitimate" motherhood and childhood) might remove the reproductive consequences of premarital or extramarital license. The army's wartime success with chemical prophylaxis also demanded attention. "We must not overlook the possibility," warned Bigelow shortly after the war, "that the marvelous progress of sanitary and medical science may some day control the health problems of sex without improving morality."[70] Such a prospect was particularly alarming, concluded Eliot, because "the accepted code of moral prohibitions seems to have little basis in conduct other than fear of results."[71]

Eliot's response to these trends pointed the way for mainstream sex education. He rejected the old-fashioned scientific and moral education as ineffective, and likewise discarded a second option, acquiescing in the flapper's quest for sexual experience, as against the public interest.[72] Instead, Eliot proposed that reformers "foresee, formulate, interpret, absorb, and socialize the new state of affairs," to create "a new code of morals which will not be antisocial."[73]

The sex educator Max Exner demonstrated the ways in which, by the end of the 1920s, many authorities had heeded Eliot's demand. "Petting," wrote Exner in a widely reprinted 1926 pamphlet, "is play at love." "It is mock love," Exner continued, and therefore poor training for a fulfilling marriage.[74] In *The Question of Petting*, Exner did not decry premarital sexual experimentation as immoral and physically debilitating, as an earlier generation might have, but rather condemned petting first because it was not a true "interplay of personalities," and second because it would interfere with one's marriage in the future. Thus Exner granted young people their demand for fulfillment, but he defused the dangers of selfishness and premature sexual activity by explaining the ways in which they endangered marriage and social adjustment.

One of Exner's allies was even more explicit in reconciling sex education with the youth culture's new motivations. "Instead of saying to young people, 'Thou shalt not!'" explained sociologist Hornell Hart in the *Journal of*

*Social Hygiene,* "we are beginning to say something like this: "You are seeking for fulfillment of your personality, for release and integration of your
powers and purposes. You are wondering what sort of sex behavior will
promote these ends . . . We find the evidence piling up that in our civilization the people who engage in premarital and extramarital sexual intercourse run heavy risks of broken friendships, of unforgettable disease, of
social contempt, of disintegrating personalities, and of the loss of the deepest and finest values of the love relationship!" This conclusion, Hart admitted, was "strikingly similar" to St. Paul's admonition against licentiousness,
but the method of reaching it was "totally different, and that difference is
crucial."[75]

Exner and Hart both echoed a widespread conviction that young people
were now motivated less by religious fervor or a sense of responsibility than
by the desire for personal gratification. What else, indeed, had created the
revolution in manners and morals? But rather than condemning this desire
as mere selfishness, as their forebears would have done, Exner and Hart incorporated it into their justifications of premarital abstinence. Man and
woman, they argued, achieved the greatest personal satisfaction only within
marriage; sexual activity outside this relation was but a debased imitation
of the real thing. It was unfulfilling.

The sex educators' new message rested on a novel interpretation of marriage and the family. Spurred on by the increasing rate of divorce in the
United States, especially among the middle and upper classes, sociologists
such as Ernest Groves and Ernest Burgess had begun to investigate with
greater sophistication the role of the family in modern urban life, and their
conclusions not only provided the foundation for the sex educators' new
approach but also helped touch off the flood of marriage manuals that
commenced in the 1920s and has never subsided.[76] In 1927, Groves outlined the sociologists' guiding thesis: "We have traveled a long way from the
biological family," he explained. "Like other institutions, the family has become artificial, and now rests upon a cultural basis rather than upon original instincts or social necessities."[77]

Sociologists proclaimed explicitly that the new cultural basis for the
family was its ability to deliver individual satisfaction. "The challenge that
comes to marriage travels on the level of pleasure and demands the giving

of happiness," observed Groves. "Marriage must accept the testing of modern youth who turn toward it as a means of gratifying individual desires."[78] A philosophy of "pleasure seeking" characterized people's approach to most American institutions, he continued—"How could we expect either marriage or parenthood to keep apart from the prevailing atmosphere?"[79]

Educators and many sociologists attempted to take the sociologists' insight into the modern family a step further: marriage not only existed to gratify desires but also represented the highest possible attainment of those desires. Marriage, argued Roy E. Dickerson, one of a score of popular sex education writers in the 1920s and 1930s, is a "fellowship with the richest of individual and social values."[80] "The underlying truth here," Dickerson noted, "is that mates find in their relationships to each other a mysterious sense of completeness . . . There is a fuller self realization because there is a larger fulfillment of the deeply rooted need of human beings for the love comradeship." In the magazines, if not the schools, authors such as Dickerson could even praise marriage for offering "occasions of extraordinary intimacy which include for husband and wife the distinctive spiritual satisfactions derived from a high degree of atoneness [sic] with each other." In other words, sex.

Locating the deepest human satisfactions in marriage allowed sex educators to accept the new philosophy of pleasure seeking without sacrificing their central assertion that extramarital and premarital sex were forbidden. Indeed, by painting the joys of marriage so brightly, educators could emphasize how drab and poorly realized, in contrast, were the fleeting satisfactions of premarital intercourse. For example, Eleanor Wembridge of the Cleveland Women's Protective Association maintained that images and demonstrations of successful matrimony could give even the lower-class girl—who seemed to Wembridge to lack the discipline for deferred gratification and future achievement—the motivation to "curb her sex instincts." "There is probably no restraint as potent as the fact or the prospect of a happy marriage," noted Wembridge.[81] Although it rested on a basis of personal gratification, marital satisfaction seemed to demand premarital chastity.

Most sex educators went further and taught that premarital experimentation would seriously damage one's future happiness. "Education for marriage," explained Dickerson, "must include giving youth a firm grip upon this psychology of intimacy as a means of safeguarding them from thinking of sex satisfactions entirely in terms of physical thrills and pleasures and from dealing with it accordingly both before and after marriage."[82] Dickerson echoed Exner in arguing that sex education should teach that "practicing the wild-oats theory actually tends to unfit one emotionally for matrimony." Petting did this, first, by creating an "unsound attitude toward the physical side of the relationship which completely distorts one's conception of what marriage is and leads to unsound practices in marriage." Second, Dickerson proposed, petting could blight a youth's appreciation of the "fuller and higher satisfactions" to be found in marriage and instead fix in him a taste for sexual variety that could only be gratified through extramarital affairs.[83] Social scientists and sex educators dutifully gathered evidence to support their prejudices against premarital sexual experimentation.

The new approach comported well with the popularity of "mental hygiene" in the 1920s. Many educators replaced their earlier demands that young people suppress their "animal impulses" with an exaltation of the glories of "sublimating" those urges in positive directions. Similarly, sex educators no longer had to rely on worn-out moral or medical reasoning to condemn masturbation, promiscuity, and other sexual misbehaviors, for psychiatry allowed them to indict those behaviors more relevantly as impediments to mental and emotional "adjustment." Finally, by characterizing successful matrimony as an "interplay of personalities," Exner and others could point out that petting and other promiscuous activities not only lacked this quality of "personality" but also actually threatened to distort a person's future appreciation of it.

Among many middle-class Americans, this focus on meeting the individual's needs no longer seemed to be indulgence or selfishness, but merely common sense. As with all "revolutions" in the 1920s, this shift away from absolute morality had been a long time coming—Sigmund Freud and all he represented exploded in popularity in the 1920s because Americans were more than ready for the mental hygiene message. "Mental health" offered scientific justification for people who had long been inclining more toward concern with individual standards and their own fulfillment than with social duty. Further, mental health offered a new vocabulary—*personality, repression, adjustment,* and other psychiatric terms—that Americans could use to refine and give voice to their new impulses for self-indulgence.

Such arguments spoke directly to a younger generation supposedly motivated by pleasure seeking, in open rebellion against the dictates of Victorianism. But rather than reinforcing hedonism, these arguments supported traditional morality. So, after a short but suitable period of mourning for the old religious sanctions, sex educators were quick to seize on family sociology and mental hygiene as the proper escorts for their surviving moral imperatives.

Despite the similarities between their conclusions and Pauline doctrine, some reformers nevertheless fretted that their new justifications for chastity might carry rather less force than St. Paul's. The promise of individual fulfillment, some reformers feared, was a gelatinous foundation on which to build an ethical code; without a stronger substructure, the moral code seemed likely to follow the disciplines of anthropology, history, and the law in their collapse into relativism. As early as 1920, "Mrs. Grundy" had anticipated the difficulty. "You may get a little way by saying to people, 'This conduct is unsocial.' But you will not get very far unless you can say, 'This conduct is wrong.' For as to what, in personal conduct, is social and unsocial, the theorists will perpetually argue."[84] If proper sexual morality were simply a matter of doing what felt best for the individual, then who could logically oppose promiscuity and even masturbation? If marriage existed to foster interpersonal sharing, then who could oppose easing the restrictions on divorce for marriages that had soured? Freud had already begun openly to doubt whether the old sexual code was worth the trouble it caused—"Especially," he noted wryly, "if we are still so much enslaved to hedonism as to include among the aims of our cultural development a certain amount of satisfaction of individual happiness."[85]

To collapse the distinction between self-indulgence and social responsibility, reformers drew from the mental hygiene concept of "adjustment," or what one sex educator called "the best obtainable moving balance between the individual and his human surroundings."[86] In practical terms, educators intended this "moving balance" to mean that a well-adjusted individual heeded public opinion and conformed to social norms.

Thus, Bigelow and his allies circled right back to their earlier problem of relying on the community's disapproval of sexual misbehavior. In a 1924 article, Bigelow stressed that some of the most important controls of conduct were still "respect for public opinion" and knowledge of "social consequences."[87] Undoubtedly these were powerful forces for a generation being raised to value peer-group acceptance above all else, but they were also unreliable. Bigelow defined public opinion as conservative, middle-class adult opinion, which condemned premarital experimentation and lauded monogamous marriage, and he willfully ignored the evidence that adult values were becoming ambiguous and anyway meant far less to young people than the approval of their peers. As the revolt in manners and morals was showing, parts of youth society had evolved a social code that accepted and even demanded a certain amount of premarital sexual play. Even in the best of Bigelow's cases, where peer-group opinions remained reliably conservative, the emphasis on "social consequences" usually meant that authorities led in the stigmatization of sexually active young women. Now these women were no longer merely immoral but also "socially deviant" and unfit for marriage.

When Alfred C. Kinsey, a respected biological scientist, began to teach his famous marriage course at Indiana University in the late 1930s, he stood aghast at the ways in which sex educators had substituted their middle-class moral prejudices about marriage and sexuality for scientific rigor, as when Hornell Hart had claimed that evidence was "piling up" to prove that premarital sex poisoned a marriage.[88] "Science is not qualified to evaluate or pass moral judgments on behavior," Kinsey argued in 1941. "The sex instruction which is gradually creeping into our science classrooms is animated by a desire to impose particular systems of morality, and as such, does not belong in our science teaching."[89] Kinsey's own work would soon demonstrate that the connection sex educators drew between premarital chastity and connubial bliss was more wishful fantasy than fact.

Yet it was a fantasy that would last for decades, and give shape to several generations' images of premarital morality and marital fulfillment. Even as many American youths graduated from the fox-trot to the lindy hop, and continued petting in ever greater numbers, the new orthodoxy in sex education colored their vision of their own activities, helping to erase some so cial possibilities while highlighting others. Sex educators had tied their efforts to some of the age's dominant cultural trends, and though some of these trends were explicitly inimical to "civilized" sexual morality, the educators nevertheless managed to combine them without ceding the essential attributes of the Victorian moral code.

# CHAPTER FOUR

# Putting Sex in the Schools

> Boystown, Pennsylvania — 1939 — High School — male students were summoned to the lecture hall.
>
> We were then shown a seven- or eight-minute film on gonorrhea and syphilis. On the way out I asked the janitor, "What in the hell was that all about?"
>
> The custodian responded: "Keep your snapper in your pants."
>
> **A. B., Dorset, Vermont (1995)**

As his retirement approached in 1940, Maurice A. Bigelow should have taken great satisfaction in his work over the previous two decades. The "positive" sex education he had fought for since serving on the 1912 Special Committee on the Matter and Methods of Sex Education had become the accepted orthodoxy among sex education leaders and other "elite" reformers. In the nation's teaching colleges and in the magazines and journals of opinion, experts in sex education no longer dwelt on immorality and the venereal diseases but concentrated instead on the "uplifting possibilities" of the sexual impulse, and generally agreed that sex instruction for adolescents belonged in a "broad program of human relations education."[1] Even the more indulgent culture of the 1920s had found accommodation in what Bigelow called "the larger sex education."[2] From his positions at Columbia's Teachers College and in the American Social Hygiene Association, Bigelow had done more than anyone else to shepherd these liberal concepts into the public domain.

Nevertheless, Bigelow recognized that convincing his fellow reformers was not the same as implementing concrete programs. On the contrary, even after three decades of labor, he felt that his positive social hygiene program still suffered from a central misunderstanding. "From the beginning of the social hygiene movement in 1905," Bigelow recounted, "during the Great War, and in the current national health drive, the medical interest in the venereal diseases has been so dominant as to create the popular notion that social hygiene is a euphemism for control of these diseases."[3] Despite years of work by Bigelow and his allies to free sex education from its early associations with syphilis and gonorrhea, sex education programs continued to be forced into the degrading role of servant to venereal disease prevention.[4] At the end of his career, Maurice Bigelow was still searching for a way to emancipate sex education.

Although Bigelow wanted to believe that this unequal relationship between venereal disease education and sex education persisted because of inertia and popular misunderstanding, the reasons went much deeper. Every reform movement suffers from a gulf between the elite level of theory and the actual implementation of its programs, but in sex education the gulf was widened by powerful institutional and cultural forces. The decentralized nature of American education and the rising status of public health ensured that the medical interpretation of sexuality would carry more weight at the local level than educational theorists like Bigelow thought wise. Still, the divide between sex education theory and practice could have been bridged if the only barriers were institutional. More important yet in creating the divide were the cultural differences between the sexual reformers and the American people in general. Despite years of effort by the sex educators, and despite the increase in adolescent sexual activity from the 1920s on, most Americans persisted in viewing adolescent sexuality—when they considered it at all—as an aberration and a moral failure. Local educators tended to share these opinions, and when they taught their adolescent students about sexuality, they turned more readily to the public health perspective and its condemnation of promiscuity. Their message focused on preventing disease and immorality rather than on preparing for sexual maturity. Constructing a bridge between this position and a "larger sex education" was a feat that would eventually overwhelm even the best social engineers.

The troubled relationship between sex education and venereal disease prevention had become painfully obvious during World War I. Before that time, the liberal position associated with Bigelow, Max Exner, the educator and minister Anna Garlin Spencer, and others had been too underdeveloped to challenge the primacy of disease education. By the time the United States entered the Great War, these theorists had developed an approach to sex education that deemphasized venereal disease in favor of the "uplifting possibilities" of sex. However, social hygiene in the World War I era had presented the educators with a quandary: the wartime crusade against syphilis and gonorrhea brought unprecedented funding and acceptance to sex education, but this new support was inextricably tied to sex education's role in fighting venereal diseases. Leading sex educators had hesitated only briefly in making their decision. Heeding the calls of patriotism and the promise of massive public support, sex educators enthusiastically set aside what Exner called "the idealistic emphasis" and entered the service of venereal disease prevention.[5] They were well compensated for their choice: the Chamberlain-Kahn Act gave official government support and hundreds of thousands of dollars to sex education programs, and sex education's newfound respectability promised to attract even more money and adherents to the cause.

Some educators complained about the wartime preoccupation with venereal disease, but even liberals such as Bigelow never denied the necessity of preventing venereal disease; rather, they promised that prevention would follow naturally from their program of teaching biology and morality. The war had brought a difference of emphasis, not of content. Sex education leaders believed, moreover, that this change of emphasis would be merely a temporary wartime shift. When the armistice was signed, most of the leaders in sex education were confident that they could use the momentum of the war to propel their own programs.

Sex educators sought to channel the demands for sex education away from their focus on the venereal diseases for both practical and ideological reasons. Bigelow warned at the end of the war that medical science might someday eliminate the dangers of venereal disease without simultaneously improving moral standards, and a study conducted around the same time determined that "fear"—the method of instruction most favored by venereal disease educators—had actually had little impact on a test group of men reading social hygiene pamphlets.[6] Although a cure for syphilis was still two decades in the future, postwar youth seemed even less likely to be motivated by fear.

These practical considerations against venereal disease education ran parallel to the cultural shift that became apparent after the war. The more indulgent youth culture of the 1920s, with its greater acceptance of sexual experimentation and personal fulfillment, seemed to demand that sex educators set aside the venereal diseases so they could contend with broader ethical and social issues. Indeed, individual youths themselves occasionally demanded guidance from the schools: Northwestern University students complained in 1925 that the "faculty is old and fogeyish, and that sex hygiene is not given sufficient prominence," and their counterparts at Barnard College proposed a revised biology curriculum that would cover such topics as "the facts of structure, functions, development and hygiene of the sex and reproductive apparatus of the male and female," "The nature and power of the sex impulse," "The pathological effects of perverse and unsocial uses of sex in society," and "The facts underlying a satisfactory adjustment in marriage and homemaking."[7] Such demands trickled down from colleges through the high schools, until even groups of junior high school girls in the 1920s were reportedly banding together to request "talks on menstruation—their reproductive organs and explanation of many questions that were puzzling them."[8] These pressures reinforced the leading sex educators' sense of mission and their desire to return to a focus on Bigelow's "larger sex education" encompassing "all scientific, ethical, social, and religious instruction and influence which in any way may help young people prepare to meet the problems of life in relation to sex."[9]

This expansive, progressive conception of sex called for a more expansive method of sex education. The manifold purposes of the sexual instinct—its role in creating and organizing society as well as its central part in fostering personal fulfillment and social adjustment—could not be conveyed solely through a biology course, as educators had formerly proposed, let alone through a handful of "smut lectures." Instead, leaders in the movement for sex education sought to bring their new thinking about sex to the schools through the equally new method of "integrated" sex education.

Like most of the new departures in sex education, the integrated method had first appeared in Maurice Bigelow's landmark 1916 work, *Sex Education*. Now that the period of wartime hibernation was ended, a young biology instructor named Benjamin C. Gruenberg revived these ideas in a work written and widely distributed under the dual auspices of the U.S. Public Health Service and the Bureau of Education.[10] In *High Schools and Sex Education*, Gruenberg followed Bigelow in proposing that a positive sex education program should not be a separate course on sex but must consist of lessons about sexuality integrated *throughout* the public school curriculum, including in courses on biology, physical education, social studies, and literature.

Integrating sex education throughout the curriculum held many attractions. No longer would a single "emergency" course on sex hygiene arouse excessive student interest, nor would one course serve as a lightning rod for community opposition. Instead, teachers in every department in the school would incorporate sexual lessons quietly and unobtrusively. Bigelow and Gruenberg were not mere tacticians, however. They saw that the integrated method's greatest contribution would be its ability to impart ideals as well as knowledge, for sex educators had long held that character was a more potent force than information alone for ensuring moral behavior.

Integration would allow sex educators to educate the "whole child," as the increasingly fashionable language of progressive pedagogy phrased it. At the heart of the integrated course in sex education, students would gain knowledge of sexual organs and functions in the biology course, supplemented by other general science courses or teaching in physiology. But rather than relying on knowledge alone to ensure proper behavior, postwar theorists called for scientific instruction to be joined by less academic training. Physical education classes, for example, were useful for teaching health and personal hygiene, as well as important lessons in socialization. The best physical educator, according to Gruenberg, not only led activities but also inspired high ideals and was admirably fitted to help boys and girls through their most intimate "problems," such as menstruation, seminal emissions, and masturbation. More broadly, civics, or the social studies, could be enlisted to instruct students in "worthy home-membership" and social ethics, by tracing the importance and development of the family through history and by examining the menace that prostitution and venereal diseases posed to civilized communities.

Finally, the school could teach the youth to appreciate higher ideals of love and sex ethics through the proper use of the literature course. Although Gruenberg cautioned against "the temptation to dogmatize and to impose personal or sectarian doctrines" through literature, inspired English teachers were certainly not immune to the same compulsion to indoctrinate that motivated every other sex educator. Louise B. Thompson, an English instructor from Cincinnati, taught classical tragedies for their "abundant opportunity for emphasizing results of wrong ways of living." She also had her tenth-grade students memorize the oath of chivalry taken by Arthur's knights in *Ivanhoe,* and noted that the "eloquent answer" to Robert Burns's dissipated life "is his death at thirty-seven."[11] Another teacher expressed the need to replace the "sensationalistic trash" occupying the leisure time of too many young people with chivalric classics that would not suggest such "morbid and unholy thoughts about marriage and motherhood."[12] "Our aim," proclaimed Thompson, "is to create habits of right thought."[13]

Thompson was perhaps more explicit in her moralism than liberals like Gruenberg and Bigelow, but she was nevertheless in perfect accord with them in seeking to bring all elements of the curriculum to bear on the sexual enlightenment of the child. Educating the whole child to embrace the positive aspects of sexuality, even as he or she delayed expressing them physically, was a complex mission. Educational theorists agreed that only the integrated method of sex education promised to be equal to the task.

The "new" sex education gained a wider hearing by molding its contours closely along the dominant lines of progressive education. In place of an earlier educational concern for mental training, the National Education Association in its *Cardinal Principles of Secondary Education* (1918) had endorsed a new set of seven central goals for education, including the cardinal principles of "health," "worthy home-membership," "citizenship," "worthy use of leisure," and, above all, "ethical character."[14] These were, to be sure, admirably vague standards; their nebulousness allowed a group of Chicago biology teachers, for example, to claim in a 1920 report that their high school biology course fulfilled all seven of the *Cardinal Principles'* goals, including the "citizenship" value of teaching that "flies and mosquitoes, allowed to breed on one's premises, may prove a menace to neighbors," and the "leisure" value of fishing, hunting, bee-keeping, and poultry raising.[15] Associating the cardinal principles with sex education was perhaps less of a stretch. ASHA's Thomas Galloway, in particular, sought to draw close connections between the broader sex education and the *Cardinal Principles'* "education for life."

Galloway and other educators' efforts to affiliate sex education with a powerful progressive education movement eventually bore fruit. Whereas in 1918 interested educators had had to fight to show where sex education belonged in the *Cardinal Principles,* by 1932 the NEA's department of superintendence would devote an entire chapter of its tenth yearbook, *Character Education,* to the importance of sex instruction.[16] Citing the many "sex problems" of "this modern generation," including the new position of women, contraceptives, sex in the media, and "differences of opinion on matters of conduct upon which there was once . . . a practical unanimity," the committee of school superintendents noted that perhaps nothing caused more "human misery" in the United States than did the "maladjustments" that grew directly out of the "failure to achieve the highest values in love, sex, and family life."

To remedy this failure, the superintendents now recommended that educators recognize students' universal desire for sex guidance and social acceptance: "Young people," explained the committee report, "want to be able to make friends easily . . . understand their own feelings . . . understand the conventions of the group," and "are eager to build a love life which is unsurpassed in beauty but they need to learn how this is done."[17] Only a positive, integrated sex education of the sort that Bigelow, Gruenberg, and Galloway had proposed would meet these deep needs.

The NEA's support was gratifying, but between the time of the *Cardinal Principles* and *Character Education,* educators were more pleased with evidence that they were making progress where it really mattered—in the nation's schools. Although discussion about sex education continued to outstrip implementation during the 1920s and beyond, postwar advances in implementation were apparent in the nation's normal schools and university departments of education, where reformers built on the foundation laid by the Chamberlain-Kahn Act during the war. Sex education for normal school students and other teachers in training had always been a less controversial issue, for these students were typically above high school age and therefore less suggestible. Teacher training, however, was no less critical to the new thinking about sex education, for integrated sex education depended heavily on enlightened public schoolteachers.[18] Further, leaders hoped that the availability of capable teachers would cause school board opposition to sex education to melt away. Sex educators were therefore pleased when a survey shortly after the end of the war found that 75 percent of responding normal schools were giving their students some form of sex education, and 92 percent of the normal school principals felt they *should* be offering instruction in this area.[19] Of the schools offering sex instruction, approximately half meant to prepare some graduates to teach some manner of sex education, mostly in biology, while the other half intended sex teaching more for the personal benefit of the normal school student and included in their teaching tally physicians' lectures and "mothercraft" courses on how to rear children.[20] Whatever the normal school's goals, such figures, along with the NEA's renewed support for sex education in teacher training institutions, were encouraging signs.

Sex education's success, however, depended on its acceptance in the public high schools. Although reliable information on the extent to which sex education was taught in the public schools is scarce, the United States Public Health Service sponsored two useful surveys on the status of the subject in 1920 and 1927.[21] Broadly, the two investigations discovered in each year that 40 and 45 percent, respectively, of the responding senior high schools offered their students some form of sex education. Even allowing for the filtering effect of the survey procedure (only 54 percent of all high schools responded to the questionnaire in 1920, 34 percent in 1927, and supporters of sex education may well have been more likely to respond), those percentages translated to approximately 2,500 senior high schools in each year definitely taking action in sex education. Ignoring the likelihood that the nonresponding high schools were far less likely to offer sex education, investigators projected that the actual number might well be double that figure.[22] Before the war, even the lower level of implementation would simply have been inconceivable.

In keeping with the new concern over integrating sex education into the curriculum, Newell Edson, the Public Health Service's primary contributor to the studies, concentrated less on the total number of schools with sex in-

struction than on the relative status of integrated and "emergency" sex
teaching within those schools. Including in his definition of "emergency"
teaching any approach from outside lectures by physicians, nurses, and
ministers to exhibitions of the Public Health Service's "Keeping Fit" poster
series, Edson found that emergency sex education was offered in 25 percent
of schools in 1920 and 16 percent in 1927. The decline cheered Edson and
his 1927 collaborator, Lida J. Usilton, for they believed it was the result of
schools' moving to an integrated sex education program.[23] Whether or not
this was true, the percentage of responding schools reporting the integrated
method did increase from 15 to 29 percent, which meant an increase in absolute numbers from 1,005 to 1,665 schools. Efforts to popularize the integrated approach seemed to be working.

Integrated sex education did not appear with uniform regularity
throughout the curriculum, but the courses that did include sex managed
to touch on major issues in the larger sex education.[24] First in the frequency
with which they treated sexual themes were the biology courses, which were
twice as likely to examine sexual matters as the second-ranked subject, social studies. Fully a quarter of respondent schools with biology classes enlisted them to teach something about the integrated program's most common subjects, eugenics and reproduction. As important as biology in their
treatment of venereal disease, menstruation, and seminal emissions were
all of the courses in physiology, physical education, and hygiene taken
together, especially when the classes were sex-segregated. Social studies
classes were naturally most valuable for their treatment of the "social aspects" of sex, which in 1920 signified prostitution and venereal disease, but
which had broadened by 1927 to include "the value of monogamy, guidance of emotions and impulses, sex attraction," and "boy-girl relationships," among other weighty subjects.[25] Fourteen percent of all social studies courses dealt at some point in the school year with these and other
aspects of sexual relations. Such figures cheered the proponents of integrated sex education.

The total statistics give a clearer picture of sex education's content. Of
1,665 schools Usilton and Edson found teaching integrated sex education
in 1927, 1,306 taught something about "eugenics and heredity," 1,154
about reproduction, 850 about "social aspects" of sexuality, 571 about ve-

nereal diseases, and approximately 420 about "internal secretions" and menstruation. Finally, 171 schools claimed to include material on seminal emissions in one course or another.[26]

Some investigators perceived gaps in the integrated approach. Fewer than 4 percent of courses on general science and home economics touched on sex. Schools were underutilizing these offerings, maintained Edson and Usilton, for such courses were usually given in the first year of high school, "which is the most propitious time for clearing the confusion and dispelling the distorted ideas of youth."[27] And though the researchers followed the educational path laid out by Bigelow and Gruenberg, they unfortunately did not seek information on the extent to which sex education was taught in the English classrooms. In general, sex was appearing far more often in the regular curriculum, but its surfacings were as sporadic as one would expect for a subject whose implementation was largely informal and uncoordinated.

The prevalence of integrated teaching depended to some extent on the size of the school, the authors found. Large schools, with enrollments of more than five hundred students, were more likely to offer sex education in the first place, and their lessons on sex were significantly more likely to be integrated into the curriculum.[28] "Larger schools," Edson and Usilton postulated, "probably have more teachers among whom can be found those of the personality and skill to do such work well," but an equally valid explanation was simply that larger schools were more likely to have a differentiated curriculum. A large, urban high school was more capable than a one-room, rural school of offering biology, physical education, and the other "modern" electives that so often served as vehicles for integrated sex education. And though the authors did not explore the subject, their figures also suggested a gap in the implementation of sex education between urban and rural schools, for small schools with low levels of sex education were more characteristic of sparsely settled farming districts, while populous facilities tended to serve cities or large suburbs.

Educators appeared unconcerned with the discrepancy, however, as they had always felt urban youths needed sex education more than their rural counterparts. In this respect, the reformers' invocation of the dangers of the city was not simply a metaphorical expression of social dislocation or nativism but a recognition that city dwellers might lack sexual knowledge in a way that rural youth, reared among openly copulating farm animals, did not. Progressive educators suspected, in any event, that the future of secondary education lay with the large, differentiated schools and not with their underdeveloped rural counterparts.

"Integrated sex education in the high school," concluded Edson and Usilton in 1927, "has shown a healthy growth in every part of the United States since 1920."[29] Many sex educators surpassed the authors in a premature declaration of victory. By moving away from the "pathological and the perverse," asserted Max Exner in 1929, "sex education has made rapid strides toward its appropriate place in education and character training."[30] Similarly, by the late 1930s Benjamin Gruenberg confidently identified a "general disposition" of the times to accept that the secondary schools must take over "progressively new functions" such as sex education.[31]

Despite this confidence, the implementation of sex education in the 1920s and '30s was only partially successful. A gradual waning of support after the Great War implied that sex educators had failed to some extent in transferring the momentum of the anti–venereal disease crusade to their own program. Attempts to measure the amount of teaching, for example, demonstrated a decline in interest and support. The response to Edson and Usilton's second survey bespoke an erosion of interest in the topic of sex education: in 1920, 54 percent of all principals had found the governmental questionnaire important enough to answer; the 1927 survey elicited replies from only 34 percent of the high schools, and the absolute number of replies declined by 700 even though 5,000 more high schools had come into existence.[32]

A more tangible sign of fading support by the end of the decade was the U.S. Public Health Service's withdrawal from sex education.[33] The service had contributed greatly by funding surveys and publications such as those by Edson and Gruenberg, and had lent much support and prestige to ASHA and other organizations in the movement. With the emergency of the war receding into distant memory, Congress no longer felt the need to appropriate funds for the Health Service's more controversial projects. The Depression, looming on the horizon, would cut away what meager financial support remained for the sex education movement. Contrary to Exner's belief, sex education was no longer making "rapid strides."

The erosion of federal support laid bare the significant differences among state approaches to sex education. Edson and Usilton found 85 percent of the high schools in Utah claimed to offer sex information either in the state-mandated biology course or in the popular high school physiology course, while only 15 percent of Massachusetts public high schools reported any activity at all in sex education.[34] Broadly, states in the West tended to favor sex education more than anywhere else, and the South was generally below even New England in discountenancing the innovation. Even within these figures, the decentralized structure of American secondary education meant that sex education for any given school was more or less dependent on local conditions.[35] Rather than a national consensus on the necessity of sex education, inspired individuals and strong local social hygiene societies were the driving forces behind sex education.

With the decline of the nineteenth-century evangelical approach to social reform, most reform movements in the twentieth century have seen their ultimate goal as not just the inspiration of individual activists but the permanent implementation of their programs. Activists have desired to transfer responsibility from individuals onto less transient bodies, such as professional bureaucracies, government agencies, the Constitution, or even the public schools. Thus embedded in a stable environment, a reform could perpetuate itself without proponents' constantly needing to arouse public sentiment and constantly worrying that the movement would go to the grave with them. This longing for permanence animated the reformers' campaign to place sex education in the public schools, but they proved unable to make the educational program self-perpetuating.

Weaknesses in sex education's implementation arose, ironically, not so much from direct public opposition as from the ways in which integrated sex education allowed teachers to convey the public's indifference or hostility toward the course. The integrated program that educators had conceived in part to avoid community censure was ultimately too obscure, uncoordinated, and diffuse to ensure its own survival.[36]

Integrated sex education had a paradoxical effect on sex education's acceptance in the schools. The integrated approach generally avoided arousing public antagonism of the sort the "Chicago experiment" had met in 1913, for teachers blended sexual content into their courses without notifying the school board or the community beforehand that this innovation was taking place.[37] But the secretive approach to curriculum change did little to build community sentiment in *favor* of sex education. Thus, sex educators missed a chance to educate parents and the local public about the purposes and methods of integrated education. In the absence of aroused public support, or even public knowledge, the decision to implement sex education was left to individual teachers.

This delegation of authority to the teacher turned out to be less wise than sex educators expected. In a *Pedagogical Seminary* article in 1921, Henry S. Curtis, an educator from Ohio, foresaw that depending solely on random teachers would be a fundamental error for integrated sex education: "Sex," he maintained, "is always avoided by those who deal with it incidentally."[38] While Curtis supported the general approach of integrated education, he also recommended that high schools hire a "supervisor of sex instruction" to coordinate the undertaking and to ensure teacher participation, for the supervisor, unlike a general biology teacher or a social studies instructor, would have an occupational interest in perpetuating the program. The supervisor might even teach a separate, supplementary social hygiene course as a regular part of the curriculum. Educational theorists, however, were wedded to the integrated idea and rejected Curtis's proposal, even though survey results throughout the decade would justify his concern that this system relied too heavily on teacher initiative. Teacher support was at best a sporadic and transient force.

Indeed, without a designated teacher occupationally responsible for sex education, several factors militated against teacher involvement. Teachers who integrated sex education into their course work took time away from other course subjects, and they received few external rewards for teaching material that was potentially uncomfortable and embarrassing. Moreover, these teachers risked being fired for including a subject that was not even central to their discipline. Integrated sex education had little besides altruistic satisfaction to recommend itself to the ordinary teacher; the relative scarcity of integrated sex education testified to the insufficiency of such motivations.[39]

Even where schools claimed to be teaching integrated sex education, the actual content of the courses depended primarily on the multifarious preferences of different teachers. Although leading sex educators were working hard to standardize materials and promulgate guidelines for teaching, implementation of their work was far from coordinated. One of the objections to "emergency" sex education was that it encompassed an overly wide range of activities, including anything from one lecture per week to one lecture per year. Sometimes it would consist simply of displaying the Public Health Service's "Keeping Fit" posters, with their obscurantist invocations of manly vigor and spermatic parsimony.[40] But integrated sex education gave no more guarantee of completeness. Usilton and Edson's 1927 survey found that fewer than a quarter of schools claiming integrated sex education taught about menstruation and internal secretions, and only 10 percent claimed to say anything about seminal emissions.[41] Fewer than half of the integrated schools touched on venereal disease, and though most of the institutions gave lessons about reproduction, chiefly in biology classes, Usilton and Edson were ambiguous about whether these lessons ever involved *human* reproduction. Indeed, the relative prominence of "eugenics and heredity" and "social aspects" in the integrated curriculum suggested that teachers tended to shy away from the more overtly sexual and embarrassing subjects in favor of topics less obviously carnal.

Ordinary teachers simply did not share the sentiments of the leading sex educators or their allies in the mental hygiene movement. They seemed slow or unwilling to take in what Bigelow called the "larger view of sex education." Toward the end of the 1930s, for example, one sex educator was still complaining that "sex rarely comes up as an issue in school other than as a problem."[42] Reasons for this had been suggested by a 1928 Commonwealth Fund study comparing the attitudes toward student misbehavior of 511 classroom teachers with a sample of mental hygienists and "students of character at Teachers College."[43] Setting the standard for the study, mental hygienists were most concerned about student unsociability, suspiciousness, depression, and resentfulness—the classic characteristics of "maladjustment" in the mental health canon. In contrast, classroom teachers rated "heterosexual activity" the most serious of all student behavioral problems, followed closely by stealing, masturbation, and "obscene notes and pictures." Truancy, the teachers' next most serious offense, was a distant fifth, followed by forty-five other misbehaviors.

The classroom teachers clearly found sexual activities to be the most serious problems, for these activities, according to the study's unsympathetic author, attacked the teachers' "moral sensitivities." Many teachers' deep discomfort with sexuality, evinced by the Commonwealth study, makes the shallowness of integrated sex education more understandable and sheds light as well on otherwise bizarre incidents, as when a superintendent of schools in one city attempted to halt masturbation among the boy pupils by ordering their trouser pockets to be sewn up.[44] Although the integrated approach depended on teachers who accepted sex as a potentially positive force in adolescent development, this attitude had not yet penetrated far into the pedagogical mind. No wonder, then, that Benjamin Gruenberg called for teachers to engage in a "severe and persistent effort" to overcome "the repressions and inhibitions and misunderstandings that are our portion for having spent our youth during a certain transitional period of society."[45] The teacher's reluctance and alleged "prudery" continued to stand in the way of integrated sex education.

The teachers' reluctance was understandable. Teachers in the public schools were no different from the students' parents or the general public. They shared the public's "repressions" and prejudices, and passed these on in the classroom. Moreover, teachers in any field tended (and perhaps still tend) to resist novelty. "The fact is that teachers, instead of being innovators, are often extreme conservatives with regard to the curriculum," explained Charles H. Judd of the University of Chicago, in his influential report to the President's Research Committee on Social Trends. "It is far easier for a teacher to administer without variation a course in which he or she has been trained than to respond to social demand for a new course. It therefore happens in many cases that the social influences have to become vigorously articulate before teachers will yield and reconstruct the curriculum."[46] Ironically, by attempting to sneak integrated sex education into the school without a public fight, its proponents forfeited even the chance to build what Judd called "articulate social influences" in favor of the new teaching. By not developing such outside pressure, sex education leaders allowed pedagogical inertia to drag tenaciously on their integrated program.

Public support and institutional strength did exist, however, for a certain kind of sex education. The "emergency" sex education that Bigelow and his allies had left behind in theory survived in practice. Although their funding, too, was drying up as the First World War receded into memory, state and local public health boards were often the only authorities with the money and motivation to initiate sex education programs. Transcending local school districts, and representing institutional persistence and a bureaucratic sense of mission, public health agencies were the critical agents in every large-scale sex education program during the 1920s and 1930s. Despite years of work by Bigelow and his allies to free sex education from its early associations with syphilis and gonorrhea, sex education programs would continue to be forced to serve the needs of disease prevention. The threat of venereal disease, not the potential for sexual fulfillment, remained the engine driving most sex education initiatives after the war.

Public health bureaucracies in individual states typically remained preoccupied with disease prevention as they overrode local indifference and opposition to sex education. Statewide programs for high schools in Kansas and North Carolina, for example, were creations of public health authorities who sought to warn youths against venereal disease and sexual vice, and Alabama's director of venereal disease control in the State Department of Health, W. C. Blasingame, appeared throughout the 1920s to be the sole mover behind sex education in that state.[47] Reminiscent of an older educational orthodoxy, Blasingame's program called for physician-lecturers to deliver a delicate hygiene lesson to mixed assemblies at every high school in the state before the speakers split up the audience to give male students a "heart-to-heart talk" about continence, the "effects of dissipation," and the "prevalence and seriousness of the venereal diseases."[48] Female students remained a mystery to Blasingame: "We have never learned just what should be taught to young girls," he confessed.[49]

Occasional weaknesses in execution did not diminish the public health bureaucracy's commitment. "Although there is an evident tendency everywhere to regard sex education as a part of the larger field of character education, and therefore its development as a task for educators rather than health officers," wrote Surgeon General Hugh S. Cumming in 1926, "the Public Health Service and the state boards of health continue to regard this work of sufficient relevancy to venereal disease control to justify certain projects."[50] Cumming accepted in theory that sex education should someday become the exclusive concern of educational authorities. "But in the meantime," he noted, "the health agencies must continue to stress certain facts which have a hygienic as well as a conduct aspect."[51]

Only rarely did the competing interpretations of sex education coexist. Sex education for the African American community in the South was one of the few instances in which the program evolved from a focus on disease to a broader concern for human relations. Partly because of inflated statistics on the prevalence of venereal disease among African American troops during the war, ASHA and the Public Health Service began directing special educational efforts toward the black community in the 1920s.[52] Franklin O. Nichols, an African American social worker, led ASHA's program to many successes in the black colleges and normal schools of the South: Howard University, Tuskegee, Hampton Institute, and other institutions in Virginia, North Carolina, and Georgia hosted many more physician's talks and summer-school courses than did white schools. To reach the vast majority of African Americans who did not attend college, state boards of health, like that in North Carolina, sent out social hygiene field cars to show educational films even in the most remote communities. In 1921 the U.S. Public Health Service estimated that these efforts had carried the social hygiene message to more than half a million African Americans.[53]

In this work, black leaders such as Nichols were motivated not solely by health concerns but also by their desire to improve the African American's personal character and public reputation through inculcating more "respectable" middle-class standards of sexual behavior.[54] These concerns allowed black social hygienists to advance past the venereal disease campaigns and take the lead in offering courses on marriage and the family—Max Exner asserted in 1929 that Negro colleges and normal schools had for the previous five years been at the forefront of activity in "sex-character education."[55] Thus, sex education for African Americans showed the capacity to evolve over time, but the motivations behind this evolution were perhaps unique to the black community, and support for the innovative programs was still buttressed by public health concerns.

Any attempts to extend sex-character education to more white students soon ran into the Great Depression. The financial crash hit volunteer groups like ASHA hard—its national budget by 1936 had fallen to a pre–World War I level of $100,000.[56] At this point, ASHA was virtually the only national organization supporting an integrated, positive sex education program, and the loss of funds largely stilled its institutional voice.

This silencing, however, did not disturb Franklin Roosevelt's surgeon general, Thomas Parran. A public health physician appointed in 1936, Parran had long been upset with what he felt was ASHA's timidity and excessive moralism. Shortly after his appointment, therefore, Parran bypassed the older social hygiene organization and called for medical experts in public health to commence a new crusade against syphilis that would frankly confront the disease as a medical matter and not a moral failure. Further circumventing ASHA and the sex educators allied with it, Parran proposed a renewed commitment to making sex education a part of this antisyphilis crusade.[57]

Parran soon squeezed enough money from Congress to implement his plans. Through a provision in the Social Security Act and the 1938 National Venereal Disease Control Act, Parran's Public Health Service funneled millions of dollars to state boards of health to aid in syphilis prevention. Disbursed by a physician who found moralizing and "delicacy" to be causes of, rather than solutions to, the venereal disease problem, these funds did not trickle down to the few integrated sex education programs that had survived the first years of the Depression. As one sympathetic social hygienist noted, "Not a few physicians want no dilution of their science and art of medicine with any admixture of what they term sentiment and morals."[58] With Parran's backing, and with the renewed vigor of many state boards of health and local social hygiene societies, emergency venereal disease instruction programs proliferated across the nation.

With such inspiration, the fight against syphilis was vigorous. A number of public health physicians successfully lobbied their state legislature to pass laws mandating venereal disease education for high school students, and elsewhere state boards of health sent out traveling lecturers to all the schools.[59] Complaining of the Parent-Teacher Association's long-standing pusillanimity regarding sex education, the Wisconsin State Board of Health, for example, sponsored one male and one female social hygiene lecturer to instruct, "without blush or guffaw," their respective sexes at a series of high schools.[60] Nor was ASHA immune to the influence of Public Health Service funding and national concern over syphilis: despite a nod toward training for marriage and repressing prostitution, the association from 1937 onward threw the vast majority of its resources onto the medical side of social hygiene.[61]

This reallocation of resources, and Parran's educational crusade against venereal disease in general, did not sit well with mainstream sex educators, who found themselves and their programs shunted aside in favor of the surgeon general's campaign. According to Bigelow, this was the same old story. "From the beginning of the social hygiene movement in 1905," Bigelow recounted, "during the Great War, and in the current national health drive, the medical interest in the venereal diseases has been so dominant as to create the popular notion that social hygiene is a euphemism for control of these diseases." Bigelow felt that Parran's venereal disease fight was a much more specialized task than school sex education.[62] The time had come to proclaim that the two were logically and factually quite separate.

At the same time, Bigelow was optimistic—perhaps overoptimistic— that parents and educators had come to support "a broad program of human relations education which will give sex its logical place." "Many of these persons," he added, "see no basis for such a needed program in social hygiene, which to many intelligent citizens has become a 'euphemism for control of venereal diseases." Considered in this light, Bigelow concluded, "Venereal disease education and sex education should be separated, except for some cross references as in the 'sex-character' aspect of sex education."[63] In thus condemning a 1940 joint report on venereal disease education produced by ASHA and the Public Health Service, Bigelow attempted once again to sever a bond that had been forged by powerful institutional and cultural forces.

Just as Thomas Parran failed to disentangle his "scientific" health crusade from what one historian has called the "stereotyping moralism of syphiliphobia," so Bigelow was unable to liberate sex education from its dependence on medicine.[64] Indeed, evidence suggested that the average high school teacher, through whom any sex education had to pass, continued to conflate medicine and morality in a manner that deeply dismayed proponents of each. Rank-and-file teachers maintained their belief in the face of strenuous efforts by sex education leaders to disentangle the two concepts.

Although leaders in sex education tried to accentuate the "positive" aspects of sexuality, especially marital sexuality, actual teachers in the class-room proved unwilling to accept adolescent sexual impulses as romantic or even validly sexual. Rather, they echoed the parents in their community in treating premarital sexual activity as a medical problem removed from the emotional realm but still, somehow, susceptible to moral condemnation. Little common ground appeared to lie between such a position and the "larger sex education." Just as the NEA's committee on character education had lamented in 1932, sex education in the schools remained "generally limited to occasional cruel discipline of a victim of poor education."[65] As happens so often in social reform, the leaders' intentions and the actual re-sults of their programs turned out to be little more than passing acquain-tances.

# CHAPTER FIVE

# Domesticating Sex

> Young people report, as a result of this course, less inclination toward promiscuous petting, a greater love for children, better habits of money management, . . . and a better understanding of the problems which generally arise in marriages of mixed religions.
>
> **A high school principal in Michigan**
> **on family life education (1958)**

If the 1930s had been inhospitable to what Maurice A. Bigelow called the "larger sex education," then World War II seemed unlikely at the outset to offer any greater welcome. Bigelow and his allies expected that the "current emergency" of war would only intensify the social hygiene movement's shift toward a medical mission at the expense of its broader social aims.[1] For a while their predictions would prove correct, as social hygienists threw themselves into the central task of preventing venereal diseases among American soldiers by any means necessary. But the social disruptions of wartime—promiscuity and delinquency among civilians, and hundreds of thousands of splintering families—also began to compete for Americans' attention. Improbably, the events of World War II would eventually free sex education, however temporarily, from the demands of venereal disease prevention and push sex educators and social hygienists toward the fulfillment of Bigelow's most fervent hopes.

Such a shift toward the larger sex education was not immediately apparent in the military. When the United States entered World War II, military authorities discarded their moralistic concern for soldiers' sexual behavior even faster than they had during World War I. Military authorities made clear that their troops would be governed by a unique set of moral rules.

"The men in a successfully trained army or navy are . . . taught in a harsh and brutal school," wrote Captain Joel T. Boone, of the Navy Medical Corps, in 1941. "They cannot, they must not, be mollycoddled, and this very education befits nature, induces sexual aggression, and makes them the stern, dynamic type we associate with men of an armed force . . . Imagine, if you can, an army of impotent men."[2] Boone's phrasing was uncommonly pungent, but he echoed the general sentiment among military men that genteel standards of morality did not apply to soldiers during wartime. Their acceptance of "sexual aggression," however, did not mean the officers also accepted the syphilis and gonorrhea that might come with the men's search for sexual relief. On the contrary, another Navy physician, Leo A. Shifrin, emphasized that the armed forces were fighting "a war of survival against two common enemies, the Axis and venereal diseases."[3] In this struggle, military efficiency by any means was paramount, and the resulting program contrasted strongly with the moralistic approach that was common in the civilian world.

The venereal disease control program in the armed forces did include elements from mainstream sex education, including the practice of substituting "socially redeeming" activities for more degraded leisure-time pursuits. "Good times in good company" became the Army's "positive" social hygiene message, and along with the military's attempt to provide "wholesome recreational activities" akin to what the Commission on Training Camp Activities had provided in the First World War, this approach probably played some role in limiting the spread of venereal disease through the ranks.[4] At any rate, movies, table tennis, and chaperoned dances helped to dispel the crushing boredom of camp life.

But the military achieved its greatest success with a sex education program that differed in certain essential ways from what social hygienists were teaching in the high schools and colleges. To disabuse the men of ignorance about venereal diseases, medical officers exhibited posters, distributed social hygiene pamphlets, and screened a series of memorably explicit training films, including *Sex Hygiene, Know for Sure,* and *Tactics for Male Hygiene.*[5] Physicians also traveled from barracks to barracks to deliver equally frank lectures on syphilis and gonorrhea. Soldiers during World War II and in later generations summed up the message of these talks as "KPIP": keep

pecker in pocket. Flying in the face of twenty years of sex education orthodoxy, the written materials and lecturing physicians did not stress the importance of morality or personal character development but rather relied
heavily on creating a fear of venereal infection.

Fear was an effective theme in the military as it seldom had been for civilians, because the armed forces backed it up by making effective prophylaxis available. "In our experience," wrote two physicians in the Army Medical Corps, "fear operates less as a deterrent to promiscuous sex exposure
than it does as a motive for inducing the individual to take prophylaxis."
While almost 40 percent of enlisted men in one survey claimed to have become "more continent" as a result of their venereal disease lectures, more
than 70 percent also claimed the lectures' primary effect had been to convince them to become "more careful in the consistent use of prophylaxis."[6]
Continence was no longer the sole aim of the "smut talks."

The military tried as well to make prophylaxis more convenient than it
had been in World War I. "We must understand," Commander Shifrin explained, "that we cannot ask these men to go on their liberties with bottles
of argyrol and permanganate solution, urethral syringes, and other medica-
tion bulging from their pocketless Navy trousers." Rather than such un-
wieldy means, Shifrin continued, "the use of the condom, which is sold at
all Naval establishments at a very reasonable price, is impressed upon all of
them." Kits of three condoms, sold for ten cents at commissaries or distributed for free by units, became so popular that one historian estimates
soldiers picked up 50 million condoms per month during the war. After an
initial upward spike in the early days of the war, the army's rate for contracting venereal diseases eventually fell to more or less the civilian rate.[7]
By accepting what many considered to be immoral behavior, the army
achieved great success in its program to enhance the health and efficiency
of the troops.

While many found sexual aggressiveness in soldiers during wartime to
be acceptable—even desirable—such promiscuity among civilian women
caused nothing but alarm and moralistic censure. The war seemed to have a
direct impact on female sexual activity. Authority after authority came forward to lament the "girl problem," or the propensity of young women—
particularly those working in war-related industries—to throw themselves

patriotically at soldiers and sailors.[8] Social hygienists initially had difficulty distinguishing such behavior from prostitution but eventually came to realize that, in the vast majority of cases, the women never asked for or received money.[9] This realization did not, however, lessen the opprobrium they heaped on the promiscuous girl. On the contrary, investigators found casual promiscuity to be in many ways more alarming than prostitution. Prostitution they could at least understand as an economic exchange, but this new trend in sexual behavior portended a more thorough breakdown in feminine social standards.

The official response was stern. Proving that the wartime toleration of promiscuity hewed closely to the double standard, authorities carried on a vitriolic publicity campaign against "loose women" and backed their rhetoric up with action. In the communities around domestic army bases, the government's Division of Social Protection, under the former gangster-hunter Eliot Ness, came down with a heavy hand on prostitutes and other suspected carriers of venereal diseases, including unescorted women and girls out after curfew. Police forces in dozens of communities stepped up their investigations of commercial and amateur "vice," and redoubled their efforts to corral "delinquents."

At the same time as local authorities and military officials brought the full weight of the law down on promiscuous women, educators and social scientists were beginning to argue that individual youths were perhaps not entirely to blame for their delinquency; echoing Bigelow from before the war, some observers noted that the family strongly influenced sexual behavior. Perhaps, suggested Evelyn Millis Duvall, a sympathetic educator, the high rates of youthful promiscuity and delinquency they saw were consequences of the war's impact on the family and deserved to be treated as such. Duvall listed just a few of the conditions she saw behind the disintegration of the family during wartime: the "separation of family members, bereavement and soul-shaking anxieties, working mothers, shifts in discipline, hurried romances and hasty marriages, war babies, new moral codes and the myriad of other characteristics of war-torn families." "The conditions of this war," explained an ASHA pamphlet in 1944, "are causing the breakdown of family groups far beyond anything that was known previously, and it must be expected that . . . the conditions leading to delinquency, promiscuity and venereal disease will increase proportionately."[10] Concerns about the health of the family were further amplified by the wartime surge in the divorce rate—including a 1945–46 spike that would not be equalled until the 1970s.

The disordered state of youth and the family took on an added meaning against the backdrop of European dictatorship. Led by Lawrence K. Frank, a committed social democrat who had an enormous influence on psychological research in America from his positions at the Laura Spelman Rockefeller Memorial and other endowments, a group of psychologists, sociologists, and educators began to argue during the war that German aggression could be linked directly to Teutonic habits of child rearing. "Baffling social problems," explained the American Association of School Administrators (AASA) in a 1941 report heavily influenced by Frank, "are the large-scale expression in human conduct of what children have learned during the process of acquiring the socially sanctioned ways of living."[11] In Germany and Italy, American psychologists concluded, the parents' method of breaking the child's will to ensure shame and obedience had predisposed millions of youths to sacrifice themselves on an altar of dictatorship. Already, the prevalence of youthful misbehavior in America suggested that many youths at home were similarly aimless and malleable. If Americans would avoid a similar fate, the AASA warned at the dawn of the war, "The family as a cultural agent needs to be guided and reassured as never before." These connections suggested that social hygiene should widen its scope.

The support that existed for a broader sex education and social hygiene movement, however, was not yet sufficient to draw ASHA and its allies away from their wartime preoccupation with promiscuity and venereal disease. Several leaders in sex education surely felt a pull toward the problems of the family, but sex educators and social hygienists in general had always done best for themselves when they kept their social concerns inextricably bound up with their medical mission. Syphilis and gonorrhea represented a more tangible danger than did poor child rearing. As the war continued, however, a singular medical discovery threatened finally to break the connection between venereal disease and promiscuity.

Midway through World War II, scientists discovered that penicillin was a convenient and effective treatment for syphilis and gonorrhea.[12] Government researchers accelerated their research on and production of various strains of penicillin, and by the end of the war many public health officials proclaimed proudly that the venereal diseases were destined to go the way of tuberculosis and yellow fever. The wartime successes with penicillin and with massive distributions of condoms seemed to offer the victory over venereal disease that social hygienists had dreamed of since early in the century. That victory, however, also threatened to strip the social hygiene movement of its ostensible purpose.

Conservative ASHA social hygienists viewed the new therapeutics with a trepidation that went beyond mere caution. Of the condom, they simply said no more: a military necessity during the war, the condom was too closely associated with birth control for ASHA to come out in favor of civilian use. Both Catholic opposition and their own discomfort with the sexual freedom suggested by the condom prevented the association's leaders from supporting this fairly basic mechanism for public health.

Social hygienists likewise evaluated penicillin with extreme caution. Dr. C. Walter Clarke, who had been pivotal in the professionalization of social hygiene in the years from 1910 to 1930, allowed that the discovery of antibiotics was indeed "one of the greatest advances of our time," but he also questioned frankly whether these drugs would solve the problems of syphilis and gonorrhea or make controlling them still more difficult. He cautioned that the new therapeutics would lead to what public health officers eventually referred to as "revolving-door infections." "Under penicillin treatment a person can be cured of gonorrhea and get a new infection, all in the period of one week," Clarke explained. "As a matter of fact, case records in rapid treatment centers and clinics abundantly show that many patients are infected, cured and infected over and over again." To Clarke, medical technology's fundamental weakness was obvious: "Neither penicillin nor any other therapeutic substance offers a solution to the problems of conduct which spread these diseases."[13]

*The problems of conduct which spread these diseases:* here indeed was the basis of ASHA's reluctance to embrace penicillin. Starting with Dr. Prince Morrow at the dawn of the century, social hygienists had typically viewed syphilis and gonorrhea less as discrete disease entities than as metaphors for social breakdown: sexual emancipation, widespread license, a revolt among youth.[14] The social hygiene movement's early vigor had depended equally on its medical and moral missions. Now, just as Thomas Eliot and Maurice Bigelow had predicted during World War I, a medical advance threatened finally to eliminate the metaphor—and with it the fear of venereal disease that had served for so long to buttress sexual morality.

Dr. John Stokes spoke for Clarke and many others when he complained that effective medical treatment for venereal disease "may inaugurate a world of accepted, universalized safeguarded promiscuity."[15] Stokes apparently did not perceive the irony in a public health officer's complaint that antibiotics might indeed protect the public health. His interpretation demonstrated the extent to which the public health establishment had come to concern itself not simply with health and disease but also with proper sexual behavior.

Penicillin seemed to strike at the social hygiene movement's very reason for existence. With the loss, however temporary, of venereal disease as an effective metaphor for social disintegration, public health authorities in ASHA and related organizations questioned what their future role should be. In the absence of a physical health threat, could they or should they focus directly on sexual and social disorder?

Not surprisingly, ASHA's leaders soon concluded that social hygiene and sex education still had critical roles to play, regardless of penicillin's impact. Dr. William F. Snow unveiled one part of ASHA's new position at the National Conference on Postwar Venereal Disease Control, held in St. Louis in late 1944. Snow, an association stalwart, proposed that social hygienists and sex educators should thenceforth concentrate more squarely on safeguarding the American family. Such a shift in emphasis, Snow explained, was merely an extension of what public health activists were already doing. "Syphilis and gonorrhea and the promiscuous sex habits which spread these diseases are a grave threat to the family as an institution as well as to the public health," he noted. Conversely, Snow also argued that the diseases were themselves evidence of deeper trouble among American families. Venereal diseases, Snow said, were "symptoms" of preexisting family breakdown, "suggesting poor sexual behavior, marital maladjustments, psychiatric problems, and in many instances, substandard or abnormal environmental conditions for families and children."[16] A responsible public health organization would have to strike at the causes, as well as the symptoms, of venereal disease and promiscuity.

Snow's call for a new focus on promiscuity and maladjusted families was clearly a strategic move. By expanding his definition of "public health" beyond the boundaries of physical health to include mental and social well-being, Snow sought a role for sex education and social hygiene that could not be performed by a dose of penicillin. Sex educators could broaden their alliances beyond the public health profession to include home economists, marriage counselors, psychologists, and others in the helping professions.

ASHA thus joined with a growing chorus of educators, social scientists, and family experts in criticizing America's traditionally haphazard, laissez-faire approach to the family. In the name of safeguarding the family, a growing body of such experts had fought since the 1920s to professionalize and standardize family life. They based their mission on the conviction that the American family was, by itself, an inadequate institution. "Actually parents represent the last stand of the amateur," wrote Evelyn Millis Duvall, director of the Institute for Family Living, in a characteristic formulation at the end of the war. "Every other trade and profession has developed standards, has required study and practice and licensing before releasing the student into his work . . . Only one profession remains untutored and untrained—the bearing and rearing of children."[17] After a decade of working in the area of family relationships, Duvall had become convinced that the family needed the same expert guidance that society already provided for manicurists, physicians, attorneys, welders, plumbers. Growing numbers of sociologists, psychologists, educators, and other experts in family living were coming to the same conclusion.

However, proposing to protect and improve the family was one thing; creating a concrete program to accomplish these tasks was another matter altogether. Once World War II was over, ASHA leaders and their allies realized that simply clapping promiscuous women in jail would treat only the symptoms, not the causes, of family breakdown. To get at the roots of family dysfunction, ASHA leaders decided to emphasize the association's educational mission. But the older tradition of sex education, rooted as it was in nature study, biology, and disease pathology, was hardly equal to the new task. For the first three years after Snow proclaimed ASHA's new emphasis on the family, sex educators in and out of ASHA cast about for new models.

Fortunately, sex educators had before them two likely examples—an older tradition of "marriage education" that was taught at hundreds of colleges throughout the nation, and more recent high school courses on "family relationships," such as that offered at Toms River High School in New Jersey. In 1926, a group of male seniors at Boston University had petitioned Ernest R. Groves, a young professor of sociology, for advice on marriage and sexual relations, and Groves had responded with the first ever college elective course on marriage.[18] Groves instructed his male students primarily in the mental hygiene of the family, how to meet the right woman, how to seek fulfillment within the marital bond, and how to rear obedient children. Word of the course spread, and over the next several years Groves and a growing coterie of colleagues in sociology, psychology, and eugenics introduced marriage courses in colleges throughout the country. By 1939, even the conservative University of Utah boasted courses in "matrology" and "patrology."

These college courses embodied middle-class America's rising hopes for fulfillment in marriage. Although husbands and wives in the nineteenth century had certainly not been strangers to romance and intimacy, they seldom would have claimed that the central purpose of marriage was to satisfy individual needs for companionship and pleasure. In justifying marriage, they would have ranked such "selfish" needs somewhere below economic necessity and the duty to procreate. By the 1920s, however, the declining economic role of the family, the wider availability of birth control, looser restrictions on divorce, and a complex of other subtle developments were causing many middle-class young people to expect more from marriage— more romance, more intimacy, more communication. Perhaps students competed for spaces in the college marriage courses because instructors like Groves promised, on some level, to aid them in realizing these expectations.

At the same time as these courses reflected changing perceptions of courtship and marriage—and constituted a novel mission for universities —the movement for marriage education also drew support from academics worried about changing sex roles. By the 1920s, female enrollment in colleges and universities had increased well over 500 percent from the turn of the century, and many of these students seemed bent on finding careers for themselves afterward.[19] Although lower-income women were still far more likely than middle-class women to work for wages, over the course of the 1920s and in the Depression decade that followed, women at most social levels and of all ages increasingly worked out of the house. Fearful that educated women, in particular, might choose to forgo their marital and reproductive duties, marriage educators generally agreed with eugenicists such as Paul Popenoe, who advised female college graduates "not to be misled by talk about 'careers,' but to head straight for matrimony."[20] By making a housewife's role seem more "scientific" and worthy of study, marriage education could make college learning and a woman's traditional duty compatible—even mutually reinforcing.

Appropriately, the most thoroughgoing effort in marriage education appeared at an all-female institution, Russell Sage College, from the mid-1930s onward. The college's president, J. Laurence Meader, placed at the heart of the school's mission its program called the Art and Science of Homemaking. The college, Meader explained, sought "to prepare each one of its 685 students to create and maintain a happy, satisfying, successful home."[21] To accomplish this, Russell Sage combined elements of marriage education (the art of homemaking) and home economics (the science of homemaking). Young women in the college were to learn the advanced skills necessary to run a household, social skills, a "right attitude toward the home," and, in a gesture toward the old ideal of the university as an academic institution, "sufficient interest in things intellectual to enable our graduates to become good companions to themselves and intellectually interesting to others." Finally, small groups of students were to meet in the living room of the Hall of Homemaking to join with President Meader and his wife in "frank discussion of the intimate and personal problems of home life."

In the two decades before World War II, the marriage educators' evaluation of the family spoke to a great many middle-class Americans, both in and outside the university setting. By 1939, American colleges, junior colleges, and universities were offering at least two hundred forty regular courses on marriage and the family, including the fateful Indiana University course on marriage begun in 1938 by an entomologist named Alfred C. Kinsey.[22] Prominent educators such as Groves not only spoke to large university and academic populations but also—through parenting magazines and advice columns in mass-circulation periodicals—reached an audience numbering in the millions, and arrogated for themselves great cultural authority over the conventions of courtship and marriage.

During World War II, educators began to teach variations on the university courses in selected high schools. Traditionally, home economics classes already covered certain aspects of the female side of family life, but now a handful of educators sought to broaden the curriculum and reach boys as well as girls through units offered in biology and social studies, or through stand-alone courses in family life. One of the most influential of the World War II experiments was Elizabeth S. Force's Family Relationships course at Toms River High School. Located in Toms River, New Jersey, a small, semirural community of about five thousand inhabitants, Toms River High School served a white, largely middle-class community.[23] The quiet town seemed largely immune to big-city social problems, but, as Mrs. Force explained, in 1941 a number of local business owners "found many of the high school graduates lacking in certain personality traits and ignorant of certain elementary rules of courtesy. It was felt that if these deficiencies could be overcome, the youth of the community would be more valuable as employees."[24]

The business owners asked the board of education to implement a course in "etiquette" for the ill-mannered youths, but the school system's supervising principal, Edgar M. Finck, quickly expanded the concept of improved interpersonal relationships to encompass far more than mere business courtesy. Arguing that unhappy homes had caused such problems as divorce, juvenile delinquency, and the occasional premarital pregnancy among high school girls, even in Toms River, Finck convinced the board that schools had a responsibility to prepare students for their home relationships. "He pointed out," Force recalled, "that if strong families were important to Toms River and to the nation, that if responsible parenthood was vital to the rearing of children, then individuals must receive a specific kind of education and training."[25] Finck was a canny salesman, and his plea resonated with general sentiment about the family during World War II. The board of education responded enthusiastically and recommended an elective course in family relationships. The high school turned to Elizabeth Force, an English teacher and longtime resident of Toms River, to convert Finck's proposal into reality, and she more than fulfilled expectations. Family Relationships quickly became one of the high school's most popular courses: after enrolling mostly girls during the war years, the course soon attracted equal numbers of boys and girls, and during the following decade almost two-thirds of all Toms River students took the class in their junior or senior year.

In Force's hands, the Family Relationships course became an innovative addition to the curriculum. In a classroom designed to resemble a living room, with paneled walls, carpeting, and linen draperies, students from all of Toms River's academic tracks discussed issues of courtship and mate se-lection, "getting along" with family members, child rearing, money man-agement, and the many demands modern society placed on marriage.[26] Other aspects of married life received more circumspect treatment. Al-though Force did not ignore sexual matters—indeed, she employed films, pamphlets, and books to deal with students' sexual questions as they arose —she maintained that "Family Relationships was pretty much an 'above the belt' matter."[27] "The word 'sex,'" she further explained, "did not rear its head to confuse the parents as it had done in some instances, thus destroy-ing at inception potentially fine programs."[28]

Quite aside from the course's content, the methods of instruction Force employed were novel and would distinguish the Toms River approach from many of its epigones. Reflecting the subject's relevance to the wider community, Force often called on a "citizen faculty" of ministers, lawyers, doctors, bankers, and other pillars of the town to offer classes on their re-spective discipline's lessons for family life (though the local theater man-ager's talk to the class on "the need for thoughtful and considerate manners in a theater and the parents' responsibility to inculcate such behavioral patterns" was perhaps more guidance than the students really needed).[29] Force's own approach to teaching revealed her affection for progressive ed-ucation. Rather than distribute a ready-made textbook, she gave the stu-dents mimeographed courses of study that they made into personal "scrapbooks" as each student wrote observations in it, pasted in clippings on family life from newspapers and magazines, and took notes on agencies that would be useful in the future. As she sifted through these notebooks each weekend, Force planned the next week's curriculum based on the direction of questions and interests she found therein. Finally, Force encouraged the students to evaluate for themselves the flood of popular literature on home life, and to study with a critical eye portrayals of the family in advertising, movies, and the radio. In spite of this profusion of lessons, the teacher did not delude herself into thinking the course had covered all future possibilities. Instead, Force explained, she tried to stimulate the students' eagerness for further learning and tried to prepare them to think for themselves. "We sought to build a basis for insight," she concluded, "so that the pupils might have a background from which to draw conclusions of their own in their own situations."

Marriage education and the Toms River experiment appealed strongly to sex educators seeking a new role for themselves after the war. By 1947, ASHA's leaders had followed up on William Snow's 1944 recommendations and proclaimed that their organization's central mission would be "education for personal and family living." The association even took on Elizabeth Force as a consultant for its new program.

Nevertheless, the sex educators' programs in the first postwar years continued to be heavily weighted toward the problems of sexuality and "sex delinquency," and the educators' invocation of "the family" remained more a rhetorical strategy than a conscious program. In fact, an ASHA subcommittee entrusted with educational change drafted a list of principles in 1947 that contained the exact same wording as a 1944 plan for sex education, except the subcommittee now substituted the phrase "education for personal and family living" in place of "social hygiene education." "Education for personal and family living," proclaimed the 1947 ASHA subcommittee report, "is based on the thesis that the sex factor in human living, as it affects personal development and especially in its relation to marriage, parenthood, the home and the family, merits a dignified place among other topics of deep human interest." Echoing Maurice Bigelow's longtime arguments for a broader sex education, subcommittee members hoped that the new teaching would help youths "to see the relation of sex to personality development, human happiness, complete family life and the fullness of individual living."[30]

In practical terms, "education for personal and family living" continued to mean a strongly prescriptive program for sexual restraint. In the late 1940s, for example, ASHA collaborated with New Jersey public health and educational officials to list nine elements of knowledge they hoped a course in human relations and family life would pass on to adolescents, including

4. General Social Etiquette.
5. Meaning of genuine manhood and womanhood.
6. Origin and values of our social conventions.
7. Interpretation of the difference between "biological maturity" and "full maturity" or adulthood.
8. The value of posture in relation to the individual's health and personal appearance.
9. Recognition of fallacies about sex conduct.[31]

These factual lessons were already heavily laden with moral messages, and the educators supplemented them with another list of possible approaches teachers could take to improve student behavior:

A2. By providing information which will guide the attitudes of adolescents toward wholesome decisions concerning conduct . . .
A7. By helping individuals to adjust wholesomely and successfully to the opposite sex (normal heterosexuality).
A8. By developing a respect for self which will restrain youth from influences which result in vice and disease . . .
C2. By developing a respect for the moral laws and customs of society . . .
C4. By awakening a responsibility for eugenics.

The sex educators were moving beyond merely warning adolescents about syphilis and gonorrhea, but they did not discard the tone of moral instruction they had inherited from their predecessors.

By the 1950s, the center of gravity for the sex educators' program began to shift further toward family living. This shift arose partly out of new interpretations of the family generated by marriage experts, sociologists, psychologists, and educational leaders in and out of ASHA, and even more out of fundamental changes in American family life.

By the first years of the 1950s, no one could ignore the fact that the United States was in the middle of a "baby boom" that would have enormous demographic and ideological consequences. As postwar prosperity swept the nation, older couples who had deferred childbearing during the Depression and the war began to make up for lost time, and they were joined by younger Americans who optimistically married earlier and reproduced sooner after the wedding. These couples produced 3.4 million babies in 1946, 3.9 million per year by 1952, and more than 4 million per year for the decade after 1954—almost half again the birth rate of the 1930s. It seemed as if everyone were in on the rush to form a nuclear family: by 1960, more than 90 percent of all women over thirty either were or had been married, and only 8 percent of women who had married in the 1950s remained childless.[32] Maternity-wear fashion spreads began to show up in mass-circulation women's magazines.

Marriage experts and, most likely, the parents of the baby boom themselves, harbored high expectations for family life—giving rise to what the sociologist Kingsley Davis called in 1951 "the cult of marital happiness."[33] Laypeople and social scientists alike had begun to consider the ideal family as a repository for human satisfactions that were increasingly unavailable outside the home. Although this idea had roots in the "companionate" ideal of the 1920s, the cult of marital happiness in the 1950s was unprecedented. As the historian Elaine Tyler May points out, the "legendary family of the 1950s," isolated but contented in Levittown suburbs across the nation, did not represent a return to tradition but rather embodied "the first wholehearted effort to create a home that would fulfill virtually all its members' personal needs through an energized and expressive personal life."[34]

Women pursued the duties of motherhood—child rearing, housework, involvement in volunteer organizations such as the Congress of Parents and Teachers—with a zeal that left many older feminists in despair. In return, according to marriage experts and many of the mothers themselves, mothers could expect a deep sense of accomplishment, social respect, and a more expressive and fulfilling relationship—including sexual satisfaction—with their husbands than previous generations of wives could have hoped for. Not that a young woman had much of a choice. "No matter how brilliant she is intellectually or how important a career she may have," explained a pair of advisors in a 1952 issue of *Parents' Magazine*, "she doesn't feel completely fulfilled until she has had at least one child."[35]

Family living experts suggested that the home could also be a haven for men from what many at the time agreed was the brutal regimentation of the working world. Not only would the home resonate with the personal affection and warmth that was absent at the husband's office, but it would also function as an arena in which he could exercise his masculine authority without a phalanx of middle managers supervising his every move. The modern husband and father would find the family to be his joy as well as his responsibility.

Husbands and wives each sought satisfaction in the home, but the baby boom family revolved, not surprisingly, around the children. The sheer number of children in the 1950s made their centrality practically inevitable, but children and child rearing also came close to becoming an ideological preoccupation during the period. Subscriptions to *Parents' Magazine*, the central publishing outlet for marriage and child rearing experts, skyrocketed from 750,000 to more than 1.5 million in the first decade after World War II, and even general-interest magazines began to celebrate the joys of parenthood, as experienced by Hollywood celebrities as well as "average" parents.[36] Americans of all classes, but especially the rapidly expanding middle class, harbored great expectations for family life.

And yet, at the same time as the culture celebrated the nuclear family, an undercurrent of fear about family dysfunction carried over from World War II and, if anything, grew stronger during the early baby boom. Although marriage experts, sociologists, and psychiatrists surely had professional reasons for stressing this darker side of American family life, cultural anxiety about the family went beyond these experts' attempts to create a need for their services. This anxiety was, in some ways, the flip side of praise for the baby boom family—if the well-adjusted nuclear family lay behind all that was good in American culture, then a disrupted family life was equally responsible for broader social problems. "Whether we start with the child who goes right or the child who goes wrong," argued a New York professor of psychology in 1951, "we inevitably wind up in the home."[37] At the beginning of the 1950s, recalled a pair of educators, many leaders in ASHA, the National Congress of Parents and Teachers, and the field of family sociology were becoming "increasingly aware of the intimate connection between the outward manifestations of various maladjustments and the kind of family living largely responsible for these manifestations."[38] Already during World War II, experts such as William F. Snow and Lawrence K. Frank had ascribed promiscuity, juvenile delinquency, and even youthful fascism to family dysfunction, and events since the war had done little to change their minds.

The most striking sign of family weakness seemed to be the "epidemic" of juvenile delinquency that struck the nation in the first years of the 1950s. "The Kids Grow Worse," lamented a typical headline in *Newsweek*, and a number of well-publicized cases in 1953 and 1954 served to inflame public opinion about the deplorable state of youth.[39] In 1954, four "above average" boys in Brooklyn were arrested for the thrill killing of an old derelict, and confessed as well to beating other defenseless victims, horsewhipping two adolescent girls, and setting fire to another man. In Philadelphia, a thirteen-year-old boy was charged with fifty robberies, rival gangs rioted intermittently in the streets, and one "girl gang" was reported to have overpowered other girls and forcibly cut their hair. Statistics seemed to support the anecdotal evidence about delinquency. A Senate subcommittee studying juvenile delinquency in 1954 reported that the number of offenders passing through juvenile courts annually had grown from 300,000 in 1948 to 385,000 in 1952, and predicted those figures would reach 750,000 by 1960.[40] Whether "delinquency" among youth was actually on the rise is debatable: investigators may have uncovered frightening statistics and damning anecdotal evidence simply by becoming more aware of social groups they had previously overlooked. But the cultural preoccupation with adolescent misbehavior embodied the fear among many Americans that parents in the postwar era were failing their children.

Equally threatening as youthful violence, the rising generation seemed to have abandoned its sexual morals somewhere in the backseat at the drive-in. More than a few commentators likened the adolescents' sexual drive directly to the destructive power of the atomic bomb. Juvenile delinquency consisted not merely of major and minor crimes but also, for girls in particular, of so-called status offenses—especially sexual activity.

Much of the concern over adolescent sexual activity revolved for a while around the publication in 1948 and 1953 of Alfred C. Kinsey's two landmark surveys, *Sexual Behavior in the Human Male,* and *Sexual Behavior in the Human Female.*[41] So fascinated were Americans with Kinsey's work that word of *Sexual Behavior in the Human Female*'s publication in 1953 pushed off the front pages news of the verification of the Soviet hydrogen bomb and Mohammed Mossadegh's surrender in Iran.[42] But fascination did not necessarily bring with it comprehension. Although Kinsey, a respected Indiana University zoologist, noted that these were studies of several generations of Americans, contemporaries seized on Kinsey's revelations as evidence of the Cold War adolescent's sexual irresponsibility.

From in-depth interviews with some 12,000 people, Kinsey and his Indiana research team concluded that generations of Americans had not simply failed to follow the accepted standard of sexual morality, but in fact had failed so spectacularly as to call into question the moral code's very validity as a social ideal. Kinsey's reliance on the memory of the people he interviewed and his naïveté about statistical sampling met criticism at the time and after, but his figures on American sexual behavior nevertheless provided a significant glimpse into an elusive, private world. In his first volume, on the male, Kinsey found that the great majority of American men had had coitus before marriage, from a low of 67 percent of college educated men, to a high of 98 percent of men who had finished only grade school.[43] Kinsey also uncovered evidence of nearly universal masturbation and widespread same-sex sexual behavior among adolescent males of all classes. Strikingly, the only sexual behavior with full social approval— coitus within marriage—accounted for fewer than half of the American male's sexual experiences.

To a society long accustomed to the "double standard" of morals for men and for women, this evidence of male sexual "misbehavior" was surprising, but not shattering. When Kinsey's research on female sexual behavior was published five years later, however, it aroused a tempest of indignation, including canceled speaking engagements for Kinsey, anti-Kinsey sermons, and congressional threats to rescind the Rockefeller Foundation's tax-free status for its role in funding part of investigation. The information that caused such outrage had been suggested in the earlier *Male* volume. Although sexual reformers could take some comfort in the findings that recent generations of men had only half as much sex with prostitutes as their forefathers had at the turn of the century, Kinsey maintained that the rate of male sexual "outlet"—Kinsey's zoocentric term for orgasm—had nevertheless remained uniform from generation to generation.[44] In the 1953 *Human Female* report, Kinsey made the implication explicit. Just as observers during the 1920s had feared, unmarried women who were *not* prostitutes were taking up the slack left by the decline in prostitution—or perhaps they were responsible for the decline in prostitution in the first place. Kinsey noted that the female rate of premarital petting to orgasm had been rising steadily for each generation born after 1900.[45] Further, young women in each subsequent generation were becoming sexually active earlier in their adolescence.[46] If the female rate of nonmarital sexual experience still did not rival the male's, it was nevertheless high enough to cause considerable alarm.

Some commentators observed that all of this youthful misbehavior occurred within a global context that did little to foster moral stability. Running throughout the *Preinduction Health Manual*, a nationally distributed high school curriculum created in 1951, was the recurrent theme that America's cold war with the Soviet Union was going to last for at least another twenty years; both the disruptions of military mobilization and the fear of nuclear annihilation threatened further to weaken social cohesion.[47] An editorialist in 1951 underlined the irony of the situation: "National defense can strengthen us. Or its pressures and dislocations can insidiously weaken us . . . Nothing could please the ironic enemies of democracy more than to witness the corrosion of American family and community life in the very course of our efforts to defend both."[48]

All of these danger signs pointed toward the family. "Families," explained Bernice Milburn Moore, a Texas home economist, in an interpretation typical of the early 1950s, "carry the first responsibilities for the development of personalities capable of handling a democratic government and of living in a democratic society."[49] Conversely, if young people failed to develop properly for a democratic society, the fault lay largely with the family. In 1951, for example, Sheldon and Eleanor Glueck published an influential study for the Commonwealth Fund that traced the differences between "good" children and juvenile delinquents. In almost all the children the Gluecks studied, social class and intelligence played no role in pushing a child toward delinquency; rather, delinquents "were reared to a far greater extent than their neighbors in homes where the 'under-the-roof culture' was bad—homes of little understanding, affection, stability or moral fiber by parents usually unfit to be effective guides and protectors or desirable models."[50] Family experts as well as casual commentators considered the rising tide of youthful misbehavior to be evidence of declining family strength.

Educated observers often singled out families that deviated in obvious ways from their own white, middle-class pattern of behavior, but many social scientists also seemed to suggest that *no* modern family was capable of meeting all of its responsibilities without help. "The accelerating pace of social change," argued one social scientist, "robs the contemporary family of the comfort and security of old guidelines, creating confusions, conflicts, and tensions."[51] Such sentiments had already spurred Ernest Groves and other family sociologists into action in the 1920s, and the passage of time had seemingly only intensified their relevance.

According to growing numbers of family and childhood experts in the early 1950s, both the rising expectations for family life and the rising evidence of family dysfunction suggested that American families needed outside support. But many experts on the family, such as Elizabeth Force and Conrad Van Hyning, another ASHA leader, also found to their dismay that a democratic society placed definite limits on an outside authority's ability to help:

He cannot tell parents that they are failing in their relationships with their children unless the child's behavior or need becomes of public concern, or violates rules or laws of school or community to the degree that his need for help is unmistakable.

He cannot counsel husband and wife on marital problems until they ask for help or seek separation or divorce. He cannot intrude upon a family, however serious its situation or shortcomings, until it flagrantly violates standards of responsibility and behavior.

"Help was being provided by social agencies, public and voluntary, and by such individual practitioners as psychiatrists, psychologists, marriage counselors and others," recalled Force and Hyning. "But this help came *after* the family or the child or the youth was already in serious trouble."[52]

Leaders in the study of family life began to think more seriously about an educational program that would act as *preventive* medicine. How much better to teach children and parents to get along in the first place than to turn to the police and juvenile courts after the fact. How much better to teach young men and women about marriage before the wedding than to rely on divorce proceedings afterward to show them where they went wrong. What was needed, maintained Sheldon and Eleanor Glueck, was an "intensive instruction of each generation of prospective parents in the elements of mental hygiene and the requirements of a happy and healthy family life."[53]

With many educators, family sociologists, psychologists, and the National Congress of Parents and Teachers supporting the change, ASHA in 1953 therefore took the lead in transforming sex education into what came to be known as family life education, or FLE. At the most basic level, supporters intended FLE to "raise the standards of home life and enable people of all ages to live life more constructively."[54] A Jewish community leader in New York underlined more clearly FLE's characteristic combination of optimism and anxiety: schools must offer compulsory courses in preparation for parenthood, argued Edwin J. Lukas in 1951, with the design of "building 'happy, fully adjusted people and keeping to a minimum the kind of behavior that causes trouble for the community and misery for the individuals involved.'"[55] Thus, ASHA drew closer to Elizabeth Force's direct focus on family living and the problems of adolescence, and attempted to relegate sex education to a small corner of the FLE curriculum.

In making this change, ASHA found strong institutional backing as well as ideological support. Family life education fitted well into the education profession's changing conception of secondary education. At the end of World War II, Dr. Charles A. Prosser, a leading educator from Minneapolis, had electrified the national Conference on Vocational Education in the Years Ahead with what came to be known as the Prosser Resolution, in which he declared that the top 20 percent of high school students should

receive a college preparatory curriculum, the bottom 20 percent a vocational curriculum, and the middle 60 percent "will receive the life-adjustment training they need and to which they are entitled as American citizens."[56] Faced with burgeoning high school enrollments, Prosser, the U.S.
Office of Education, and countless committees and school officials came to
support "life-adjustment training," for they considered the great mass of
high school students to be incapable of following a more "academic" curriculum; to prevent the middling students from dropping out, the schools
would meet their perceived needs for information on mental and emotional health, leisure time, socializing, and other immediate concerns of
daily living. FLE was, in many ways, life-adjustment education carried on
under a different name.

Combined with the growing visibility of the baby boom family, the
movement for life-adjustment education prompted private foundations as
well as government organizations to offer support to experiments in family
life education. In 1953, for example, ASHA's leaders began to sense interest
from the Mary Reynolds Bagley Foundation, set up by the tobacco heiress
to fund programs in social welfare. "Dear Esther," wrote ASHA's Ray H.
Everett to his colleague Esther E. Sweeney in the fall of that year, "Believe
your 'educational futures' theme is far more apt to hit pay dirt than was
your earlier suggestion . . . (and, when I say 'pay dirt,' I mean it literally as
well as figuratively.)"[57] Beginning in 1953, the Bagley Foundation (which
requested anonymity for its sponsorship) granted ASHA almost $100,000
annually to set up regional FLE projects in the Midwest, Mid-Atlantic, New
England, middle states, and Rocky Mountain areas.[58] The main purpose
and method of each project differed, but all of the "Bagley Projects" were
devoted fundamentally to educating teachers and developing curricula for
family living. ASHA consultants, including Elizabeth Force, crossed the
country holding meetings and coordinating advisory councils to arouse
and meet the demand for courses in family living. ASHA seemed to be re-
covering fairly well from the shock of penicillin's discovery.

Not all sex educators followed ASHA into family life education, however.
Despite a general sense that sex education should now be subordinate—that
FLE was related to sex education "'in the same way that a comprehensive
mathematics course is related to the binomial theorem,'" as one expert put

it—sex education programs of all varieties nevertheless continued in the nation's schools.[59] The same old smut talks—lately enlivened with new anti-
venereal disease films developed for the army in World War II—continued
in thousands of schools, sometimes cheek-by-jowl with courses in reproductive biology or with integrated programs in sex education. Most memorable, according to men and women who took such courses in the postwar
era, were the venereal disease films that featured, in the words of one former
student, "babies born with crusted eyes as a result of gonorrhea; both males
and females in the tertiary stage of syphilis; drooling and walking with that
strange gait that comes from tertiary syphilis; brain damage; open, running
sores; and on and on." "The truth is," recalled one woman from Tennessee,
"they scared a lot of us out of teenage pregnancy." She recalled that even
such a course "helped to straighten out all the misinformation I had picked
up at slumber parties or from reading forbidden novels under the covers."
Many male students were less pleased with the effects. "For weeks after the
showing of that film to junior girls," complained a graduate of Tilden High
School in Brooklyn, New York, "it was impossible for any junior or senior
boy to arrange a date with a junior girl."[60]

The localistic nature of American education—and American values—
guaranteed that a national portrait of sex education programs would present only an irregular, almost random pattern of persistence and progress.
But at the leading edge, where decisions were not based simply on inertia,
sex education was metamorphosing into family life education.

Despite their general harmony on the goals of FLE, supporters had
difficulty agreeing on what constituted a proper education for family life.
Opinions differed even within a single organization, such as ASHA. At the
beginning of ASHA's collaboration with the Bagley Foundation, Conrad
Van Hyning invited the rest of the upper-level staff to give him a description of family life education.[61] The result was confusion. One staff coordi-
nator placed understanding of students' "sexual nature" first in her list of
goals, while another suggested dropping the sexual aspect altogether. In
discussing methodologies, one ASHA leader endorsed FLE's teaching of
scientific facts while another disparaged facts entirely in favor of conveying
only "wholesome attitudes."[62] Outside of ASHA, coordinators from the
National Congress of Parents and Teachers maintained their own separate

interpretations of FLE, and a wide range of family sociologists, marriage counselors, professors of education, and psychologists all contributed to the cacophony of definitions. Understandably, then, ASHA allowed local participants a great deal of latitude in defining FLE for themselves, and so the meaning of "family living" varied from region to region.

Such diversity notwithstanding, the course in Marriage and Family Living at Elgin High School in Elgin, Illinois, may be taken as representative of the leading developments in family life and sex education. In the mid-1950s, several departments contributed to the family life program at Elgin High, including the departments of biology, "mental hygiene," and "social problems," but the centerpiece of Elgin's approach was a senior course called Marriage and Family Living, which met separately with boys and girls once per week. Marriage and Family Living, explained R. S. Cartwright, Elgin High's principal, broke down into four parts: Anticipating Marriage, Physical Aspects, Adjustments in Marriage, and Parenthood.[63]

The Anticipating Marriage segment met the students' most pressing questions about dating and courtship. "Students are grateful," Cartwright noted, "to have adult guidance in discussions that range from dating etiquette to the relationship between such intimacies as petting and the sex urge."[64] Like their predecessors in sex education, and like other FLE teachers around the country, Elgin instructors took a strongly prescriptive approach to these matters and informed students that excessive premarital intimacies were virtually guaranteed to harm their relationships in the future. Thus far, family life educators were well within the traditional boundaries of sex education.

But FLE teachers in Elgin and elsewhere went well beyond the older approach to instruct their students in positive strategies for avoiding intimacy while still having a good time. To preserve their students from the emotional harm and social stigma that would follow premarital experimentation, teachers spent any number of sessions recommending social alternatives such as wholesome movies, bicycling dates, lunch and picnic dates, double dating, and, most reliable for heading off sexual liberties, group dates.[65] Looking ahead to the successful completion of dating and courtship, students examined "the meaning of an engagement, who gets married and to whom, [and] the spiritual aspects of marriage." At the final session, a clergyman of the students' choice visited the classroom to discuss broader spiritual issues as well as the practical procedures of marriage ceremonies.[66]

Elgin's Anticipating Marriage unit seemed directed primarily toward attitudes and knowledge, but in many schools preparation for marriage became essentially an introduction to consumerism. A family living class in the mid-1950s at Council Grove High School in Council Grove, Kansas, exemplified this approach.[67] After examining dating, courtship, and divorce, the class traveled to local stores for lessons in buying engagement and wedding rings and choosing china and crystal for the home. They planned and budgeted a mock wedding, and listened intently as local bankers explained home buying. Students worked out family budgets after repeated field trips to grocery stores for pricing. Finally, noted Una Funk, the Council Grove family life teacher, "Local merchants show[ed] students the furniture and equipment needed to start a home, giving pointers on how to buy wisely," and an insurance agent set up family policies for the class. Funk's "realistic" program in family living seemed to have crossed over into an invitation for guided consumption.

In his published description of the Elgin program, Cartwright subtly omitted the title of the second unit, Physical Aspects, but these sessions seem clearly related to sex education. Teachers covered "the physical aspects of marriage; venereal diseases and promiscuity; and prenatal growth and development," and they showed students the film *Human Reproduction* to reinforce the messages. By their senior year, Elgin students had already received some information about the physical changes of adolescence and fetal development in biology and mental-hygiene courses, but now the subjects were gathered together in one place. Just as a clergyman closed out the first unit, a local physician attended the final session of this segment to answer student questions. Although typical student queries revolved around the relationship between sex education and the divorce rate, and the origins of premarital physical examinations, Cartwright reported, "This is always a lively session—frequently students don't even hear the bell ending the class!"[68]

Student interest, however, did not always mean that a school would include sex education in its family living program. With its sex education coordinated between the lower grades and the senior marriage class, Elgin offered a fairly thorough treatment of sex for the time, but in some states and cities, such as neighboring Chicago, sex education was actually illegal in the public schools. In light of such laws, and recognizing that FLE's opponents often attempted to reduce debate over the curriculum to the inflammatory issue of sex education, even ASHA deemphasized sex in all its materials and let local officials determine for themselves how much sex education was appropriate.[69] "Since sex education is the bete noir of agreement among groups," counseled Elizabeth McQuaid, an ASHA staff member, at the outset of the Bagley Project in 1954, "we should not attempt to include in a definition [of FLE] any preference we may have for teaching it—where, when, by whom or to whom."[70] With even the nation's foremost sex education organization in retreat, schools could not be blamed if they chose not to emulate Elgin High.

After covering the physical aspects of sex and marriage, Elgin's Marriage and Family Living course concluded with its Adjustments in Marriage and Parenthood units. Cartwright particularly appreciated the results of these segments: "As students learn some of the responsibilities of parenthood," he observed, "they gain a new appreciation of Mom and Dad." In these sessions, teachers attempted to explain "common conflicts in marriage, facts and feelings about divorce, what holds a marriage together, [and] the legal side of marriage," and led students in an exploration of child-care and parenting styles, as well. "We attempt to prepare our youngsters for happy marriage," Cartwright explained, "by dealing with the factors which make for happiness or unhappiness in marriage, the problems of newlyweds, [and] the importance of cooperation and mutual willingness to make personal adjustments."[71]

Cartwright's invocation of "cooperation" was not accidental: FLE leaders hoped to soften the boundaries of sex roles so that marriages would be more "companionate" and less patriarchal. "Companionship, with a firm foundation in love, is considered the most desired goal in marriage," explained one educator in 1951. "Companionship means comradeship between a well-matched pair . . . Mutual sharing is considered the basis for the enrichment of the personality of each by the other."[72] Judson T. Landis, one of the national leaders in FLE, clarified where the change must take place. "Popular literature still assumes today that the mother rears the children and the father earns the living," Landis complained in 1957. "But if families are to be successful in providing a climate for effective personality growth, then fathers must carry their full share of the load."[73]

Family life educators were intensely interested in the question of sex roles. At the time, Margaret Mead, Erik Erikson, and a wide range of other psychologists and social scientists were arguing that masculinity and femininity were not innate qualities but were largely learned attributes. Traditionally, Americans had believed that masculine and feminine traits were biologically based and fundamentally different. Growing up, for a boy, meant allowing his masculine characteristics to unfold naturally; for a girl, growing up was similarly a process of giving expression to her innate femininity. In the postwar revision of traditional wisdom, boys and girls each partook of masculine and feminine characteristics, and they did not naturally grow into male and female roles but rather *achieved* them through individual effort and a supportive environment.

The foundation leader Lawrence Frank, for one, tried to find comfort in the loss of certainty about the biological basis of masculine and feminine roles. Regarding the "essential bisexuality of every individual," Frank thought this insight "might be of real help [to adolescents], because it would serve to show that it is not only unnecessary for each boy and girl to strive to attain the traditional stereotypes of masculine and feminine, but it is a definite handicap and source of anxiety."[74] Adults could benefit as well. If traditional sex roles were not innate, then fathers could feel more comfortable playing an active role in home life and child rearing, as many marriage and family educators recommended.[75] In general, Frank hoped that the new thinking about sex roles would soften the edges of gender stratification in American society.[76]

Despite Frank's prominence, his was almost a solitary voice calling for the reform of gender roles. Most educators and social scientists did not question the validity of traditional sex roles but instead grew fearful that an unsettled family life might hinder young people from growing into their "proper" sex roles.[77] Indeed, many observers explicitly blamed gender confusion among youth for a wide variety of adolescent misbehavior. Adolescents who lacked clear male and female role models in their parents seemed much more likely to experiment with disapproved behaviors, such as drag racing or promiscuity, as they sought their own definitions of masculine and feminine. Other commentators feared that as the young man "grope[d] around to discover his role as a male," he would "slip into promiscuity or homosexuality."[78] In the classic Hollywood exploration of juvenile delinquency, the 1955 film *Rebel without a Cause*, James Dean's misfit character clearly reacts against sex-role confusion at home: not only is his mother domineering but his father's emasculation is so palpable that he appears in one scene wearing an apron.[79]

Notwithstanding calls for fathers to share the load, FLE did little to challenge traditional gender assumptions. On the contrary, family life educators typically sought to reinforce the boundaries between male and female, and they began this mission as early as elementary school. "The little boy and girl begin to learn attitudes that will assist them in becoming happy, healthy, and wholesome men and women," noted one educator. "In typical, conventional idiom, it can be said that the little boys will be taught to play the role of gentlemen . . . Little girls assume the role of little ladies. In our culture, many of them love most to prepare to be young ladies, debutantes, fiancees, brides, mothers, and citizens."[80] In discussing dating and sexuality for high school students, educators continued to portray the boy as the eternal aggressor and the girl as the party responsible for setting limits. Many women in the 1950s who recognized the injustice of this double standard, such as the young poet Sylvia Plath, nevertheless heeded the enormous social pressure to remain "nice girls" and remained content only to "lean enviously against the boundary and hate, hate, hate, the boys who dispel sexual hunger freely."[81] Like other young women, Plath knew that the school authorities would blame her, and not the young man, for sexual improprieties.

Even where educators stepped away from strictly traditional lessons, as when they taught that fathers should involve themselves more in child rearing, they were primarily concerned that fathers be available as masculine role models for their sons. "When they reach the teens you need a man on the job," counseled *Parents' Magazine* in the early 1950s. "For then, adolescence rears its troublesome head in your formerly peaceful domicile."[82] Family life educators attempted at most to bend certain traditional rules in order to leave intact the more fundamental divisions between male and female.

FLE in this form was popular with the students. Perhaps because family life educators tried to meet student demand so directly—some schools structured their curricula explicitly around student requests—FLE fulfilled at least part of its task of maintaining interest in school for Charles A. Prosser's middle 60 percent of students. Noting that FLE was an area in which "most parents do a very poor job," Elgin High School principal Cartwright reported, with much satisfaction, "Our students term it the most valuable practical knowledge they have received in high school."[83]

For a while, ASHA's leaders considered the Bagley Project in family life education to be one of their most valuable undertakings. After eight years, ASHA could point to nearly one hundred city and county school systems that had implemented family life courses as a direct result of the Association's guidance, to say nothing of hundreds of related school systems that had been indirectly stimulated by the regional projects. Almost one hundred colleges and universities, as well, including teachers' colleges, had cooperated with the association to add courses in family living, and teachers, educators, and community leaders by the thousands had attended more than one hundred workshops and institutes sponsored by ASHA.[84]

Measuring classroom success was harder. Although most educators took for granted that a connection existed between what they taught and what the students learned, in the 1950s a number of researchers using sophisticated testing and sampling techniques began to deny that "common sense" was a sufficient basis for linking education causally to a variety of social behaviors. Some sociologists began to question whether any particular educational program could have a meaningful effect on student behavior. Drawing on a growing body of social psychology theory about character development, including Robert Merton's work on "reference groups," critics argued that the determinants of human behavior were far more complex and deeply ingrained than most family life educators were willing to admit.[85] Such doubts about education's instrumental value prompted supporters and detractors of various educational programs to attempt to measure with greater sophistication the programs' effects. As the dominant approach to instrumental education in the 1950s, FLE became the first to go under the microscope.

Researchers quickly learned that measuring the behavioral results of courses in FLE or sex education was extraordinarily difficult. Evaluation of FLE's effects was hampered, above all, by the difficulty of isolating the course's influence from other variables, and by the problems of timing the evaluation and defining the nebulous positive values to be measured, such as marital happiness or fulfilling use of leisure time.[86] Even "objective" data, such as a decline in arrests for juvenile delinquency in a community offering FLE, might reflect lighter law enforcement rather than any change in behavior among youth.

The strongest supporters of family life education confessed that they were never quite sure themselves of the relation between their courses and their students' future behavior. Evelyn Millis Duvall told the story of a tenth-year class reunion for students who had taken a course called Marriage and Family. Confounding expectations, she said, the only boy to fail the course returned with "an attractive wife who seemed to adore him, three happy children and the air of a successful marriage." With the perfect irony that makes one question all such anecdotes, the girl who had earned a straight A in the same course returned, in Duvall's words, "a disillusioned spinster full of criticism for the course, its professor and the false promises it raised in her unhappy bosom."[87] Duvall raised the story not to question the instrumentalist model of FLE and sex education but to criticize the academic system of grading that evaluated only how much information students remembered and not how well they could put their lessons into practice. Behavior, in Duvall's eyes, was still the key. Seeing such problems, a small number of family life educators in the 1950s did try to argue that the difficulty of evaluating behavioral effects had no bearing whatsoever on the validity of the program—after all, courses in American history did not depend on measurable personal development for their justification—but their hearts nevertheless continued to lie with Duvall and the instrumentalist model.[88]

Like the sex educators before them, family life educators were convinced that their courses made an impact on students' behavior, but in the end they could support this belief only with weak correlations and hopeful assertions. Francis J. Brown of the American Council of Education, for example, contended in a 1954 speech to ASHA that it was "reasonable to assume" that the baby boom was "due to the increasing emphasis upon marriage and family life in the curriculum of our high schools and colleges," but reasonable assumptions were Brown's only evidence.[89] Most educators made less ambitious claims, but even these rested on a tenuous connection between FLE and student behavior. The best studies of FLE's effects demonstrated at most that students who had taken courses in family living did, indeed, know more about the course material at the end of the semester than did students who had not taken the class, but by the family life educators' own admission, this accumulation of knowledge meant little without evidence that it would lead to well-adjusted behavior in a student's adult life.[90] Friendly critics could complain about the ways in which sex education and FLE had been "oversold" as solutions to social problems, but for practical and ideological reasons most family life educators continued to rely comfortably on the "common sense" notion that students would actually apply their lessons.[91]

The problems with evaluation did not lessen the outside pressure educators felt to maintain the instrumentalist model. In 1961, after almost ten years of work on the Bagley Project in FLE, educators in the American Social Health Association could point to the great numbers of seminars, workshops, and courses they had created, but they also had to recognize that, given the paucity of evidence about any program's impact on individual students, teachers, and parents, all this activity did not necessarily mean progress.[92] The association's position was made more difficult by the Bagley Foundation's understandable demand, after several years of funding, for some solid measurement of the project's social effects.[93] When funding for the Bagley Project was to run out in the early 1960s, the boards of several foundations pressured ASHA to find more of a "hook," such as the reduction of illegitimacy or delinquency, on which to hang its FLE program.[94] But no amount of wishful thinking could substitute for solid measurement.

In the eyes of some critics, more damaging than FLE's possible lack of impact was its omission of certain critical information. On the question of sex education, family life education represented more of a retreat than an advance for ASHA and its allies. "Family life education has become a relatively common commodity in schools and colleges," observed Frances and Robert Harper in a 1957 Marriage and Family Living article. "But where, pray tell, are the clear and forthright voices on problems of sex? The only lucid, steady, and cogent sounds we have heard on the matter have not, for the most part, issued from family life educators." This omission was not trivial: "To offer family life education without a full examination of sex information, sex attitudes, and sex emotions," argued the Harpers, "is like trying to teach nutrition without any reference to gustatory urges or practices."[95]

No doubt certain legal prohibitions and the personal inclinations of educators played a large role in their avoiding sex education, just as FLE leaders claimed, but the neglect of sex also grew out of the nebulousness of the family living concept itself. Family life education continued to be a grab bag of concepts from tangentially related disciplines with no unifying orthodoxy.[96] "Some schools and colleges purport to teach family life education when they are really teaching courses in citizenship or human relations," complained ASHA's Edgar C. Cumings in 1958. "Others teach courses in homemaking—admittedly a part of family life education—with emphasis on the more or less mechanical factors inherent in good family living. Still others teach courses in 'charm' or personality development in the name of family life education."[97] FLE could enter the school through home economics or social studies or biology, so no academic discipline claimed sex as its province, and few institutional guidelines encouraged teachers to include the potentially disruptive subject in their family living courses.

On the contrary, the leaders in family life education—ASHA chief among them—intentionally deemphasized sex in an effort to shake free of their social hygiene past and win wider acceptance for the family living program. "It would be easy to get a whirlwind up over a course on sex," a professor of education had written to Walter Clarke in the late 1940s, "but even the bigots have to search for a handhold wherewith to tear apart teaching done for 'family living.'"[98] Clarke seemed to heed these words, for during the 1950s ASHA muted its public support for sex education in favor of a vaguely defined educational program that may or may not have included information about sex.[99]

As Clarke's correspondent had suggested, downplaying the program's sexual aspect was at first primarily a strategy to sneak sex education into the schools, past "allegedly reactionary and unenlightened administrators, parents, and citizens at large." According to this plan, once FLE became strong enough educators "could then bravely and boldly arise and declare sex to be an important human relationship and educational objective." Strategic retreats, however, can become habitual. After years of downplaying the controversial subject of sex, many ASHA educators were quite ready to jettison the topic altogether. "There is," the Harpers lamented in 1957, "in fact, evidence that the passing years have brought a decline, not a rise, in boldness regarding the sexual aspects of marriage and family courses."[100] By the end of the 1950s, the former leader in sex education had largely fallen silent, and few other voices broke the stillness.

While family life educators were often conspicuously silent about sex, on all other questions of practical daily living they found they could seldom say enough. In practice, FLE courses always tended toward the more mundane details of daily living. Balancing a checkbook, applying for a job, learning to date, planning a wedding, finding a hobby—these became the central concerns of many family life classes. Like Una Funk, whose Council Grove High School course included jewelry and furniture shopping, family life educators found themselves doggedly including direct instruction on every conceivable situation a high school graduate might meet in daily living.

In their preoccupation with the trivial, family life educators were at some level simply meeting student demand. In Denver's program called Home and Family Living, noted a pair of observers, "Boys and girls in all five schools want to know how to attract dates, how to act, how much dates cost, where to go, how to deal with parental differences of opinion and standards about dating, how to deal with 'blind' dates and a host of other questions relating to the all-important interest of young people."[101] In a generation whose average age at marriage had dropped to just above twenty years, young students felt fully justified in pressing for practical information on marriage and setting up house. Educators concerned about the "holding power" of the public schools responded readily to what they considered their students' immediate interests.

Family life education's tendency toward the mundane was more than a response to student demand, however. It was, first of all, ordained by the psychology on which family life education was based. The practice of teaching quotidian "life skills" was a logical result of studies pioneered by the psychologist Edward L. Thorndike earlier in the century and revived after World War II. Building on rudimentary tests that seemed to explode the theory that education was a "discipline for learning," Thorndike and his followers had claimed that education could not train the human mind generally but could only pass on specific skills for specific situations. When the life-adjustment education movement began to revive these ideas, I. L. Kandel, the editor of *School and Society*, complained that such an approach overloaded the curriculum with trivia. Life-adjustment education, Kandel argued in 1947, "implies that all the contingencies which human beings are likely to encounter in their lives must be anticipated and education adjusted to them. Among these contingencies are dating, marriage, mating, rearing of children, work experience, vocations, and all the social issues which make up the day's headlines in the newspapers." Noting that Thorndike's followers had derived this position from an "easy misinterpretation" of research, Kandel decried the educators' preoccupation with "instruction that brings immediate returns." Behind such a relentlessly practical program lurked what Kandel called "a species of anti-intellectualism."[102]

Kandel's complaints were insufficient to hold off the renaissance of Thorndike's theories. In the years after World War II, a growing militancy among educators and other experts in family living breathed new life into this literal-minded educational philosophy. These educators and academics were convinced that their research into psychology, sociology, and family relations had given them the definitive wisdom about familial stability and personal fulfillment. Behind their embrace of Thorndike lurked a palpable fear that students might somehow misapply this wisdom. In the spirit of the Prosser Resolution, many educators believed that greater enrollments had "diluted" the talent in schools, so a lower proportion of students had the intellectual power to generalize from broad principles. Thus, in Kandel's words as he lampooned the life-adjustment educator's condescending view of high school students, "Nothing can be left to chance on the assumption that no individual is likely, without appropriate courses of instruction, to have sufficient intelligence to meet the 'life situations' which may arise."[103] Better to teach young people exactly what they were supposed to do when they became adults, for supporters of family life education did not, in the end, trust the students' ability to reason for themselves.

In a sense, family living was deemed too important to allow students to act on their own interpretations.

Family life educators were equally concerned that students might *willingly* diverge from their "common sense" interpretation of family life and morality. As educators observed the broadening of the secondary school population in the postwar era, they grew alarmed at the diversity of the students' backgrounds. More families than expected seemed impossibly distant from the FLE ideal. "Many of the teachers who described their work in this area spoke of encountering attitudes toward various social problems that represented startling departure [*sic*] from the standards usually accepted," explained investigators into the Denver Home and Family Living program. "These children must also be introduced to other ways of thinking and to demands of a larger society which does not condone the mores of sub-groups if these depart to any great degree from those of the group as a whole."[104] Family life educators believed they were thus acting in the best interests of the coming generation. Too many American families, in their opinion, unwittingly crushed their children's spirits or damaged their psyches. Sometimes they damaged much more: investigations into juvenile delinquents almost always uncovered vicious child abuse by the delinquents' parents. Rather than allow these families to pass on their idiosyncratic and possibly harmful values, educators hoped to impose the middle-class standards they felt gave individuals and families the best chance of success.

The FLE ideal might have seemed especially distant from the average American family because it was modeled not merely on middle-class standards but on a peculiarly prosaic version of those standards. The portrait that family life educators drew of the "healthy" family was a smooth, banal image. In 1959 Gerald R. Leslie, a professor at Purdue University, criticized FLE for its uninspired combination of middle-class assumptions and emotional flatness. "In family life education textbooks," he observed, "there are never families of six children or barren couples, and they never live in three rooms or in a house that badly needs paint. There are no full ash trays . . . Children aren't grimy or sticky . . . Teenagers don't slouch or swear or have cigarettes hanging out of the corners of their mouths . . . Fathers don't lounge around the house in their undershirts (or shorts) or remain unshaven on the weekend."[105] In perfect families as drawn in FLE, Leslie concluded, domestic bliss followed naturally: "Once again, note that these families have an emotional range that runs roughly from a kind of cow-like contentment to a mild, unending joy which results from living with such a splendidly tempered group."[106] The vacuousness of this portrait was not merely a consequence of uninspired textbook writing; it was integral to the family life educator's ideal of a rational, carefully controlled home life. Indeed, FLE's focus on the practical aspects of home life, such as cooking, cleaning, budgeting, and personality development, was a conscious strategy to combat what one supporter decried as the "Hollywood conception of marriage and the family," with its precarious foundation in the "romantic cult."[107]

The educators' mistrust of individual choice begins to suggest the irony that lay at the heart of family life education. Although family life educators lauded the family as a haven from a regimented, bureaucratic society, their fundamental purpose was nevertheless to standardize and rationalize home life along what educators considered to be scientifically approved lines. The public schools have perhaps always served to shape students for social roles, but seldom before had they been so baldly in the service of social tinkering for middle-class values and conformity.[108]

FLE thus represented a significant expansion of the educator's mission. Previously, social hygienists had complained that parents were generally unprepared to teach their children about sex, but not until now did reformers suggest that parents' incapacity extended to almost all aspects of home life. After praising the family for its role in passing on values, personal standards, and moral principles, one ASHA director nevertheless proclaimed it the schoolteacher's duty "to help the child acquire the proper image of good family life"—an image presumably unavailable in the child's own home.[109]

Whereas authorities had earlier been primarily in the business of proscribing certain kinds of behavior, they now undertook to outline positive satisfactions for the family to realize. Family life education offered the first representation of the family as a site for total personal fulfillment, both for men, who supposedly could no longer look to work or public life for satisfaction, and for women, who were considered to be confined already to the family circle. Marriage counselors and family life educators informed young married couples that a home lacking intimate communication, companionship, consuming and educated devotion to children, and a host of other positive qualities was a deficient home indeed. When they addressed adult audiences, some family experts even suggested that married couples had better achieve a high level of sexual satisfaction, too, if they wanted their marriage to succeed.

These higher standards for family life were a positive expression of rising expectations for marriage in the 1950s, but higher standards could also be a burden. Most young couples could not expect to achieve such an elevated level of family living on their own, and so, according to the experts on the family, they should seek out family life experts to aid them with communication, child rearing, sexual adjustment, and all the other elements of a successful family life. The public schools, argued a group of early FLE supporters, should stimulate "a more widespread demand for the social services that have come into being to help people in the modern world," such as psychiatrists, marriage counselors, "the nursery school, child guidance clinic, mental hygiene clinic, juvenile court, community center, family welfare society," and a host of similar agencies.[110] In assessing the results of a high school course in family living at the end of the 1950s, one professor of social work asked the students how willing they were to seek help from social agencies. "We assumed," noted the professor, "that a high degree of willingness to seek intervention would show a healthy attitude about family life." The results were reassuring: half the class, for example, had come to favor involving community agencies to help with "family quarrels," whereas a large majority of students in an outside control group opposed such intervention.[111] Well-adjusted families of the future would be like patients with a host of life-support tubes running from their bodies.

As they compounded the areas in which their competence was necessary, family living experts simultaneously narrowed the limits of acceptable behavior. Educators and social scientists measured family life against their own values of rationality, emotional temperateness, and cooperation, and stigmatized deviations from this genial, middle-class pattern as unhealthy. Already in 1948, a friendly critic had pointed out that ASHA's pamphlets on "Education for Personal and Family Living" strongly implied that "'healthful, wholesome personal relations' are pretty much the same for all decent people," and family life educators during the next decade did little to change that impression.[112] Although they might have denied the implication, family experts were in fundamental agreement with Leo Tolstoy's dictum that all happy families resemble one another, while each unhappy family is unhappy in its own way.

The movement for family life education was the high point of the American educational system's attempt to train adolescents to conform to middle-class family life standards. At a time when tremendous economic growth was actually expanding the middle class and equally spectacular demographic growth was fostering the popular impression that marriage and child rearing were the central activities for any reasonable American, FLE's mission seemed almost unassailable. But at the same time as family life educators sought to press youth into a particular behavioral mold, American sexual behavior and morals were quietly changing in ways that would in the next decade smash the mold into barely recognizable shards.

# CHAPTER SIX

# Fighting the Sexual Revolution

> Q. Are students in Family Life courses taught the techniques of sex?
>
> A. No. Sex techniques have no place in our Family Life and Sex Education program . . . We answer questions honestly and factually, but we do not encourage the students to linger on the discussion of such matters.
>
> Paul Cook, superintendent of schools,
> Anaheim, California (1969)

The American Social Health Association's retreat from sex education into family life education came at a critical moment in American sexual history. Even as the declining incidence of syphilis and gonorrhea during the 1950s was leading many educators to believe they could ignore or downplay the sexual component of FLE, the elements of a "sexual revolution" were beginning quietly to coalesce.

The first shot fired in the sexual revolution is impossible to determine, but as early as the beginning of the 1950s evidence of a more overtly sexual public culture began to appear. The so-called *Kinsey Reports* on male and female sexual behavior that appeared in 1948 and 1953 not only seemed to prove that an unthinkable number of Americans failed spectacularly to live up to middle-class standards of sexual morality, but their scientific aura also allowed previously staid periodicals and persons to chat openly about sexual "outlets" and "frequencies." Equally influential, Hugh Hefner's *Playboy* magazine debuted in 1953 with a nude Marilyn Monroe in the centerfold. More literary and mainstream than cheap "girlie" magazines, more overtly sexual than its ancestor, *Esquire* magazine, *Playboy* sprang from Hefner's conviction that millions of American men, at least, were ready for a more public expression of sexuality.

Hefner's creation was to have the same ripple effect as Kinsey's books in shifting public discussion toward greater sexual frankness. The immediate sensation made by such otherwise very different novels as Grace Metalious's *Peyton Place,* published in 1956, Vladimir Nabokov's *Lolita,* which was published in this country in 1958, and the American release of an unexpurgated edition of D. H. Lawrence's *Lady Chatterly's Lover* in that same year could be attributed in part to their sexual frankness. Hollywood, reacting as much to the financial threat of television as to the artistic promise of greater "realism," also began in the 1950s to treat more explicitly sexual themes.[1]

Even as the public culture grew more overtly sexual, the moral unity among family sociologists, family life educators, sex educators, and other authorities on sex was beginning to crumble. Over the course of the 1950s some of these educators were tentatively developing ideas about sexuality that would become central to the sexual revolution of the next decade. As one such educator, Lester Kirkendall, moved from a position as elementary school principal in his hometown of Oberlin, Kansas, in 1927, to his ultimate destination as a professor of family life education at Oregon State College from 1949 until 1968, he came to focus on the sex educators' central concern: premarital and extramarital intercourse. In the course of his research, however, Kirkendall also came to dissent from sex education and family life's rigid demands for extramarital chastity.

Initially Kirkendall studied the differences during World War II between soldiers who engaged in extramarital intercourse and those who remained chaste. At this time he did not question society's prohibition on promiscuity but only sought more effective means to enforce the prohibition.[2] Like many of the more liberal social hygienists at the time, Kirkendall concluded that repression and threats generally did little to deter men from sexual indulgence. He came to believe that only better interpersonal relationships and individual social adjustment would lead to less promiscuity, less prostitution, and less venereal disease. A more sympathetic psychological approach would make the taboo against promiscuity stronger, not weaker.

In 1950, when he published *Sex Education as Human Relations* and a number of similar articles, Kirkendall still condemned premarital and extramarital sex, but he also focused more on the psychological meaning of the sexual exchange.[3] Sex, according to Kirkendall, had three functions: the first was reproduction, the second was physical satisfaction, and third was sex as a "communicative, unifying factor." Sex could perform this third and vitally important function, Kirkendall argued, "only as psychological and personality values are associated with it."[4] Thus Kirkendall came to view sexual relations more broadly as part of social adjustment, and like his colleagues in FLE he praised sexual exchanges as integral to marital fulfillment.

Sex before marriage was a different matter. Kirkendall still condemned premarital sex, but he translated the problem into social and psychological terms. Contrary to what Kinsey would soon proclaim in 1953 in *Sexual Behavior in the Human Female*, Kirkendall in 1950 argued that premarital sexual experimentation did nothing to help couples make satisfactory adjustments in marriage and might even impair marital relations.[5] With a similar regard for interpersonal relations, Kirkendall also disapproved of the "exploitative" nature of petting. "Those who indulge in harmful and exploitative sex behavior will still have to be controlled," the author concluded, "but they will be regarded more as immature and unsocial personalities than as sinners."[6] Kirkendall seemed to have exchanged moralistic condemnation for psychological condemnation.

Over the next decade, however, Kirkendall's observations of adolescents and young adults began to push him toward a greater acceptance of premarital sex. To arrive at this new position, he merely needed to carry his apotheosis of interpersonal relations to its logical conclusion. In a controversial article written in 1960 for *Marriage and Family Living*, the official organ of marriage educators and social scientists concerned with the family, Kirkendall first took the fairly conventional position that "Man's supreme satisfactions and his greatest miseries come from his successes and failures in his interpersonal relations." Kirkendall thus found "morally good" those acts that improved the capacity for interpersonal relationships, and "morally bad" those acts which destroyed the quality of relationships between persons.[7] So far, the author was on solid ground, but as he pursued this path further, he began to step away from the accepted tenets of FLE and sex education.

In the absence of clear evidence that premarital intercourse per se harmed marital adjustment, Kirkendall proposed that the more important questions to ask about premarital sex were what was its meaning for the participants, and how did their conduct affect their present and future human relations. Kirkendall had not "progressed" so far in his thinking that he lauded premarital sex, but his new framework of values nevertheless lifted the absolute opprobrium from the act. "We must . . . be able to face the possibility," Kirkendall advised, "that ways may be found to use sex in premarital relationships in a positive, meaningful way. This we will be able to do if we can focus on the really important issue—the creation of sound interpersonal relations."[8]

Kirkendall thus elevated the value educators placed on "adjustment" and human relations above the value they placed on chastity. This stance was to make Kirkendall the target of vicious abuse later in the 1960s, but he had derived his position only from tensions inherent to the marriage education project. Kirkendall was not alone in taking this path away from the older certainties about chastity. Many sociologists and other authorities on the family, including a conspicuous body of sex and family life educators, were soon to follow the same trajectory. Those who did not go so far as to endorse premarital sex at least ended up calling for a less judgmental moral posture. By the early 1960s, when a small minority of youths began to revolt openly against older sexual standards, the grown-ups would no longer be united to quell the rebellion.

Indeed, the sexual revolution among youths grew directly out of these cultural and intellectual changes in the 1950s. While Hugh Hefner and the family life educators each created their separate images of ideal social and sexual behavior during that decade, adolescents and young adults of the baby boom generation constructed their own meanings for love and marriage out of the varied materials of public messages and lived experience. Often the conclusions they drew were entirely conventional, but as the 1950s passed into the 1960s, many young people, especially those at the nation's colleges, came to dissent with increasing vigor from the inherited middle-class moral code and embrace instead those elements in Kirkendall and others' work they found most congenial. When some of these college-age youths came to question publicly the taboo on premarital sex—the central prohibition of the dominant sexual code—the real revolution had arrived.

"We've discarded the idea that the loss of virginity is related to degeneracy," explained a senior from Ohio State University in 1964.[9] Previous generations had often honored chastity more in the breach than in the practice, as Kinsey's work amply demonstrated, but many of the baby boomers were open in calling for an end to society's condemnation of premarital sexual experimentation. Some of the "advanced" college students decided that even their predecessors' more indulgent sexual behavior had about it the hint of something shameful. "Radcliffe girls think petting is dirty because it is teasing," noted a psychiatrist at Radcliffe Health Services in 1964. "They feel if you are going to do that, it is better just to have intercourse."[10] With those casual words, more than a century's worth of sexual prohibitions was overthrown.

Contrary to charges at the time and after, this questioning of premarital virginity's value was not an expression of hedonism; the basis of the "morals revolution" was simultaneously more comforting and more confounding. "If two people are in love," maintained a University of Chicago student in the early 1960s, "there's nothing wrong with their sleeping together, provided no one gets hurt by it." In 1964, a *Newsweek* cover story devoted to the "Morals Revolution on the U.S. Campus" backed up the student's claim: "Undoubtedly, the key to the new morality is the widespread belief that a boy and girl who have established what the campus calls a 'meaningful relationship' have the moral right to sleep together."[11]

Such radical notions prompted many Americans to call for the nation's schools to formulate a response, but sex education by the early 1960s was virtually moribund. In particular ASHA, the traditional leader in sex education (now called the American Social Health Association), had been muffling its support for sex education under the vague heading of family life education, which might or might not include education about the sexual side of life.[12] By 1962 ASHA's commitment to "local preference" on curriculum content had come so close to outright silence about sex and venereal disease that public health officials at a series of gatherings on the West Coast felt compelled to push Edgar C. Cumings, ASHA's regional director, to declare publicly whether the organization was, finally, in favor of sex and venereal disease education.[13] Cumings protested that ASHA still supported teaching these subjects, but the point had been made. ASHA and similar institutions by the early 1960s seemed to have abandoned sex education.

At this juncture, Dr. Mary Steichen Calderone stepped in to become the orphaned subject's guardian—or, as the national press soon dubbed her, its "grandmother." As medical director of the Planned Parenthood Federation of America since 1953, Calderone had had a front-row seat for the postwar changes in American sexual life; at the same time, she and the federation had been receiving hundreds of letters each year, most of them, in Calderone's opinion, evincing a stunning ignorance about sexuality. Calderone was convinced that sex education in America was doing woefully little to prepare young people for their lives as sexual adults.

Since attending a conference in 1961 on marriage and the family sponsored by the National Council of the Churches of Christ, Calderone had remained in contact with a small core of educators and researchers, such as Kirkendall, who felt as she did that the time was right for a "breakthrough effort" in the area of sex education.[14] Like Kirkendall and many other professionals in the field, Calderone in the early 1960s was beginning to receive a flood of invitations to speak or write on changing sex standards; further, she was growing increasingly dissatisfied with her salary at Planned Parenthood, particularly because she was carrying the entire educational load of an association that had no separate staff in public health nursing or health education.[15] She was ready to jump.

Thus, at a separate meeting during the Groves Conference on Marriage and the Family in 1963, Calderone proposed the creation of an organization that would deal exclusively with the broad aspects of human sexuality. The next year, at the age of sixty, Calderone launched SIECUS, the Sex (later Sexuality) Information and Education Council of the United States. It was an audacious name for an organization whose New York office consisted solely of Calderone, a secretary, and a typewriter perched atop a couple of orange crates, but SIECUS's elite membership gave it instant credibility. Along with Calderone and Kirkendall, charter members of SIECUS included Wallace C. Fulton, a past president of the National Council on Family Relations; William Genné, director of the Family Life Department at the National Council of Churches; and Clark Vincent, who was chief of the Professional Training Division of the National Institute for Mental Health.[16] A start-up grant from the Commonwealth Fund underscored the respectability of the enterprise.

Respectability notwithstanding, SIECUS members from the beginning had to defend themselves against accusations from colleagues in the National Council on Family Relations that they were improperly "pulling sex out of context."[17] Indeed, SIECUS placed its focus on sex up front in its vague but hopeful statement of purpose: "To establish man's sexuality as a health entity"—that is, SIECUS would dignify sexuality by a scientific approach, explore its potential for reproduction, creativity, and responsible use, and disseminate useful information on sexuality to professionals and society at large.[18] Calderone denied, however, that an exclusive focus on sexuality in any way limited SIECUS's purpose. "Sex is not just something you do in marriage, in bed, in the dark, in one position," she explained. "Sex is what it means to be a man or a woman."[19] Further, the family life experts' complaints that SIECUS might lack gentility carried little weight with a woman who had spent the previous decade leading Planned Parenthood's fight against the taboos on discussing birth control and abortion.

In addition to emphasizing frankly the sexual components of life, SIECUS planned to convey Calderone's positive view of sexual energy. "We must block our habit of considering sex as a 'problem' to be 'controlled,'" she had admonished in 1963. "Emphasis must be on sex as a vital life force to be utilized." Kirkendall, moving toward his later position, fully agreed. "The purpose of sex education is not primarily to control and suppress sex expression, as in the past," he explained, "but to indicate the immense possibilities for human fulfillment that human sexuality offers."[20]

In an equally strong break from the inherited tradition of sex education, Calderone and her allies claimed that sex education's purpose was not to force sexual standards on anyone but merely to make information available to help young people and adults reach their own decisions. For youth, in particular, SIECUS leaders denied that one uniform moral code could apply; rather, sex educators would respect young people's right to choose for themselves from what was becoming, in the early 1960s, a buffet of competing moral systems.[21]

Although SIECUS's forthright, nonjudgmental, and occasionally celebratory approach to sexuality was a radical innovation for the time, Calderone's brainchild also embodied a liberal response to sex and adolescence characteristic of the 1960s. Like ASHA and the earlier generation of family life educators, SIECUS claimed as its primary mission the conservation of the American nuclear family. But like increasing numbers of social scientists and educators concerned with youth in the 1960s, SIECUS leaders and their eventual allies concluded that the only way to preserve the family and aid in personal development was to discard their predecessors' timidity about sex and their moralistic prescriptions.

In its combination of libertarianism and praise of family, SIECUS bore the unmistakable likeness of its founder. Born in New York City in 1904 to the former Clara E. Smith and the photographer Edward Steichen, Mary Steichen grew to maturity in the kind of bohemian affluence that can mark the families of particularly successful artists.[22] She was, in addition, reared a Quaker, and her religious devotion played a large role in shaping her public commitments in the years to come.

As a freshman at Vassar College in 1921, Steichen had her first encounter with sex education as it was then practiced, but the event was hardly an epiphany. In the required freshman hygiene course, a college physician inaugurated the annual notorious "sex" lecture with the sage admonition, "Now, girls, keep your affections wrapped in cotton wool until Mr. Right comes along," before touching briefly on the facts of reproduction.[23] Steichen was unimpressed.

After Vassar, the brilliant young woman foundered. For three years Steichen attempted to become a professional actress before accepting that she would never make it to the top ranks. Her first marriage, too, fell apart—a disaster she later attributed, in part, to "sexual repression." Because she was from a wealthy family and because this was New York in the 1920s, Steichen began seeing a Freudian analyst, who advised her to enter medical school.

In 1932, when she began to study medicine at the University of Rochester, Steichen started down the path to her destiny. Dr. Mary Steichen Calderone (she married Dr. Frank Calderone in 1941) emerged from her medical training with a deep commitment to the public health profession as a force for change in society. Limited as a woman to a narrow range of choices for medical practice, Calderone toiled for ten years as a physician in the Great Neck, New York, public school system. In 1953, however, she received an offer to become medical director for the rapidly expanding Planned Parenthood Federation of America. Worried colleagues advised her she might lose her reputation by working for the controversial organization, but Calderone was undaunted. "I have no reputation to lose," she said.[24]

Although the libertarian objectives she pursued in much of her medical career were to differentiate her clearly from less controversial counterparts at ASHA, Calderone's commitments at Planned Parenthood and afterward nevertheless grew out of her Quaker faith and a sexual ideology that was becoming, among the college-educated middle class, commonplace and even conservative. "Companionate marriage," in the broad sense of a relationship characterized by mutuality and personal fulfillment rather than legal obligations and a responsibility to reproduce, had been a cultural ideal since at least the 1920s, when Calderone attended college and was married for the first time, and the ideal thereafter guided her approach to sexual matters. As the medical director of Planned Parenthood from 1953 to 1965, naturally Calderone supported the right to birth control, and like her colleagues in that organization she justified that right by appealing primarily to women's right "to develop unhampered a constantly deepening relationship with their husbands," by expressing their love without "fear of an unwanted pregnancy."[25] Even as Calderone in 1958 organized the nation's first major national conference on abortion, she combined her support for a relaxation of abortion laws with a stress on "preventive medicine," such as sex education, to encourage "higher standards of sexual conduct and . . . a greater sense of responsibility toward pregnancy."[26] In her career at Planned Parenthood, Calderone assigned great importance to sexual freedom, but only insofar as it buttressed the marriage relationship.

A similar combination of freedom and responsibility motivated Calderone's commitment to sex education in the public schools. From her earlier years as a school physician in Great Neck, Calderone had derived the conviction that schools shared the duty of helping young people find fulfillment in their human relations, including their sexual adjustment.[27] This duty, however, did not include inculcation in moral absolutes, for Calderone agreed with a growing chorus of social observers that American culture was far too dynamic and diverse for educators to impose any predetermined moral code on students. At any rate, it had been Calderone's experience—shared by increasing numbers of educators—that young people responded unenthusiastically to blatant moral prescriptions.

In her own talk to Vassar undergraduates in 1964, some forty years after she had graduated, Calderone made it clear that despite her own religious devotion, she intentionally steered her sex education talks away from such words as "ideals, morals, sacred, and so on." She did not discard all standards, however. While condemning sex outside of marriage, Calderone had arrived at a position much like that of her ally, Kirkendall, in which sexual relations were good or bad insofar as they were "nonexploitive" and served to enhance the meaningful relationship between two people. Indeed, a proper sex education, in Calderone's opinion, would convey both the "facts of life" and "some glimmering of awareness of how the gift of sex can be used *for* each other by two people in the primary relationship." But Calderone disagreed with Kirkendall's final proclamation that a man and a woman could achieve a meaningful, nonexploitive sexual relationship outside of marriage. Calderone focused particular attention on the meaning of the sexual relationship for women. Only time, Calderone maintained, the waiting, the investing, the self-disciplining of time, would allow a person to enter marriage as "a whole person," and not, in her telling phrase, "as one who has been nibbled at by bits and pieces given away prematurely."[28] Young people possessed sexual freedom, but they had to exercise it within the boundaries of responsible self-fulfillment.

A fulfilling marriage remained Calderone's primary goal for women and men. This commitment left Calderone, despite her association with sexual liberalism, profoundly ambivalent about the sexual revolution of the 1960s. In the end, the doctor told the assembled Vassar freshmen in 1964, "I have a passionate desire that young people, who are today so free, not only should understand and respect, but also should aspire to and achieve, the permanent man-woman relationship" of marriage. Thus Calderone had, by her own admission, come almost full circle. "Now girls," she concluded in her Vassar address, "keep your affections wrapped in cotton wool until marriage."[29]

The popularity of SIECUS and sex education in general in the 1960s derived as much from this vestigial moralism as from the educators' innovations in methods and messages. Although opponents would later charge that SIECUS members and their allies had pressed sex education programs on an unwilling and unwitting public, SIECUS would have accomplished little without the rise of a nationwide panic about the sexual revolution. Concern over sexual changes provided the real energy for a proliferation of sex education programs; SIECUS and related organizations tried to stimulate and channel this energy, but by and large they merely followed popular demand for some kind of public response to the sexual revolution.

Few questioned the existence of this "revolution." "We are all in a period in which the sexual mores are changing," Kirkendall told the Association for Higher Education in 1964. "We have, therefore, a choice to make. Will the changes occur through a war of attrition, a sort of guerrilla in-fighting, with youths engaged in a kind of civil disobedience campaign and the adults in essence refusing to acknowledge that any issue exists? Or will we discuss the problem openly and, hopefully, arrive at some consensus in which sex is integrated along with the rest of our capacities in a genuinely humane concept of life and its purpose?"[30] In his hopes for the future, Kirkendall took a rosier view than most, but his analysis of the sexual scene of the early 1960s nevertheless mirrored adults' increasing concern that young people were instigating a sexual revolution.

Commentators in every outlet from educational periodicals and public health journals to popular magazines and television specials echoed Kirkendall's description of a generation gap in sexual mores, and thousands of worried parents took up the cry. Articles on "sexual ethics," particularly those on premarital sex among young people, multiplied from the early 1960s to the middle of the decade, and a similar distribution occurred for pieces on venereal disease among teenagers. Conspicuously, *Time* and *Newsweek* each devoted cover stories in 1964 to the sexual and moral revolutions taking place at elite American colleges.[31] Other books and electronic media emulated those magazines' enticing combination of sociological investigation and prurient exposé, aided by the remarkable willingness of "sexual revolutionaries" on campuses from Harvard to Ohio State to Berkeley to proclaim the birth of a new morality.

These cultural changes rested on large demographic changes. As many members of the baby boom generation reached their late teens and early twenties, they began to reverse their parents' trend toward early marriage and child rearing. The median age at first marriage for women began a slow, steady climb past 20.5 years beginning in 1963, and in 1964 the median age for men crept above 23.0 years for the first time since 1948.[32] Delayed marriage for this generation did not necessarily bring with it chastity. Beginning in the mid-1960s, according to two historians, the incidence of premarital intercourse among white females, in particular, began to "zoom" upward; ultimately, white female rates were to narrow substantially "the disparity between them and their male peers."[33]

Some college students at this time also tried to cast off the traditional institutional restrictions on their behavior. At the same time that many youths in the 1960s were becoming aware of themselves as a separate generation with separate interests, they mounted challenges to a time-worn set of rules on parietal visits, sex-segregated living, and such nonsexual subjects as student input into education, off-campus living, and dress codes. For reasons of economic convenience as well as conscience, most colleges and universities were to capitulate to almost all of the student demands by the end of the decade.

A revolution also seemed to be taking place in the public visibility of sexual matters. A series of U.S. Supreme Court decisions on obscenity in the 1950s and '60s had removed some of the legal strictures on disseminating sexually explicit materials, and the media's new stress on frankness in sexual themes seemed to make sexuality more public than ever. "Words like coitus, orgasm, penis, vagina, erection, ejaculation are used fairly freely— to be sure sometimes with the intent to shock," noted a generally favorable contributor to the *PTA Magazine* in 1967. "Formerly taboo topics like homosexuality, masturbation, contraception, and abortion are discussed at public forums, in newspapers, and in popular magazines."[34] Political movements to loosen many of the legal restrictions on contraception and abortion only added to the din of sexual discussion.

Parents, educators, and community groups took their cues particularly from the popular literature's conflation of public health concerns and moral anxiety. "Parental panic," noted John Kobler in the *Saturday Evening Post*, "has given the revolution [in sex education] its main impetus."[35] Kobler's 1968 article, which became one of the most widely read examinations of the sex education movement, came late enough in the movement to present a kind of confused summary of sexual anxieties:

National statistics tell part of the story. Venereal diseases among teenagers: over 80,000 cases reported in 1966 . . . Unwed teen-age mothers: about 90,000 a year, an increase of 100 percent in two decades.

One out of every three brides under 20 goes to the altar pregnant . . .
illegal abortions performed on adolescents run into the hundreds of
thousands. One of the findings that decided New York City's New
Lincoln School to adopt sex education was a poll of its 11th-graders
on their attitudes toward premarital intercourse: The majority saw
nothing wrong with it . . . Newspaper reports of dropouts and run-
aways, of drug-taking, sexual precocity and general delinquency intensify the worries of parents.

But these evils are only the grosser symptoms of a widespread social upheaval. Communication between the generations has stalled
("Don't trust anyone over thirty"), and moral values once accepted
by children because Mom and Dad said so have given way to a morality of the relative ("What's right or wrong? It all depends on the particular situation, on the individual").[36]

To his list, Kobler might well have added anxiety over the birth-control pill
and sex crimes, but his shorter enumeration adequately represented the
problems that led parents to pressure school boards for solutions to sexual
troubles among adolescents. Community leaders sought to use education
as a "vaccination" against these symptoms of social decay.[37]

Given their fears of sexual rebellion and its consequences, many parents
began to believe that sex education might be the proper response to the
younger generation's moral decline. Roper and Gallup polls conducted
throughout the postwar decades consistently found the number of Americans favoring some kind of sex education in the high schools to top 60 percent; this support peaked in mid-1968 at 71 percent.[38] Even if many teachers were still reluctant to undertake sex education, many of the more
cosmopolitan school superintendents were also predisposed to heed parents' wishes for sex instruction in the schools.

Professional sex educators were naturally delighted with the popular interest in their subject but ambivalent about community expectations. Leading educators were well aware that no study yet had found sex education or
family life education to have a measurable impact on students' behavior, let
alone on broader indices of social dysfunction. Kirkendall decried the tendency of parents to look on sex education as "disaster insurance," but a

prominent contributor to the 1964 omnium-gatherum, the *Handbook of Marriage and the Family*, warned of trouble if the instigator of a sex or family life course "refuses to 'sell' it as a cure for divorce, delinquency, and other great social issues."[39]

The temptation to make such claims proved irresistible, even for the leading sex educators. Had not the original impulse for sex education grown directly out of social hygiene's promise to "solve" the problems of venereal disease, prostitution, and sexual misconduct? Fifty years had not greatly changed the educators' mission. For all her emphasis on a positive approach to sex, even Mary Steichen Calderone found her major spur to action in the rising incidence of teenage venereal disease, high rates of divorce for young people, and high numbers of teenage pregnancies. Sex education, she felt, could be "preventative medicine."[40] Certainly some sex educators explicitly denied that sex education would "solve" anything. But by interlacing their articles and speeches with statistics on illegitimacy, teenage marriage, and sexually transmitted diseases, they nevertheless implied strongly that their program had at least a tangential bearing on remedying the problems. Whatever their ambivalence, SIECUS members and other leaders were not about to apply the brakes to sex education's gathering momentum.

"America seems to have suddenly discovered an urgent need for sex education," John Kobler reported in 1968, "and is galloping off in all directions at once to meet it."[41] A number of sex education programs predated the family life education crusades of the 1950s, and with SIECUS members barnstorming the country, small grants for sex education coming from the U.S. Commissioner of Education starting in 1966, and, above all, parental concern with the morals revolt, thousands of other communities came to imitate those programs.[42]

In Chicago, for example, the public schools had been largely bereft of sex education ever since Superintendent Ella Flagg Young went down to defeat over the issue in 1913. Right next door, however, parents in the well-to-do suburb of Evanston, Illinois, got a comprehensive sex education curriculum installed in the community's kindergarten through twelfth-grade classes in 1956, and the program flourished for the next nine years while Chicago schools remained silent on the subject. Finally, in 1965, a Chicago school board member, citing great increases in teenage venereal disease and in the number of girls dropping out of school because of pregnancy, secured an appropriation for the city school superintendent to formulate a program.[43] By 1969 Chicago had courses emphasizing "the values of the family as the basic social unit in our society, particularly as responsible sexual behavior relates to the family," in more than two hundred elementary schools and all fifty-seven city high schools. Similar programs proliferated across the country after 1965: by 1968, Kobler estimated, nearly 50 percent of all schools were offering some kind of sex education.[44]

Nowhere was sex education taken up with more vigor than in the California public schools. Perhaps the relative newness of most California communities led many Californians to see the public schools as their primary institution of reform and community order. San Diego had had a model program in sex and family life education since World War II, and now the rest of the state worked hard to catch up. Much of the impulse came in 1965 from the California state legislature's hearings on domestic relations, which many prominent family life and sex educators used as a public platform for airing their views. The following year, Governor Edmund G. Brown established the Governor's Commission on the Family, and charged it explicitly with the duty of developing a course in family life education. Local circumstances also led to change. Under pressure from the local Parent-Teacher Association (PTA) in 1969 to do something about divorce, illegitimacy, delinquency, and other social dysfunctions, the Sacramento County school board, for example, hired three staff advisors and invited SIECUS consultants, including Calderone and Kirkendall, to help set up its K–12 Family Life and Sex Education program.[45] At about the same time, the Oakland Unified School District cooperated with its county health organization in working toward its own K–12 integrated program in family life.[46] In San Mateo County, just south of San Francisco, the local medical society allied with educators and PTA members to create a sexually frank family life program.

These programs resembled the earlier family life education courses in their therapeutic intent and flexible methodologies, but they dwelt more fixedly on the topic of sex. Notably, the new programs often extended sex education of sorts to the elementary schools, as in Palo Alto, California, where kindergarten children were allowed to help bathe babies in class, and in the city of San Mateo, where students learned the fundamentals of human reproduction before third grade and the proper anatomical terms for the reproductive system by the end of sixth grade. In high schools, the sex education units leaned heavily on the ethical side of sexual relationships: students discussed such films as *The Game*, which tells a story about a teenage boy and girl who have sex and regret it.

Most California programs were far from radical. Although many educators agreed in principle with Sacramento County's commitment to making the programs "nonauthoritarian," in fact the courses were geared toward adjusting students to a fairly traditional standard of sexual behavior.[47] Rather than directly lecturing students to delay intercourse until marriage, teachers handed out lists of venereal disease statistics and offered cautionary tales of teenage loves ruined by social censure or pregnancy. Students were to draw their own conclusions from these loaded "facts." Although such tactics undermined their claims to neutrality, teachers were not thereby perverting the sex education impulse. From the beginning, parents and administrators had sought deliberately to use sex education to shore up youthful morals. The multiplication of courses, materials, and interest in the 1960s was largely an expression of this will to uphold traditional morality.

By 1968 Calderone's decision to create SIECUS seemed to be entirely vindicated. Not only had hundreds of programs already commenced, but also the publicity they were receiving promised to bring hundreds more school systems into the fold. Publicity, however, was an unpredictable machine. Even as sex education programs were receiving their most favorable notices ever in the national press, conservative activists throughout the country were awakening to the intruder in their midst.

The year 1968 was to prove particularly fertile for conservative backlash. A series of shocks had been building tension throughout the decade. For the previous three years, U.S. involvement in Vietnam had been increasingly polarizing domestic opinion, and an antiwar movement made up most conspicuously of student political radicals and counterculture "hippies" had grown more and more visible and militant. The spring 1968 Tet offensive in Vietnam caused the so-called liberal establishment to begin questioning the nation's Vietnam policy as well, prompting many conservatives to decry the liberals' "caving in" to student radicals. Polarization over issues of poverty, race, and law and order seemed to deepen when Martin Luther King's assassination on April 4 touched off riots in more than a hundred cities. A great many Americans, particularly conservatives, were losing patience with antiwar activists and with what seemed like rampant criminality in the nation's ghettos. When Chicago mayor Richard Daley endorsed a "police riot" against hippies and antiwar protestors during the Democratic Convention there in August, the result was not national sympathy for the unarmed protesters but an outpouring of support for Daley.

To radicals and conservatives alike, the sexual revolution seemed to be of a piece with the antiwar movement and the counterculture. Whether or not they had plowed through Herbert Marcuse's turgid *Eros and Civilization,* many college students had concluded that sexual repression was somehow intimately related to America's modern, mechanized, and warlike culture; sexual liberation, conversely, could become part of the struggle against an oppressive civilization. Vietnam protest posters urging Americans to "Make love, not war" were only the most obvious example of this fusion of political activism and sexual liberation in the late 1960s. Many campus radicals proclaimed the unity of sexual and political revolution, and many conservatives began to take them at their word.

During the spring of 1968, controversies over sex education began to flare up in northern California and a handful of other locales, but the greatest battle was fought in Anaheim in southern California, which was home to not only a comprehensive sex education program but also a peculiar confluence of right-wing networks. It was, noted an observer for the *Village Voice,* "the exact point where the two contending forces were concentrated."[48]

Comprehensive sex education in the Anaheim Union High School District had grown out of an earlier failure in sex education. The junior and senior high schools had been teaching rudimentary classes in sex education for a number of years when in 1962 a group of parents, led by a local Catholic priest, criticized the use of a film in which a coach discussed masturbation. Rather than remove the film, the school board commissioned an opinion survey that revealed that more than 90 percent of the parents in Anaheim felt that sex education of some sort should be given in junior and senior high schools.[49]

Buoyed by such support, however vague, the school board had a citizen's advisory committee aid the district's school nurse, Sally Williams, in developing a course in family life and sex education (FLSE) for grades seven through twelve. By 1966, almost every student in the Anaheim junior high and high schools was studying an age-appropriate five-week FLSE curriculum. SIECUS was not involved in setting up the curriculum, but the comprehensive program was so much in accord with Calderone's goals that she soon hired Sally Williams as a SIECUS consultant.

Like any other academic subject, FLSE was an age-graduated, cumulative program. In some ways the curriculum actually began in elementary school, as children up through the third grade learned about families, physical growth, and babies. This information formed the foundation for students in fourth grade to sixth grade to learn about the great changes awaiting them at puberty—especially menstruation for the girls and general pubertal changes, such as the onset of nocturnal emissions, for the boys. Students in seventh through ninth grade were exposed to the more controversial sexual subjects: intercourse, masturbation, dating, petting, homosexuality, venereal disease, and a handful of other topics. With these preliminaries out of the way, the later high school curriculum consisted largely of marriage education, as students learned more about courtship and engagement, marital adjustment, family planning (contraceptive methods), and child rearing philosophies.

Much of the curriculum strongly resembled the older family life education courses, but Sally Williams's program broke with this tradition in its methodology and much of its content. Despite the occasionally explicit subject matter, all FLSE classes were coeducational. In the older approach to sex education, classes had normally been segregated by sex, but family life education in general had been coeducational, and Williams and many others chose to apply this aspect of FLE directly to sex education. Williams insisted from the beginning that if the course were to realize its goal of improved interpersonal communication and, ultimately, more stable marriages, then boys and girls must learn in the same classroom. Leaders proclaimed that no subject would be too delicate or embarrassing for teachers to compromise on the coeducational method.

Mixed-sex classrooms were all the more important to educators because the Anaheim classrooms, like so many classes in this new wave of sex education, were "dialogue-centered." Sex education in the 1960s had been carried along on the wave of educational reform that sought to replace "teacher-centered" classrooms with "student-centered" learning.[50] No longer did the teacher simply lecture passive students: "The teacher serves as a catalyst," Williams explained, "creating a classroom where honest communication can take place between students."[51] Through discussion, debate, small-group projects, and role playing, students spent far more time speaking to one another than listening to a teacher. Williams hoped that boys and girls could thus reach mutual understanding on such subjects as dating etiquette, sexual standards, and sex roles.

Dethroning the teacher was more than just a pedagogical technique; it was part of FLSE's attempt to reject sex education's tradition of blatant moral prescription. "Experienced teachers know that young people simply drop a mental curtain when the moralizing and sermonizing begin," noted Williams. Further, she argued, "This approach hardly prepares young people to deal with a complex and uncertain world where standards of all kinds are in a state of upheaval. And finally, whose code is to be taught in the schools of this pluralistic society? The minute a school tries to establish a code about masturbation, for example, or premarital sex, petting and necking, dating, and other such subjects, it is placing itself in a precarious position." Rather than take what Williams called a "tell-them-what-is-right" approach, Anaheim's curriculum tried to prepare students "to decide on a set of values that they choose for themselves." The dialogue-centered classroom gave students "an opportunity to question adult beliefs about what is moral, to examine the reality of adult behavior, and to discuss their own beliefs with their peers."[52] On the surface, at least, this change in emphasis represented a radical break with the past.

Dialogue and moral neutrality began early in the Anaheim curriculum. In the ninth grade, for example, students examined dating standards and sexual morality to find an understanding of "the divergence between actual behavior and personal and societal moral codes." Recognizing that the ninth-graders felt "very close to adulthood and that they want adult experiences," teachers held a "Great Debate" in which teams of students debated the pros and cons of sexual intercourse before marriage. Similarly, students in the tenth grade were trusted to evaluate petting and premarital sex for themselves against a list of criteria for moral behavior that Lester Kirkendall had generated: did these behaviors lead to such positive outcomes as "Integrity in relationships" and "Broadening of human sympathies," or were they more likely to foster "Duplicity in relationships" and "Exploitation of others?"[53]

FLSE attempted to foster a similar questioning attitude in regard to sex roles and family structures. Like some other family life educators since World War II, Sally Williams saw sex roles more as social conventions than as inherent characteristics, but she took this insight further than her predecessors to encourage a mild revision of traditional sex roles. Students in junior high, for example, engaged in a role-playing exercise in which they took the parts of family members in the colonial era, when the father was more clearly "the head of the household, taskmaster, teacher, minister, decision maker." After reading a document arguing that many 1960s families "are operating as true partnerships of husbands and wives," students broke into small groups to discuss the relations of authority in their own families. Similar exercises continued through the high school years. In most grades, students also reexamined sex roles in American society, as in the tenth-grade unit on "The changing male and female roles." Here students separated into smaller groups of boys and girls to create lists of masculine and feminine characteristics before entering a full-class discussion on their differing interpretations of sexual roles.[54] In this pre–women's liberation era, such revisions were mild indeed, but they nevertheless embodied Williams and her allies' attempts to shake free of their forebears' unquestioning sexism.

In keeping with this tone of liberalism and moral neutrality, Anaheim's FLSE program sought to dispel myths that masturbation was physically harmful and offered a treatment of homosexuality that was, for the time, sympathetic. Explaining that students might know masturbation better by other names, such as "playing with yourself" or "jacking off," the seventh-grade booklet's section on special problems of puberty offered the advice that "the dire consequences that are commonly believed to follow from masturbation are almost entirely fictitious . . . Actually, any harm resulting from masturbation, according to the best medical authorities, is likely to be caused by worry or a sense of guilt due to misinformation." As part of the broader ninth-grade unit on "sexual deviations," students learned that homosexuality "has been known throughout human history and occurs in many societies." While noting that homosexuality was not approved or condoned, the study guide explained that "occasional sexual interest in others of the same sex or periods of great interest frequently occur in adolescents who do not become homosexuals in adult life." Although students viewed a ten-minute film, *Boys Beware*, which pointed out the dangerous patterns that homosexuals might use to approach young boys, curriculum materials also noted without comment that many legal scholars and church officials supported removing private sexual behavior between consenting adults from the list of crimes. Indeed, the problem of homosexuality seemed not unrelated to other problems of sexual repression in American society. The ninth-grade study guide quoted approvingly a SIECUS publication that called for "adequate sex education of both parents and children, so that the homosexual can understand himself better and the community can free itself of its punitive attitudes toward all sexuality."[55] In FLSE, homosexuality was still a statistical "deviation," like exhibitionism and rape, from the married, heterosexual norm, but Williams tried to steer students toward a greater sense of tolerance.

Above all, Williams sought to make Anaheim's curriculum frank and straightforward. How could students create their own moral framework if educators did not give them the fullest possible information? As with moral neutrality, sexual explicitness began early. Williams developed a description of sexual intercourse for seventh-graders, for example, that attempted to answer their questions with satisfactory detail but "without inviting more questions related to technique." After preliminaries suggesting that sexual intercourse was shared only between married couples, the handout delved into the act itself: after the couple kiss and embrace, "the woman's mind and body become prepared for the act of intercourse. The vagina becomes soft and moist. Meanwhile, the man's penis has become erect or hard so that it may enter the vagina easily." After a "pleasurable sexual climax, or orgasm," the male's sperm "is ejected or released into the upper part of the woman's vagina" and a "new life" may perhaps begin. "When two married people, deeply in love, have intercourse, they communicate their love in this intimate and joyous way." FLSE did not go so far as to display pictures of the sexual act, but this description—and its suggestion that an orgasm was a pleasurable sensation—went well beyond portrayals in earlier sex education materials. By the time students reached the twelfth grade, they were fully prepared for a unit on family planning that not only covered the theoretical issues of family size and the historical roles of Margaret Sanger and Anthony Comstock but also discussed the practical methods of birth control in great detail. The examination of birth control devices concluded with the admonition, "Any method is better than none"—a recognition, however tacit, that many of the students might engage in premarital intercourse.[56] The contrast with ASHA, which had largely avoided even mentioning contraception for half a century, could not have been clearer.

Despite the official emphasis on suspending moral judgment, however, most of the FLSE teachers were, like Calderone and her allies, deeply interested in supporting a more traditional scheme of moral values. Sally Williams stood squarely in favor of abstinence from premarital petting (what one of her handouts called "the first steps of intercourse") as well as premarital coitus. The program materials avoided overt moralizing but repeatedly invoked venereal disease, pregnancy, half-truths from behavioral science, and disapproving social standards to help students arrive "freely" at a rational understanding of sexual ethics.[57] The in-class Great Debate over premarital intercourse, for example, came only after the ninth-grade students had listened to tape recordings of "personal stories of young people involved in premarital pregnancy, nonmarital intercourse, and teenage marriages," so that they could "realize the ramifications caused by premarital relationships and teenage marriages."[58] Further, the discussion guide on which students based their debate was heavily biased toward the conclusion that premarital sex was wrong. "Physical union before marriage is very, very seldom a preview of sexual love within marriage," the discussion guide explained. "When it is one of many promiscuous encounters, to the boy it is merely an exciting sensual episode during which he is interested only in his own satisfaction. It has no other meaning, no past, no future . . . it may leave an after-taste of shame or disgust or worry about inadequate technique or abilities. This can affect their sexual relations for years, even for life."[59]

Students read further about society's double standard of morality, which

condemned young women for taking the sexual liberties that had always
been available to boys. The lessons suggested not that this was unfair to
girls but that it was another very good reason for them to remain chaste.[60]
As well, numerous curriculum materials at every grade level after elementary school warned of the disasters of premarital pregnancy, and as noted,
teachers did not explain contraception until the students' senior year. The
Anaheim curriculum thus echoed Mary Steichen Calderone's own combination of liberalism and moralism in response to the sexual revolution.

The combination seemed to work, for a time. Sally Williams and Paul
Cook, the Anaheim school superintendent, soon found themselves in great
demand with other schools and the national press. SIECUS and other organizations held the Anaheim course up as a model for school districts seeking to cope with the sexual revolution. For three years, Anaheim's FLSE
program continued without controversy.

During the 1967–68 school year, however, Anaheim conservatives began
to sit up and take notice. The conservative reaction began quietly. One conservative Catholic parent, Eleanor Howe, had her private misgivings about
the course partly confirmed by her two sons, who attended high school in
Anaheim. At some point during the school year, Howe went to their school
to view the curriculum materials herself, and she was shocked by what she
considered to be overly explicit sexual descriptions and overly sympathetic
treatments of homosexuality and masturbation. Still more damning, in
Howe's eyes, was the near absence of moral injunctions. "It wasn't so much
the information," Howe later recalled. "It was the shift in values."[61]

During the summer of '68, Howe distributed inflammatory excerpts
from the course, held parent meetings in her home, and eventually joined a
local organization named MOMS, or Mothers Organized for Moral Stability, to take up the fight against sex education. Anaheim proved a fertile field
for her activism. Although there was nothing unique about the mostly religious women who gathered in Howe's living room to plot their strategy,
Anaheim possessed a strong network of support for conservative activism.
Conservative Republicans ran the community's major institutions, Disney-
land and nearby Knott's Berry Farm, and helped set the political tone for
the area as a whole. As of 1966 the John Birch Society boasted of 3,000
members in Anaheim. The remnants of the California Citizens Committee,

an organization created to support Barry Goldwater's 1964 presidential
candidacy, helped coordinate the opposition to sex education and lent the
struggle greater prestige in the media. A number of local churches, too,
provided meeting places and moral backing for MOMS. The winds of religious conservatism in the district were strengthened by the *Anaheim
Bulletin,* one of a string of "Freedom Newspapers" that the conservative en-
trepreneur R. C. Hoiles had purchased around midcentury to warn "right-
thinking Americans" of the threat from "Jewish conspirators and other
subversive enemies of the American nation."[62] The *Bulletin* soon took the
lead in attacking the Anaheim curriculum and its creators, and roused the
opposition with constant articles and editorials about the latest sex education atrocity.

Under Howe's prodding, members of MOMS began to recount traumas
the course had inflicted on their own children, including a teacher's shocking students by writing obscene words on the blackboard, and another
teacher's supposedly asking a junior student in class what he would do if he
someday came across his own son masturbating.[63] A program that would
sanction such behavior, opponents maintained, was contrary to what parents in the district wanted from their schools. Howe and the other mothers
were finding ample raw material in the curriculum to arouse concern.

It took the work of professional activists, however, to forge this animosity toward sex education into a semicoherent philosophy of opposition.
Earlier in 1968, Gordon V. Drake had stumbled across the issue of sex
education almost by accident. A former professor of education who had
taught at small colleges and a fundamentalist Christian seminary, Drake
had more recently been making a living as a pamphleteer for the John
Birch Society and for the Reverend Billy James Hargis's fundamentalist organization, Christian Crusade. Like his employers, Drake had been warning for years that Satan was seeking earthly dominion through the medium
of a world communist conspiracy and its offshoots, which included secularism, American liberalism, and "progressive" education. Although Drake
seemed to find hints of communist intrigue throughout American life, he
had until this point always considered sex education and adolescent sexuality to be only minor factors in America's slide toward Sodom.

Drake's audience convinced him otherwise. His first major piece for the

Christian Crusade, *Black Board Power: NEA Threat to America* (1968), charged the National Education Association with turning youths against their parents and toward secularism and "groupthink." Drake soon became aware that readers and activists responded most strongly to one particular section of the pamphlet—the chapter on the NEA's involvement with sex education. He obligingly expanded his brief examination of sex education into a separate forty-page pamphlet. The result was incendiary.

*Is the Schoolhouse the Proper Place to Teach Raw Sex?* became an underground best-seller. By Drake's estimate, it sold more than 90,000 copies, at fifty cents apiece, within three months of publication.[64] The money was a godsend for the Christian Crusade, which had lost its tax-exempt status for mixing too much politics with its religion, and Reverend Hargis capitalized further by taking Drake on the revival circuit through the South and West, where the two men spoke to rapt audiences about the sex educators' plan for social domination.[65]

At some point in the summer of 1968, Drake's pamphlet fell into the hands of the Anaheim sex education opponents, and Drake and Billy James Hargis carried their religious revival into Orange County in the fall of 1968. Although no more than a small vanguard of sex education opponents ever accepted Drake's indictment in full, the Christian Crusade pamphleteer nevertheless gave to MOMS and related organizations a wealth of unsubstantiated anecdotes, a framework of analysis, and a target for their rage.

Drake crafted his indictment by weaving classic right-wing themes with an imaginative, semipornographic portrait of education. He first offered his readers an edited version of actual sex education techniques and programs and recounted sex education "horror stories" of less reliable origin. Ironically, Drake derived most of his factual information from laudatory articles about sex education in the popular press, including *Look* magazine and John Kobler's long review in the *Saturday Evening Post.* But in Drake's capable hands the anecdotes took on a sinister shape. Drake decried the "flood of materials" being put out for sex education, including "unbelievably clever models which even include multi-colored plastic human figures with interchangeable male and female sex organs—instant transvestitism." In Van Nuys, California, he noted, a high school teacher had polled students about the variety of their sexual activities; in Evanston, Illinois, kindergartners were "exposed to the full details of the human birth process"; elsewhere, students intently watched *The Game,* a film in which a boy has coitus with a female virgin. In an unnamed community, Drake recounted, there occurred a "super-realistic classroom demonstration" in which a teacher or student applied "a condrum [*sic*] on a life size plastic phallus," while in many other mystery locations schools were installing "joint boy-girl toilet facilities without partitions" in an effort to desensitize children and free them of their inhibitions.[66] Drake's account of sex education atrocities joined the other unsubstantiated sex education anecdotes that would soon crop up in Anaheim's opposition literature and in controversies throughout the nation: a sex education teacher in Michigan "stripping" before her class, a young female sex educator raped by overstimulated male students, boys and girls sent into dark closets together for "exploration," and teachers forcing their children to take questionnaires that probed their families' sexual habits.[67] Such details helped to inflate the sense of danger in Anaheim and elsewhere.

Although Drake's "factual" accounts played a role in the opposition, Drake's central contribution was to make SIECUS stand for all sex education, and then to identify SIECUS with what Mary Calderone would soon label "a party line of lies, skillfully constructed half truths and quotes out of context."[68] At a basic level, Drake employed a tactic of guilt by association for SIECUS members. He erroneously accused several members of belonging to the Communist Party or peddling pornography, and he did not hesitate to attack SIECUS for the personal and intellectual heresies of writers whose works merely showed up occasionally in organization bibliographies.[69] And just as Calderone had charged, he uncovered damning fragments of quotations from such SIECUS stalwarts as Calderone, Kirkendall, and even the Reverend William Genné. An organization that harbored such people, Drake charged, was not to be trusted.

Drake relied on more than half-truths to make his indictment. *Is the Schoolhouse the Proper Place to Teach Raw Sex?* became a central document for the conservative attack on sex education by plugging SIECUS directly into the hot current of right-wing paranoia. With a worldview inherited in equal measure from Senator Joe McCarthy's red-baiting crusade and from deeper fundamentalist Protestant metaphysics, Hargis and his followers believed deeply that a satanic conspiracy manifesting itself as world communism threatened the United States.[70] Hargis maintained that a network of conspirators, in place since Roosevelt's "socialist" New Deal, was seeking to undermine the nation's religious and economic traditions to smooth the path for domination by atheistic communists. As McCarthy had proclaimed, this was not an uprising of the proletariat but a conspiracy populated by people of privilege—lawyers, financiers, and, especially, the educated elite in the universities, the government, and private foundations.

To draw the connection between SIECUS and the conspiracy, Drake did not have to restate explicitly Hargis's theories. He needed only to list the lofty organizational affiliations of SIECUS members and dig at their power and respectability. Drake's readers, "trained by Hargis, could put two and two together."[71] As a nonmembership organization of sex education leaders, SIECUS seemed well connected indeed to the most elite conspirators, comprising, as it did, directors of the National Education Association; the National Council of Churches; Planned Parenthood; and the U.S. Department of Health, Education and Welfare; as well as numerous professors and academic researchers—an "interlocking directorate," Drake charged, of liberal thought.[72] Hargis's followers were already aware of these organizations' roles in the communist takeover; SIECUS's coordinating role placed it at the center of the conspiracy.

Sex education, according to Hargis, was a central part of SIECUS and the NEA's "cleverly contrived plan" to "destroy the traditional moral fiber of America and replace it with a pervasive sickly humanism." Taking Calderone and other sex educators at their word that the curriculum's goal was to dispel false modesty and allow a frank and nonjudgmental consideration of sexual matters, Drake discerned a desire to eliminate completely "any inhibitions or moral and religious taboos." Eliminating inhibitions played directly into SIECUS's hidden mission: "This, obviously drives a wedge between the family, church and school—bolstering the authority of the school while casting cynical doubts on the traditional moral teachings of the home and church," Drake argued. "If this is accomplished, and the new morality is affirmed, our children will become easy targets for Marxism and other amoral, nihilistic philosophies—as well as V.D.!"[73] SIECUS, and therefore all sex educators, stood accused of paving the path to communism with the bodies of American adolescents.

All of these charges found their way into an epic confrontation between MOMS and the Anaheim school board. On October 17, 1968, Howe and her allies staged a confrontation at a school board meeting, liberally sprinkling their harangues with passages from Drake's pamphlet.[74] When the board members moved to limit speeches to two minutes apiece, opponents simply lined up at the microphones and spoke in relays for three full hours. In addition to repeating Drake's anecdotes, his attacks on SIECUS, and his philosophical indictment of sex education, Howe charged without evidence that Anaheim's own family life and sex education course was causing teenage venereal disease and pregnancy rates to skyrocket in the district and enticing servicemen to crowd around the schools in search of "easy" girls.[75]

The shaken school board finally adjourned the meeting well after midnight, but members of MOMS were far from finished. In the months after the board meeting, MOMS and its allies kept up a drumbeat of confrontations, publications, and verbal assaults on the FLSE program.

Despite Superintendent Cook's energetic refutations of opponents and what Cook called their "semi-legal pornography," the FLSE curriculum was heavily outgunned: while a large majority of parents who had been surveyed supported sex education in general, their endorsements were passive, and in many cases what they had in mind may have differed greatly from what the district was implementing. In contrast, MOMS members were highly motivated and ideologically united. Such unity made all the difference in the low-turnout election for Anaheim's board of education in the spring of 1969, and anti–sex education candidates seized a majority of the seats. The new board promptly gutted the program, demoted the superintendent to "curriculum consultant," and returned Sally Williams to her previous job of school nurse, imposing a gag order to stop her from speaking to the press.[76]

Thousands of conservatives all over the country in the late 1960s seemed to agree with Gordon Drake and Anaheim's conservative activists that "sexperts" were engaging in a conspiracy to corrupt the nation's youth through sex education. Citizens' groups opposed to sex education sprouted nationwide, their official unrelatedness belied by the similarity of their acronyms: MOMS, MOTOREDE (Movement to Restore Decency), PAUSE (People against Unconstitutional Sex Education), POSSE (Parents Opposed to Sex and Sensitivity Education), and, proof that public schools were not the sole victims of the sex educators' plot, POPE (Parents for Orthodoxy in Parochial Education).[77]

Despite Drake and his allies' accusations, untruths, and misuses of SIECUS as the "whipping boy" for sex education, Mary Calderone refused to debate her attackers. "I just won't stoop to an interchange," she told an interviewer in 1970. "I don't go on platforms with liars, deliberate liars." Calderone was perhaps too genteel for gutter politics. "She seemed to speak not with the voice of a person but with the voice of a class," remembered the interviewer, "a voice that had been bred in generations of parlor and salon gatherings."[78]

When Calderone finally deigned to answer her opponents, she chose to do it in an article for the October 1969 issue of the *Vassar Alumnae Magazine*. No doubt she gained numerous new supporters among her fellow alumnae, but this did little to refute conservatives' charges. In a move not calculated to help the sex educators' standing with conservatives, it was *Playboy* magazine that undertook the major task of refuting the erroneous charges against sex education, largely without Calderone's help.

Had she spoken out more, Calderone might still have been unable to stem the tide of opposition. By the fall of 1969, various MOMSes and MOTOREDEs had precipitated battles over sex education in at least thirty states, and had scored some stunning victories—even the school board in Toms River, New Jersey, where Elizabeth Force had made her national reputation in family life education, retreated from sex education in the face of public opposition. Further, Congress and the legislatures of nineteen states were entertaining bills to prohibit or curtail sex education in the public schools.[79] Gordon Drake had tapped into a deep well of public rage.

The forces arrayed against sex education achieved their greatest triumph in California in 1969, when the legislature repealed a law that had been passed earlier in the decade supporting sex instruction and the state board of education adopted a staunchly conservative report on moral instruction in the schools. Written by a committee that featured right-wing educators and legislators, as well as a minister from Knott's Berry Farm in Orange County, the nonbinding "Guidelines for Moral Instruction in California Schools" warned that a "moral crisis is sweeping the land," including drug use, sexual promiscuity, illegitimacy, and crime. Unlike the social scientists who discerned the causes of the crisis in poor parenting or poverty or a host of other structural and social factors, the California committee blamed the crisis squarely on "cosmopolitan" attitudes and institutions.[80] The United Nations, the Supreme Court, mental health programs in the schools, Margaret Mead, and psychiatrists who attempted to eradicate guilt and fear in children were among the primary culprits. The report devoted another thirty-two pages to an attack on the famous pragmatic philosopher and educator John Dewey, SIECUS, and Lester Kirkendall, as exemplars of a dangerous "secular humanism."

For solutions to youthful unrest, the guidelines offered a program based on the Bible, century-old textbooks, such as *Cowdery's Moral Lessons,* and the Moral Leadership Program of the U.S. Marine Corps. Governor Ronald Reagan's appointees to the state board of education added the stipulation that Darwinian evolution should no longer be taught as fact but only as a theory equal in emphasis to biblical creationism.[81] The board's allies in Anaheim were overjoyed. Sex education had provided the critical wedge for moving a broad right-wing program into law.

Despite sex education opponents' claims that theirs was a fight for local control against an elite, cosmopolitan conspiracy, opposition efforts grew out of a loose national right-wing network that had been expanding throughout the decade and included the *Dan Smoot Report,* a radio show from Dallas, H. L. Hunt's *Life Lines,* and dozens of radio preachers and anticommunist pamphleteers, Hargis and Drake prominent among them.[82] Although the John Birch Society was originally taken unawares by the attacks on sex education, in January 1969 that organization's leader declared the necessity for local front groups to organize against the "filthy Communist plot" of sex education, and by April, local MOTOREDE committees, backed by the Birch Society, had sprouted across the land.[83] All of these groups woke up to sex education's potential for inflaming the faithful and converting previously apathetic conservatives, and they helped reproduce the Anaheim controversy in hundreds of other school districts throughout the nation. Not for nothing did a Birch Society representative declare that sex education was "the best recruiting device to come down the pike since fluoridation."[84]

Indeed, the sex education controversies of the late 1960s were crucial events in the development of the religious right. Like the crusades against obscenity earlier in the decade, the controversy over sex education demonstrated to the political right the usefulness of social issues in mobilizing not only fundamentalists and culturally conservative Catholics but also previously apolitical evangelicals who connected sex education with what one sociologist has labeled the "wider culture of modernity," with its assaults on traditional sexual morality, gender roles, and religious sentiment.[85]

When some members of the baby-boom generation moved toward more premarital sex, cohabitation before or instead of marriage, and eroded gender lines, they were clearly repudiating the conservatives' social norms. Outside of the Black Panthers, perhaps, nothing upset social conservatives more than this evidence that the coming generation was rejecting in general its elders' worship of patriotism, deferred gratification, and traditional sexual ideals. The high point—for conservative observers, the low point—of political radicalism and countercultural hedonism seemed to come with the well-publicized Woodstock festival in 1969, where half a million people, mostly young, danced to music and listened to political speeches, and some cavorted *en déshabillé* for all the nation to see. One Anaheim conservative knew she could always stir up her allies by showing them the *Life* magazine issue devoted to Woodstock, for only the most acute observers perceived that Woodstock was the birth not so much of a revolutionary nation as of a profitable market in record albums and bell-bottoms.[86]

It was ironic, but logical, that traditionalists should come to see SIECUS and sex educators as allies of the sexual revolution and the broader counterculture movement of the 1960s. On the surface the conflation seems strange, for SIECUS had risen to popularity largely on the strength of its hostility to teenage promiscuity, venereal disease, pregnancy, and all-around misbehavior. Like sex education curricula in general, SIECUS's materials were heavily imbued with sexual warnings, moralistic stories, and statements of support for conventional morality. Indeed, a gay rights group in 1970 declined to support sex education in the schools, justifiably fearing that sex education would become a vehicle for antihomosexual information.[87] Further, to attack sex education as a cause of the sexual revolution, opponents had to ignore the fact that the majority of adolescent "revolutionaries" had never heard an official word about sex in the schools.

Nevertheless, opponents worked up a faith in sex education's ability to do harm that outstripped even its most fervent supporters' faith in its ability to do good. Far from cooling off the sexual revolution, argued one author, "Present concepts of sex education will only add to the boiling cauldron of permissiveness and will hasten to destroy the family unit and parental authority."[88] To some extent, sex education must have seemed to opponents merely the most proximate, manipulable aspect of society's preoccupation with sex. A small group of committed activists could take over a school board more easily than it could the Supreme Court or Hollywood. But sex education was not only a convenient target; it really was the embodiment of a new middle-class sexual ethos that was closely related to the sexual revolution.

The anger in the traditionalists' attack measured the distance sex education had traveled from the sexual orthodoxy of the turn of the century.[89] Beneath the surface of opponents' attacks on communism and secular humanism lay a traditional set of sexual and moral values that seemed increasingly marginal in the late twentieth century, compared with the sex educators' ideology. Traditionalists adhered to a nineteenth-century middle-class ideology in which sex existed primarily as a force to be controlled and repressed, intercourse was clearly for married couples only, and sexual pleasure was secondary or tertiary behind procreation and marital duty. Marriage, in this view, was a sanctified institution for creating families. In the first decades of the twentieth century, these were not marginal ideas; indeed, the same ideology had motivated the founders of the sex education movement.

By the 1950s most members of the white middle-class still clung tightly to the taboo on premarital sex, but they had also come to embrace a sexual ethos in which pleasure could be separated from reproduction, at least within marriage. As the strictly economic functions of the family continued to decline, and as birth control became more widely available after to the development of the Pill and the Supreme Court's 1965 defense of married couples' right to contraception in *Griswold v. Connecticut,* many Americans were increasingly freed to interpret sex as Calderone did, in romantic terms, as the most intimate form of marital communication, or as one of the bonds of personal fulfillment for which marriage existed. To traditionalists, this approach reduced marriage to a contractual experiment in self-actualization, and degraded both the spouses and the institution. But these new marital and sexual ideals became important elements in the new sex education.

When increasing numbers of young people in the 1960s began also to justify premarital sex and other novelties with the same language that sex and family life educators had used for decades to glorify marriage, traditionalists felt that the nation's moral degradation was complete, and that the elitist authorities on marriage and the family were fully responsible. Sex educators refused to apologize and strove mightily, sometimes against their own personal inclination, not to condemn. When SIECUS affiliates like Kirkendall and the sociologist Ira Reiss proclaimed that young people were moving toward a moral standard of "permissiveness with affection," they spoke to many middle-class Americans who believed that love and affection had the power to sanctify almost any sexual behavior, but they did nothing to still traditionalist fears that America's youths were indulging in an unholy orgy.

Sex education's moderate response to the greater public openness about sexuality in the 1960s also offended many opponents. At a time when sex seemed to be exploding onto every billboard, movie screen, and magazine, conservatives felt that the public schools, at least, should be safe havens from the revolution outside. SIECUS leaders agreed, but they interpreted the school's role as providing a "balance" against these outside influences. If the public schools simply ignored the commercialization and public promulgation of sex, in the educators' opinion, then they were inviting Hollywood and Hugh Hefner to become the sole arbiters of sexual mores. Long concerned with campaigns for public "decency," conservatives complained bitterly about the sex educators' "caving in" to the sexual revolutionaries.

In stressing the schools' duty to balance the public commercialization of sexuality, sex educators in the 1960s continued to express their predecessors' conviction that sex education was a proper responsibility for the state. At the dawn of the century, sex education had grown out of the broader movement to have the state bring sexuality under public control: the push for sex education proceeded alongside the development of state marriage licenses, secular divorce proceedings, and increased police regulation of sexual delinquency.[90] Compared with the legal sanctions against sexual immorality, sex education was a "soft" expression of state power, but the early sex education activists had nevertheless helped establish the principle that public authorities held the right to intervene in a previously private realm. Although family life educators in the 1950s dumped the explicitly sexual topics they had once treated, they simultaneously expanded the principle of public intervention. Through family life education, many educators, psychologists, and family sociologists staked a claim for the public schools to wield authority over a still wider range of personal behaviors—dating, leisure activities, mental adjustment, consumption, marriage, and child rearing, to name only a few.

When in the early 1960s the first rumblings of the sexual revolution reinvigorated the movement for sex education proper, such leaders as Mary Calderone and Lester Kirkendall did not discard FLE's claims but added them to their own renewed program of state intervention in sexual matters. Many conservatives found this expansive educational mission to be just as offensive as sex education itself. "What concerned me was that this wasn't just a sex education course," recalled an anti–sex education activist in the early 1970s. "It dealt with every aspect of a child's life. It dealt with their attitudes. In fact, the stated purpose of the course was to teach children how to think, to feel, and to act. And it covered everything, from their relationship with their parents, to their attitudes toward the use of drugs and social drinking, to their attitudes toward sexual conduct. So that concerned me."[91] Conservative opponents were hardly free from the urge to invoke state power over sexuality: Protestant fundamentalists and conservative Catholics had long been prominent in campaigns against pornography and in crusades to enforce the laws against sexual delinquency, for example. But conservatives insisted that these activities were consistent with the nation's moral heritage, while sex education was an unwelcome innovation.

Both the original vision for sex education and the expansive 1960s version were based on a peculiarly modern interpretation of sexual learning and human development that found rational learning to be more important than "natural" development. Stretching all the way back to Dr. Prince Morrow and the first days of ASHA, sex educators had argued that young people could base their sexual decisions on scientific facts. If reached early enough, with enough information, the youth would choose the path of chastity, followed by marital monogamy. This approach was a significant break from the traditional religious reliance on "innocence" to safeguard the adolescent. In agreement with the early sex educators, traditionalists at the turn of the century admitted that puberty quickened the sex drive, but they maintained that the youth's task until marriage was to repress and control this drive, not to explore and understand it. Without forcing one's attention onto sex prematurely, God would reveal a fuller understanding in due course—preferably at the time one was married. In the traditional conservative interpretation, giving sexual information to young people earlier meant replacing God's plan for development with the corrupting theories of a few university professors.

According to the traditionalist interpretation, the "timely sexual warning" that sex educators hoped to give would not cleanse the youth's morals and behavior but would hang permanently in the child's "chamber of imagery," polluting the imagination and, conceivably, leading the youth to overt acts of sexual degradation.[92] Opponents early in the century had felt that ASHA's overtly moralistic form of sex education marred the chamber of imagery; SIECUS's franker, less authoritarian approach in the 1960s did not meet with greater approval. Nevertheless, most sex educators by the 1960s were convinced that the adolescent's best protection in the sexual wilderness of modern society was not a dependence on natural innocence but a rational understanding of frank sexual facts.

Building on this understanding of sexual development, sex and family life educators from the 1950s on sought to remove sex roles and family life from the realm of the "natural" and bring them under rational, factual inquiry. In contrast to the traditional expectation that boys would unfold naturally into men and girls into women, sex educators in the 1960s continued to employ FLE's insight that masculinity and femininity were collections of characteristics that boys and girls needed to *attain*. Anaheim's FLSE curriculum, for example, asked young people to reflect on the varieties of masculine and feminine characteristics, and to ponder their uses. The curriculum guide urged teachers to help the students understand that these stereotypes were primarily social conventions. Opponents believed that sex educators thus undermined belief in the God-given stability of male and female roles, and exposed themselves as trying, again, to replace God's natural plan with an intellectualized product of social science.

Insofar as sex educators were also sympathetic to Lawrence Frank's desire to foster less rigid sex roles, they trespassed even further on traditional notions of masculinity and femininity. When Gordon Drake and others made the false charge that sex educators often forced boys and girls to use same-sex bathrooms, they were as concerned about the erosion of gender distinctions as they were about the loss of shame and privacy. And though the unisex lavatory never came into style, the 1960s was witness to a continuation of the century-long trend toward more women entering the workforce; by the end of the decade, many women would even begin to make the "radical" argument that they belonged in the workplace as much as they belonged in the kitchen. SIECUS and its allies were hardly at the forefront of this movement, but their questioning of traditional sex roles was a step toward understanding some of these larger social changes. In following years, the leading sex educators were to march alongside the activists for women's equality.

Changing gender roles also implied that the patriarchal family, with the father as the unquestioned authority, was not necessarily an eternal arrangement. Conservatives worried that here, too, sex educators were undermining a traditional institution with their academic examinations. When they saw that units of Anaheim's FLSE course would investigate "the changing family," "factors in family happiness," and questions of family decision making, fundamentalist Christian opponents became justifiably suspicious that Anaheim's FLSE course would propagate an image of the ideal family that was at odds with traditional relationships and lines of authority. FLE and FLSE were themselves hardly free of sexism, but they did echo the modern praise of companionate marriage and a sharing of spousal duties. Some curricula even flirted with encouraging democratic decision making within the family. Opponents' attacks on these ideas carried more than a hint of defensiveness. Their self-perceived status as an embattled minority added intensity to one conservative mother's complaint that it was "an invasion of privacy to have a child tell his classmates how his parents get along and how they make decisions."[93] "Natural" or not, family life, in the traditionalists' opinion, should not be measured against the sex educators' own cosmopolitan prejudices.

All of these conservative fears—of sex-crazed teens, unisex bathrooms, disintegrating families, and so forth—came to center around what sex educators actually considered the least objectionable part of their program in the 1960s, its moral neutrality. Unlike their predecessors, Calderone and her allies had chosen to teach not a series of moral prescriptions but a "framework" for making moral decisions. Obviously their neutrality was compromised at many points, but neutrality remained the official pedagogical basis of the dialogue-centered sex education course. Ironically, as it turned out, sex educators conceived of moral neutrality primarily as a way of sidestepping moral and religious controversy. "Even if it were not forbidden by law," noted Anaheim's Paul Cook, "it would be impossible to teach religious morality without involving the schools in a controversy over which particular religion's approach to morality should be taught."[94] Cook and leading sex educators decreed that the teacher must remain officially neutral on moral questions, simply giving students enough factual information to choose for themselves from among an array of competing value systems. At least in theory, the teacher would emphasize the student's moral autonomy and not hold up one moral code as superior to any other.

This novel approach directly threatened traditional concepts of morality and family authority. Whereas educators felt that they were thus preserving their neutrality on moral standards, opponents maintained that tolerance and pluralism themselves carried direct moral implications.[95] First, moral neutrality seemed an attempt to label religious considerations irrelevant. Second, as a practical matter, when teachers urged young people to make their own moral decisions, they were implicitly suggesting that adolescents need not accept their parents' authority as absolute. In a warning calculated to resonate deeply with fundamentalists and evangelicals, Gordon Drake proclaimed, "Parents are in grave danger of losing control of their children's secular and moral education."[96] Opponents did not doubt that young people, if they were given all of the relevant information neutrally and allowed to make their own decisions, would inevitably choose the low road.

Finally, the moral neutrality approach suggested that many school authorities and academics were unwilling to unite in condemning the sexual revolution. At a time when many Americans believed that the nation's youth had discarded all codes of sexual morality, the sex educators' "surrender" seemed to exemplify the moral bankruptcy of the elite establishment. And as universities and high schools during the 1960s and 1970s heeded student wishes and cut back on acting in loco parentis, they too must have appeared as allies in the youthful struggle for independence and autonomy. Conservatives were literally wrong when they blamed the sexual revolution on sex education, but their attack contained a deeper truth.

When Gordon Drake and his followers complained that SIECUS and educators in general were attempting to drive a wedge between parents and their children, they were half right. Although driving a wedge between the generations was hardly the sex educators' intent, any education—and especially the "neutral" education that sex educators professed to offer—could become a tool to help youths to separate themselves from their parents. To a generation seeking increased distance from parental domination, the moral neutrality of the sex education curriculum—however compromised in practice—must have held out the promise not of revolution or anarchy but of simple maturity.

# CHAPTER SEVEN

# The Triumph of Sexual Liberalism?

I am 19 years old and a graduate of Roosevelt Senior
High School. I would just like to say that when I was sixteen years old I got pregnant. I didn't know anything
about sex education. I didn't know anything about taking care of a baby. I wasn't taught.

**Testimony given before the Senate Committee on
Human Resources, Washington, D.C. (1978)**

Conservative attacks finally led Mary Steichen
Calderone to step down from the presidency of the Sexuality Information
Education Council of the United States in 1970, but she nevertheless began
the next decade with high hopes for sex education. Increasingly liberal
legislation and court decisions about such matters as contraception,
homosexuality, and sex discrimination suggested that the recent changes in
American sexual life were becoming institutionalized in the legal system. At
the same time, the proliferation of singles bars, sex manuals, and public
messages about sex, along with soaring rates of extramarital and premarital
intercourse and out-of-wedlock births, underlined the ways in which a sexual revolution of sorts had moved from the counterculture to mainstream
America. Calderone expected that this liberalized sexual culture would be
more welcoming to SIECUS, and that SIECUS could in turn use the continuing alarm over sexual activity to further its own mission of steering American society toward a positive, healthy approach to sexuality.

Because the movement for sex education in the 1960s had in fact been an
expression of broader social trends and not a conspiracy of Marxist sexolo-
gists, it did not completely collapse under Gordon Drake's assault. However, Drake's decision to blame SIECUS for sex education and sexual per-

missiveness in general did leave the group isolated for a time, and it took a personal toll on SIECUS members—in addition to Calderone's resigning from the presidency to become executive director, Lester Kirkendall suffered a heart attack.[1] But the attacks on sex education also reinforced SIECUS's more militant tendencies.

After realizing the futility of trying to please their most conservative critics, SIECUS members felt emboldened to take a more defiant stance on sexual issues. The organization in 1974 published a broader, more contentious set of position statements that placed SIECUS more squarely on the side of a rising sexual liberalism. The SIECUS board of directors began from the premise that sex education could not be effective "in a society which, in many of its aspects, inhibits rational assessment of sexuality as a central force in human behavior." "SIECUS's role," their statement continued, "is to identify and publicize social policies which perpetuate unhealthy attitudes about sexuality and foster alienation from self and others." Most of those pestilential policies were laws that trammeled sexual liberties or perpetuated fundamentalist beliefs. Proposing to make the 1970s into "the decade of sexual human rights," SIECUS endorsed the right of all humans to exercise personal sexual choice, including freedom of choice in such areas as sexual orientation, pornography, and unmarried minors' access to contraception.[2]

SIECUS had been inclining toward sexual libertarianism anyway, and the rising strength of sexual liberalism in the 1970s pushed the leaders in sex education still further in this direction. Ironically, the right-wing attack on sex education in the late 1960s had opened the curriculum further to precisely the kinds of sexual liberalism that conservatives most feared. Sex educators from the beginning had tried to maintain control over the curriculum by arguing that sex education could be trusted only to scientifically trained experts in medicine, education, and psychology, but Drake and his allies maintained that the public school's curriculum should be a matter for the public to decide. Once sex education entered public debate—at the nexus of larger disputes over morality, sexuality, and adolescence—returning it solely to the pages of educational periodicals became impossible. But the "public" or "community of parents" that Drake and other sex education opponents claimed to represent was always more a rhetorical creation than an identifiable majority. Conservative opponents therefore could not control which elements of this phantom "public" were to be represented in decisions about sex education. If the school curriculum was not a matter restricted to professional educators but instead was a subject for public debate and decision, then sexual liberals were as justified as religious conservatives in fighting for inclusion.

Feminists, for example, historically had found little to embrace in sex education's replication of traditional sex roles, but as the women's movement burgeoned in the 1970s, many activists recognized that they could fight on their own for changes in the curriculum. Throughout the twentieth century, women had been obtaining more education and entering the workforce in increasing numbers, but for most of that time commentators had considered the trends to be mere distractions from the woman's more natural role as wife and mother. When Betty Friedan published *The Feminine Mystique* in 1963, however, she helped launch a movement to bring society's interpretation of women's roles into line with the concrete changes women had been experiencing. In the next decade, shifting gender roles became a mainstream topic. In the inaugural issue of *Sex Roles,* an academic journal begun in 1975, the editor repeated the popular perception that "complex and rapidly proliferating changes in the norms and attitudes associated with masculinity and femininity" were leading to a "sex-role revolution."[3]

The intellectual foundation for the feminist movement and the sex-role revolution was not new: like family life educators and others from the 1950s on, most feminists argued that masculinity and femininity were not so much innate qualities as acquired characteristics. In the process of growing up, children learned about male and female sex roles from their parents, peers, and schools. But whereas earlier educators had interpreted this insight to mean that schools must help children grow into their "proper" sex-typed roles, feminists in the 1970s emphasized the pathological nature of society's traditional sex roles. Traditional sex stereotypes, Friedan and her allies claimed, pushed women into passivity and underachievement, trapping women in the lower echelons of the workforce or forcing even the most brilliant female students to exchange a professional career for the consolations of marriage and motherhood.

Women's groups in the 1970s therefore reversed the original family life educators' desire to teach traditional sex roles and emphasized instead the schools' potential to *reform* society's norms. Feminists prodded the schools to teach that women could learn the same subjects and perform the same work as men, and they pushed to eliminate sex stereotypes in school materials, such as a widely used fifth-grade reader that noted, "Girls are only smart enough to sew." Under such pressure the New York City Board of Education, for example, developed a curriculum in 1976 that was called *Changing Sex Roles in a Changing Society,* and leading sex educators, such as Lester Kirkendall, proposed that "men are going to have to learn to be more equalitarian in their sex lives, or many of them are going to be defeated."[4] Many sex educators, including Kirkendall, took the issue of reforming sex roles as their own—besides, they had long believed that hypermasculinity contributed to sex delinquency.

This is not to say that feminists fully succeeded in making over sex education into a weapon in the struggle for women's equality. Well past the 1970s, complained one researcher, most sex educators still failed to include "sex equitable sexual attitudes, knowledge, and behavior. Thus, they often reinforced the 'double standard' or inaccurate stereotypes about females and males." Sex education materials continued to idealize the heterosexual, nuclear family, and tended to portray "the male as the instinctual sexual initiator and the female as the passive, morally pure sex object." Most sex education curricula would fail even more clearly to meet a later feminist demand that "sexuality education recognize and endorse female sexual pleasure and desire."[5] Nevertheless, the fact remained that sex education was now opened up to liberal political activism in a way that would have been nearly inconceivable twenty years earlier.

At the same time as women's liberation began to coalesce into a movement, the hitherto cautious movement for homosexual rights was exploding into a new militancy triggered by the 1969 "Stonewall rebellion" in New York City. For most of the century, sex education had mimicked the broader culture in either ignoring homosexuality or condemning it as perverse or immature. American gays and lesbians through the 1960s had suffered not only from rhetorical condemnation but also from punitive legislation, the constant threat of exposure, vice raids on their gathering places, and a raft of other persecutory practices. But over the course of the 1950s and 1960s, gays and lesbians in New York, San Francisco, and Los Angeles had also been creating more visible and self-conscious communities. On 27 June 1969, when gays and lesbians at the Stonewall Inn in New York City's Greenwich Village heard the police descending on the bar for one of their usual raids, they unexpectedly decided to resist arrest and thus launched five days of rioting and a mounting determination to resist not just legal persecution but also social stigmatization.[6] Over the next decade, supporters of gay rights managed, for example, to prevail on the American Psychiatric Association to remove "homosexuality" from the list of mental illnesses in the official *Diagnostic Statistical Manual II.*

Similarly, advocates for more equitable treatment of homosexuals lobbied for sex education to rehabilitate the image of same-sex relationships. Unlike feminists, supporters of tolerance for homosexuality usually argued that sexual identity was biologically determined. In most cases, therefore, no amount of classroom teaching could induce adolescents to become homosexuals, so sex educators should feel safe in teaching about tolerance. Contrary to later conservative charges, activists did not attempt to make "propaganda for homosexuality . . . one of the hallmarks of American education"; they merely sought to prevent the sex education curriculum from becoming a government-sponsored exercise in gay-baiting.[7] By 1974 SIECUS, for one, agreed that homosexuality was a variant of "personal sexual choice," deserving of legal protection and classroom understanding rather than moralistic repression.

Although heterosexually active teenagers and young adults never developed as a separate political interest group, their behavior in the 1970s also pushed SIECUS and other supporters of sex education farther along the path toward sexual liberalism. Except for the earliest years of the social hygiene movement, sex educators had always considered much of their task to be preparing students for marriage, but over the course of the 1970s, marriage was losing its privileged position as the sole site for sexual relations. Continuing the trend that first became visible in the mid-1960s, fewer people were marrying, and they were marrying later in life. The median age at marriage for men in the late 1970s rose to a high of 25.5 years, while women were typically 23.2 years old when they walked to the altar. By the end of the 1970s, more than 40 percent of marrying couples had lived together before their wedding.[8]

Rather than put off sexual relations until the honeymoon, increasing numbers of men and especially women were engaging in sex before or simply outside of marriage. A host of commercial institutions sprang up to meet these demographic pressures, including "singles bars" in which men and women could meet casually to initiate sexual encounters, and "singles nights" at museums, bookstores, and even grocery stores. Unlike the young men and women of the 1950s, whose sexual encounters usually signaled that they were well on their way to marriage, young men and women in the 1970s were far more likely to engage in sex with no expectation that marriage would follow.[9]

Public opinion shifted in step with these changes in behavior. Whereas fewer than a quarter of Americans in the 1950s endorsed premarital sex for men and women, according to one report, in the 1970s more than half approved, though this approval rate plummeted when respondents were polled specifically about sex between "unmarried teenagers." Young people themselves, however, approved of premarital intercourse by "substantial majorities."[10] Similar numbers of Americans came to approve of cohabitation, with or without the expectation of marriage, though the reasons for this could range from sexual liberalism to the oldest kind of double standard. As one traditional gentleman remarked, "Why buy the whole loaf when you can get the slices for free?"[11]

The postponement of marriage was not responsible for all of the changes in sexual behavior. Men and women were putting off marriage until later, but they were also having sex earlier. According to the National Surveys of Family Growth and other government-sponsored inquiries, only about a quarter of eighteen-year-old women in the late 1950s had engaged in coitus, and many of those had already been married; by the end of the 1960s, 35 percent of eighteen-year-old women were sexually experienced, and by the end of the 1970s more than half of eighteen-year-old women had had sex, even as they were far less likely to be married. Age at first coitus also dropped significantly, so that the number of young women reporting first intercourse before they turned sixteen doubled from around 10 percent in 1965 to more than 20 percent in 1980. Rates of premarital sexual activity for African

American youths were higher to begin with, so their primary change came in the woman's likelihood of having begun to have sex at an earlier age.[12]

Sexually active teenagers never created their own lobbying group, but early in the 1970s a liberal coalition sought on their behalf to protect and extend the sexual rights of youth. Inevitably, this activity on behalf of sexually active youths was also to have a significant effect on the course of the sex education movement. Pledging to be realistic rather than moralistic about adolescent sexual activity, SIECUS and related organizations, including Calderone's former employer, the Planned Parenthood Federation of America, joined with such prominent liberal politicians as Massachusetts Senator Edward M. Kennedy to protect minors' access to contraception, and to obtain greater government support for sex education, family planning clinics, and other necessities for sexually active adolescents.

To build support, Kennedy and his allies proclaimed that the nation was suffering from an "epidemic" of teenage pregnancies. Activists noted correctly that the rate of teenage births out of wedlock—their real concern—was soaring. To call this an "epidemic," however, required some statistical juggling. More than half of all births to teenage mothers were to eighteen- and nineteen-year-olds—hardly consistent with the general impression of "children having children." Further, the birthrate for women age fifteen to nineteen had actually been *declining* from its all-time high of 91 per 1,000 in 1960, to 69.7 per 1,000 in 1970 and 55.6 per 1,000 in 1975. The teenage pregnancy rate remained constant despite the dramatic increase in the number of female teenagers who were sexually active. Nevertheless, those teenage women who did give birth were becoming less and less likely to marry before the birth of their children. Like older women in general, teenage women had begun in the 1960s to have a much greater percentage of their children out of wedlock. In 1960, about 15 percent of all births to teenagers were out of wedlock.[13] "By 1978," reported one Senate inquiry, "almost half of all births to women 19 years of age and under were illegitimate." This statistic harbored information that many found even more alarming: while the percentage of out-of-wedlock births for white teenagers had risen to just over 20 percent, such births made up *three-fourths* of all births to African American teens.[14] African American teenage women also had a birthrate that was twice as high as their white counterparts.

The notion of an epidemic, along with evidence of astronomically high rates of out-of-wedlock births for African American teens, resonated with another liberal crusade. Confusing cause and effect, supporters of legislation aimed at teenage pregnancy concluded that teenage motherhood contributed significantly to poverty in America. Testifying before a Senate committee in 1978, Secretary of Health, Education, and Welfare Joseph A. Califano, Jr., noted that "for hundreds of thousands of teenagers, particularly the majority who are unmarried, the birth of a child can usher in a dismal future of unemployment, poverty, family breakdown, emotional stress, dependency on public agencies, and health problems for mother and for child." "The prospects for these young women, whether they marry the baby's father or remain single, are poor," observed another investigator mentioned in Califano's testimony. "Teenage parenthood is often associated with health problems for the mother and child, poor educational attainment and employment prospects, large families, and eventual welfare dependency."[15] Prevent teenagers from becoming mothers, supporters suggested, and you would prevent many young women from falling into poverty.

Congress enshrined the epidemic of teenage pregnancy in the Adolescent Health Services and Prevention and Care Act of 1978. Although consistently underfunded, the Adolescent Health Services Act offered grants to public and private agencies to provide "pregnancy testing, family planning services, health services, family life and sex education services," and a number of other services to pregnant and at-risk teenagers.[16] Thus, the act accepted adolescent sexual activity as more or less inevitable, and sought primarily to minimize the social damage that teenage motherhood could create. In the spirit of sexual liberalism, the act also treated teenagers as legally autonomous individuals capable of making their own sexual decisions: it required grantees to counsel pregnant adolescents about the availability of abortion, and followed the trend of recent Supreme Court decisions in not requiring parental notification or consent for adolescents to obtain birth control devices or abortions.[17]

Public concern over teenage pregnancy harmonized well with SIECUS's purposes in the 1970s. SIECUS's 1974 mission statement supported the adolescent's right to birth control, and SIECUS and sex educators in general agreed with the Adolescent Health Service Act's rejection of moralization over teenage sexual activity. Mainstream sex educators maintained that their nondirective approach was the only realistic form of sex education, for it recognized that the majority of high school students would have intercourse before they graduated. Sex educators still emphasized the desirability of abstinence, but rather than pretend that adults' wishes would prevent adolescent sex, they also offered information about contraception to minimize the pregnancies and venereal diseases that might attend sexual experimentation.

The crusade against teenage pregnancy illuminated the complexity of sex education's contemporary mission. Although Mary Calderone and other sexual liberals sought to foster positive, value-neutral sexuality education, they also maintained their grip on the instrumentalist model of sex education. At the dawn of the century, sex educators had created the instrumentalist model when they justified their pedagogical experiment by pointing to the behavioral results they expected from a series of social hygiene lectures: fewer men would visit prostitutes, fewer young women would become promiscuous, syphilis and gonorrhea would fade into history. The passing of several decades had altered some of the particular goals, but the social reform model remained the most popular version of sex education. Faced with a potential epidemic of out-of-wedlock teenage pregnancy in the 1970s, sex educators naturally argued that they should play a role in curing the epidemic. At the same time, Calderone and other sexual liberals began to suspect that the instrumentalist model, with its constant demand for sexual crises to solve and urgent need for evidence of behavioral change, might in some ways undermine their more positive mission. It was difficult to praise sexual communication in one breath and explain the dangers of premarital pregnancy and promiscuity in the next. Nevertheless, sex educators rallied around this nondirective form of sexuality education, just as they rallied around the delivery of contraceptive services to teenagers, as an expression of their own faith in the power of factual knowledge and tolerance to solve social problems. By the end of the 1970s sexual liberalism was at its high tide, and it lifted SIECUS and its comprehensive program in value-neutral sex education along with it.

In the opinion of supporters of the 1978 Adolescent Health Services Act, the combination of contraceptive availability and one or more of these educational programs seemed to be working. Although unmarried teenage females were more than twice as likely to be sexually active in the 1970s as compared with the early 1960s, the overall birthrate among teens actually dropped over the course of the decade.

Not everyone was satisfied with such success, however. Perhaps inevitably, a conservative reaction against women's liberation, gay rights, adolescent intercourse, and a variety of similar offenses had also set in by the end of the 1970s. Although social conservatives included all elements of sexual liberalism in their indictment, they centered their attack on the government's involvement with teenage pregnancy in ways that would resonate deeply for sex education. Spurred on, in part, by the violent reaction against the Supreme Court's 1973 *Roe v. Wade* decision on abortion, many politically active fundamentalist Christians and conservative Catholics insisted that the birthrate in the 1970s had declined only because rising numbers of pregnant teens were terminating their pregnancies. The pregnancy rate among teens actually *rose* in the 1970s while the birthrate dropped; the difference in the two figures was primarily made up of the 300,000 to 400,000 abortions performed on teenagers each year since the *Roe* decision. To many conservative critics, this was hardly evidence that the greater availability of contraception in the 1970s was having a positive impact on the lives of adolescents.

Neither liberals nor conservatives were pleased with the number of abortions sought by teenagers, but only conservative activists were eager to employ the abortion numbers in their broader denunciations of sexual liberalism. In light of such figures, conservatives began to contend that the problem was not teenage motherhood or teenage pregnancy at all; rather, the real "epidemic" to be cured was teenage sexual activity itself. Activists resurrected the old charge that the availability of sex education, contraception, and abortion all actually encouraged adolescent sexual activity—and pointed out, accurately, that rising rates of intercourse between unmarried adolescents in the 1970s had indeed proceeded alongside the increased availability of contraception and abortion and the broader dissemination of sex education.

Although the correlation was more superficial than causal, it allowed opponents to brand many sexually liberal policies—family planning clinics, support for abortion, increased sex education—as failures. Conservatives pointed to the state of California's heavily funded Office of Family Planning (OFP) as a classic case: "Far from discouraging 'unintended' pregnancy," argued one California economist in 1982, "the OFP attempt to saturate the state with publicly-subsidized sex instruction and contraceptives has encouraged a great deal of sexual experimentation that would not otherwise have taken place. Through the highly-financed efforts of the OFP the young people of California have been brought to levels of sexual sophistication and moral 'tolerance' never before seen." An antiabortion activist went further in claiming that such behavior was the result of a conscious conspiracy among sexual liberals: "It seems apparent from the available evidence," argued Dr. James H. Ford in 1981, "that by encouraging abandonment of chastity as a means of avoiding pregnancy, Planned Parenthood and its allies have served their own purposes quite well by creating a larger new teenage clientele for their abortion and contraceptive services." Many opponents perceived an explicit connection between sex education and the explosion in premarital sexual activity. As the educational historian and political activist Diane Ravitch argued in 1982, "It would be difficult to see how teenagers could spend a semester reading how to do it right, how good it feels when you do it, and how meaningful the experience is, without wanting to try it as soon as possible." Ravitch finally highlighted the public schools' role in this crisis with questions that were as inflammatory as they were inaccurate: "Is it appropriate for the government to teach its citizenry how to masturbate? To explain how to perform cunnilingus? To reassure them that infidelity is widespread?"[18]

Such concerns played at least a partial role in Ronald Reagan's electoral victory in 1980, and Reagan's presidency emboldened conservatives to roll back sexual liberalism where they could. In 1981 Congress passed the Adolescent Family Life Act (AFLA), which quickly came to be known as the Chastity Act. In contrast to the 1978 Adolescent Health Services Act, AFLA denied funds to most programs or projects that provided abortions or abortion counseling, and AFLA mandated abstinence education and units promoting "self-discipline and responsibility in human sexuality" in the sex education programs it did fund. In an attempt to roll back the idea that adolescents were legally autonomous in their sexual lives, Congress soon passed the so-called squeal rule, which required federally funded family planning clinics to inform parents if their teenage children were seeking contraception or an abortion.[19] In the 1980s congressional conservatives— mostly midwestern and western Republicans and southern Democrats— cut funding for nondirective sex education and widened their scope to include legislation condemning feminism and homosexuality as well as teenage sexual activity. In 1981, for example, newly energized Republicans tried unsuccessfully to resurrect the Family Protection Bill from during the Carter administration: one of its provisions would have denied federal funds for schools whose curricula "would tend to denigrate, diminish or deny the differences between the sexes as they have been historically understood in the United States"; another section of the bill would have denied all government benefits for individuals who held that homosexuality could be "an acceptable alternative life style."[20] By the early 1980s, the high tide of sexual liberalism seemed to be receding.

Although it was certainly important in itself, the controversy over unwed teenage pregnancy was in some ways only a rehearsal for the struggle over acquired immunodeficiency syndrome, or AIDS, that began in the mid-1980s. The AIDS crisis deepened the politicization of sex education even further, for by inducing far more school districts to add some sort of sex education to their offerings, it multiplied the possible sites for controversy, and by making certain sexual behaviors matters of life or death, it imparted to these controversies a grim intensity. This new intensity notwithstanding, responses to the AIDS epidemic proceeded along familiar pathways: AIDS locked sex education even tighter into the instrumentalist model; it solidified the dominance of danger and disease in thinking about adolescent sexuality; and it reinforced the American faith in the schools as a tool for social reform. Despite nearly a century of formal sex education in the United States, the AIDS epidemic ultimately revealed that supporters and detractors of sex education were incapable of thinking outside these inherited boundaries.

In the spring of 1985 the *Journal of School Health*, a central organ for research on sex and sexuality education, printed its first article about AIDS.[21]

Published four years after scientists first discovered what came to be known as AIDS among a group of gay men in Los Angeles, "High School Students' Perceptions and Misperceptions of AIDS" simply reported on an attempt to measure the average high school students' knowledge about the disease; the authors did not make a ringing call for AIDS education in the schools, nor did they report that such teaching was already taking place. And yet, few could deny the seriousness of the AIDS epidemic. By 1987, the U.S. Public Health Service estimated, more than 50,000 Americans had developed full-blown AIDS, and as many as 1.5 million more were infected with the human immunodeficiency virus (HIV) that causes AIDS.[22] At that time, infection almost always meant death, for scientists had not yet developed the vast array of treatments that were to buy time for those afflicted with the disease in the later 1990s. Despite the evidence of an epidemic, many Americans in the mid-1980s found comfort in the errant conviction that AIDS was a disease affecting only homosexuals; perhaps high school students should know about it in general terms, they thought, but the disease seemed to have no real bearing on their lives.

Public health officials were soon to change their stance. Epidemiologists quickly realized that because of the long latency period for the disease, many infected adults had actually contracted HIV as teenagers: by the end of the 1980s, it was clear that a significant percentage of the 7,000 men diagnosed with AIDS in their early twenties had become infected as adolescents. By 1991 a total of 9,000 persons between the ages of thirteen and twenty-four were diagnosed with AIDS.[23] The rate of diagnosed infection among teens was to continue rising in the next decade to a high of nearly 800 new cases in 1993 alone.[24] Further, HIV infection was becoming increasingly prevalent among heterosexuals, particularly among intravenous drug users, their sexual partners, and their offspring. Increasing numbers of female adolescents were becoming infected through this route.

Although teenagers in 1987 made up only 1 percent of all AIDS cases, the congressional Select Committee on Children, Youth, and Families that year declared that AIDS was a potential "time bomb" for American adolescents. Because AIDS is most frequently transmitted through sexual contact, teenagers' sexual behavior placed them peculiarly at risk. As the congressional committee noted, before they turned twenty more than 70 percent of

American women and 80 percent of men had engaged in sexual intercourse. The sexually active teenager's lack of caution expressed itself clearly through the 1 million teenage pregnancies yearly and rates of sexually transmitted diseases (STDs) as high as one in every seven teens. Only 15 percent of adolescent girls surveyed had reported using a condom the most recent time they had had intercourse (latex condoms are the only effective barrier to HIV transmission).[25] Public health officials recognized that heterosexual HIV rates could explode in this sexually active and careless population.

Recognizing the growing importance of sex education, many politicians and public health officials readily turned to the schools for a solution. As a majority of the 1987 select committee argued, "Until a vaccine or cure is found and becomes available, education is the only tool we have to prevent the spread of this deadly disease."[26]

As with the "realist" crusade against teenage pregnancy in the 1970s, supporters demanded that AIDS education take into account the strong likelihood that teenagers were sexually active. "Testimony presented to this committee established that between 70 and 80 percent of America's youth under the age of 20 are sexually active," noted Representative Theodore S. Weiss of New York, a member of the Select Committee on Children, Youth, and Families. "Clearly, urging abstention and issuing advice on moral behavior by themselves are painfully inadequate." Instead of offering moral homilies, AIDS education would instruct youth directly about the sexual practices that held the highest risks of HIV transmission, and teach them the proper use of condoms to prevent transmission of HIV. The looming threat of AIDS made this no time for circumlocution. "When we talk about condoms," noted C. Everett Koop, Ronald Reagan's surgeon general, "the education that goes with that has to be extraordinarily explicit."[27]

Congressional liberals repeatedly prodded a Republican administration that Weiss and others considered to be "mired in right-wing conceptual morality" to devote greater resources to the fight against AIDS. President Reagan consistently cut the funds allocated by Congress for the fight against AIDS, and in 1991 the Bush administration cancelled the government-sponsored American Teenage Study, which was seeking to gather in-

formation about teenage sexual behavior and possible approaches to preventing STDs. Nevertheless, the Centers for Disease Control (CDC) began
in 1987 to disburse $310 million over the next several years to states that
would mandate AIDS education. In 1991 the CDC devoted approximately
$82.1 million to the problem of adolescent AIDS, much of it going toward
educational programs.[28] The government was waging an expensive war
against AIDS.

The combination of money and fear made an impact. By 1990, at least
forty-one states encouraged or required sex education, and all fifty either
recommended or mandated AIDS education in schools.[29] Government action rested on increasingly favorable public opinion. Although rising sexual
liberalism in the 1970s had brought the greatest jump in adult support of
sex education—from approximately 56 percent in favor in 1970 to 82 percent in 1980—the AIDS crisis was largely responsible for the next rise, to 85
percent of adults supporting sex education by 1992. A survey that focused
more narrowly on a white, rural population uncovered similar rates of approval for sex education in general, with as many as 94 percent of adults
supporting, in particular, teaching about sexually transmitted diseases, including HIV and AIDS.[30]

As pressing as the need for AIDS education seemed, the prominence of
AIDS at the same time distorted the shape of sex education in the United
States. HIV/AIDS education in many areas replaced altogether the broader
kinds of sexuality education that would include discussions of sexism, homosexuality, and ethical values. "HIV education," argued Susan Wilson,
director of New Jersey's Family Life Education Network, in 1996, "has bi-
furcated sexuality education, and in many cases it's become just HIV education, sometimes without information even about teen pregnancy prevention." As of 1989, a number of states, including Illinois and North Carolina,
took no official position on sex education but required AIDS education in
the public schools. Like many other states, Pennsylvania and Michigan
would mandate AIDS education but only "encourage" sex education. AIDS
education, concluded Wilson, had in many cases "absolutely squashed
any education about healthy sexuality."[31]

Wilson's own state of New Jersey makes an interesting comparison with
the typical state's approach to sex education. In 1979, before the AIDS epi-

demic hit, New Jersey passed a mandate for sex education that allowed local curriculum decisions but did not allow noncompliance with the law's demand for "baseline" education in reproduction, human growth and sexuality, responsible behavior, and other subjects. Over the next decade, different localities established a wide range of programs, but sexuality education in New Jersey into the 1990s was still widely characterized by a comprehensiveness of topics and a lack of overtly didactic instruction.[32] Significantly, New Jersey implemented these programs both before the discovery of AIDS and before organizations on the religious right had moved from their negative position of opposing all sex education to their more positive goal of strongly influencing the sex education students do receive in the schools.[33]

Despite the potential conflict between AIDS education and comprehensive sexuality education, the threat of AIDS quickly became the central argument in support of all sex education. AIDS achieved this status not only because it was so deadly but also because it aligned so well with tendencies that had long been dominant in sex education. Proponents of "realism" in sex education, for example, maintained that AIDS made the need for frank, nonjudgmental sex teaching stronger than ever. Since the founding of SIECUS, many sex educators had strongly supported including information about the proper use of condoms, the risk factors involved with various sexual practices, and the dangers of intravenous drug use, and they now argued that AIDS made such explicit sex education absolutely imperative. "If you deny young people information based on your morality," argued the director of a New York center for young gays and lesbians in 1991, "you are sentencing them to death. Nothing is more immoral than that."[34]

Although organizations for women's liberation and homosexual rights similarly predated the AIDS epidemic, these movements soon employed the rhetorical power of AIDS as well in an attempt to create room for their programs within the sex education curriculum. The disease's prevalence in the gay community added particular strength to arguments in favor of teaching about sexual identity and sexual diversity in the schools. Not only were gay high school students at high risk for contracting HIV, noted supporters of inclusion, but also *all* students needed to understand and tolerate better the range of sexual behaviors they would discover in the course of learning about AIDS.[35]

Advocates of sex equity also used the threat of AIDS to argue that the risk of disease made eliminating sexism all the more important. Many of these scholars and activists advanced two rationales for empowering young women in the age of AIDS: first, girls needed to be given more discretion to set the boundaries of the sexual situation, including the nonnegotiable right to demand the use of a condom or to refuse outright to have intercourse; second, and less obviously, girls needed sexuality education that would recognize their sexual desire as legitimate, for only by embracing their own sexual nature would girls be able to approach sexual situations thoughtfully and responsibly. The rising incidence of HIV and AIDS among heterosexual African American teens also buttressed arguments by educators who favored a more consciously multicultural curriculum: if sexuality education's typically white, middle-class bias made it seem irrelevant to African American and Latino youths, then those adolescents would not respond to the only educational message that could protect them from contracting HIV.[36]

Rare indeed is the educator in the AIDS era who proclaims the importance of teaching about condoms, homosexuality, sexism, diversity, abstinence—even masturbation—without reflexively gesturing toward the AIDS epidemic for justification. The life-and-death nature of the disease is obviously a pressing concern, but the sex educators' invocation of AIDS signifies, as well, their desire to remove certain elements of the curriculum from the realm of political dispute. Insofar as Americans think of the "public health" as an apolitical affair for physicians and scientists to determine, the threat of AIDS seems capable of draping the fabric of disinterested science over all manner of sex education proposals.

Despite the political uses of the epidemic, the AIDS crisis has in many ways narrowed the parameters of the sex education debate. Most obviously, AIDS has restored the fear of disease to a central position in sex education. The centrality of fear handicaps the teacher's ability to discuss more positive aspects of sexuality, for the prevention of mortal illness has become the primary rationale for sex education.

Paradoxically, the AIDS argument also harms those activists who employ the fear of disease to support their programs. By basing their arguments for teaching about sex equity or homosexuality on the dangers of AIDS, educators have largely discarded the opportunity to justify their programs on the basis of fairness or justice. Instead, they have narrowed their arguments to the technocratic issue of whether such education will or will not benefit the health of students. If an AIDS vaccine is discovered, will condoms and homosexuality lose their places in the curriculum? Less obviously, the prominence of fear and danger in AIDS-era sex education inevitably undermines some educational activists' larger goal of rehabilitating alternative sexualities, such as same-sex desire or female sexual subjectivity. How can sex education help improve the status of homosexuality, for example, when the issue is completely hedged about by danger signs?

Finally, the crises of teenage pregnancy and AIDS have demonstrated that the sex educators' reliance on physical and mental health within a framework of value neutrality leads to moral confusion and a certain amount of disingenuousness. Contrary to conservative attacks on teachers' value-neutrality or outright "radicalism," sex education teachers tend to reflect the moral predisposition of their community. Like the national leaders in sexuality education, most sex education teachers share a nagging sense that sex among teenagers is wrong. But in the absence of a coherent moral vocabulary, they are able only to discuss the many ways in which it is unwise. By making unsafe sex exceedingly unwise, AIDS has only prompted these educators to intensify their emphasis on physical danger without clarifying their own moral position.

As with the "epidemic" of unwed teenage pregnancy, the AIDS crisis seemed initially to strengthen the sexual liberals' position, but AIDS has ended up reinvigorating the conservative opposition. Sex education's opponents in the AIDS era have massed their attack precisely at the weak point of value neutrality. By focusing on the sex educators' value-neutral methodology as if it were an ethical position, critics have argued that sex education programs completely ignore the moral dimensions of sexual relations. "Far from being value-neutral, sex may be among the most value-loaded of human activities," contended William J. Bennett, the secretary of education under Ronald Reagan, in his widely reprinted 1987 essay, "Why Johnny Can't Abstain." "It does no good to try to sanitize or deny or ignore this truth." Bennett complained that mainstream sexuality education did not take the moral nature of sexuality into account. "It is a very odd kind of teaching—very odd because it does not teach," Bennett explained. "While speaking to an important aspect of human life, it displays a conscious aversion to making moral distinctions."[37]

Conservative opponents have perceived a definite set of values lying behind the modern sex education program's "neutral" facade, values surely not calculated to appeal to religious traditionalists. Prominent conservatives such as Robert L. Simonds, the president of the National Association of Christian Educators, maintained in 1993 that "liberal" educators were using their supposedly nondirective methods "to turn schools into institutions of psychological manipulation and to produce robotic students on political correctness." Worse, as the issue of AIDS became an avenue for homosexuality to be studied in sex education, this value neutrality seemed to play right into what Simonds called "homosexual/lesbian recruitment of children in the classroom."[38]

Conservative critics have not confined themselves to philosophical attacks on value neutrality. Like their predecessors in the 1960s, many of these critics still uncover (or fabricate) "horror stories" about sexuality programs, and the greater explicitness of modern sex education has made the horrors seems still more threatening. Courses that include condom education have been a particularly fertile source of anecdotes. "Many such programs, including Planned Parenthood classes," explained Simonds, "force boys to hold bananas while the girls practice putting on condoms. Many girls throw up in class, according to our parents' reports."[39] Such stories, along with tales about classroom rapes recycled from 1969, did much to fortify political opposition to the franker versions of sex education from the late 1980s through the 1990s.

Recognizing such discontent, William Bennett demanded that the public schools become a conscious agent of community morality, generally defined in conservative terms. Because most parents support premarital chastity, conventional marriage, and more traditional sex roles, Bennett argued, the schools should act as their ally in propagating these ideals. Bennett's followers have noted, further, that the schools must play this role to aid parents and children in resisting the sexually libertarian messages that dominate the media.[40]

The AIDS crisis, ironically, played a critical role in this attempt to make the public schools into a conscious moral agent. By the late 1980s, many conservatives recognized that AIDS had transformed the question of whether or not the schools should offer sex education into the question of what *kind* of sex education they should present. A number of conservatives therefore began to formulate their own value-laden programs in abstinence education to compete with SIECUS's brand of sexuality education. Indeed, once these activists overcame their initial reluctance to have what was once thought of as a "gay disease" discussed in school, they embraced the threat of AIDS for its potential to enforce a stricter chastity among unmarried youth.

As social conservatives moved from criticizing from afar all sex education to formulating their own sex education curricula, however, they found themselves as likely as liberals to confuse values with health. In the fall of 1992, Grady Webb-Wood of Jacksonville, Florida, sat down in his seventh-grade health class for sex education. Over the next forty-five minutes, Grady heard that birth control does not avert teen pregnancy and condoms fail to protect sexual partners from sexually transmitted diseases. Abstinence until marriage, the teacher stressed, was the students' only insurance against unwanted pregnancy or AIDS, and it was, further, the only moral choice for unmarried teens.[41] At the same time that Grady was hearing about the unreliability of birth control, his counterparts in the schools of East Troy, Wisconsin, were working their way through a sex education textbook containing slogans that teachers hoped were as meaningful as they were memorable: "Pet your dog, not your date!" "Don't be a louse, wait for your spouse!" and "Do the right thing, wait for the ring!" Understandably, the textbook's paraphrase of the old marine recruitment slogan—"The Public Health Department Wants You: Be One of the Proud. One of the Virgins"—left out the slogan's first imperative: "Be one of the few."[42] Presumably the younger generation would not notice the discrepancy.

Grady Webb-Wood's school in Duval County, Florida, and its counterparts in Wisconsin were among the growing number of schools embracing the "abstinence-only" sex education programs put out by conservative groups under such titles as *Teen-Aid* and *Sex Respect*. Rather than embrace the pluralist model of sex education as an overview of scientific facts and behavioral options, these programs attempted to convey an unambiguous condemnation of sexual activity outside of marriage. Fueled by federal education grants for programs that would encourage abstinence, such abstinence-based programs were offered in more than two thousand junior high and high schools by 1993.[43]

Although its Christian orientation was only implicit, the *Sex Respect* curriculum expressed the eagerness of religious conservatives to turn public schools into instruments for moral regeneration and the rebirth of traditional values. *Sex Respect*'s author, Colleen Kelly Mast, charged erroneously that mainstream sex education programs "instruct for genital activity," and pledged that her curriculum would, in contrast, uphold abstinence as a primary value. Mainstream sex educators were naturally mystified by Mast's charges: a 1989 survey found that nine out of ten educators were teaching that abstinence is the best alternative for preventing pregnancy and STDs.[44] But to look at the actual evidence of what mainstream sex education consisted of was to miss the broader political points conservatives hoped to score. By equating sexuality education with sexual indulgence and moral agnosticism, abstinence educators could interest school districts in programs that aimed to turn back sexual liberalism.

*Sex Respect* did indeed offer at least a form of sex education, and it was not without a certain old-fashioned charm in its preoccupation with chastity, but it also discarded many topics more mainstream sexuality educators considered essential, including contraception, masturbation, abortion, adultery, sexual orientation, freedom of choice, and the positive aspects of sexuality. *Sex Respect* also played games with a number of facts. Rather than note the efficacy of latex condoms in halting HIV transmission, for example, Sex Respect inflated the failure rates of condoms and other contraceptive methods; like many conservative opponents of comprehensive sexuality education, Mast proved particularly fond of confusing "natural-skin" condoms, which are generally understood not to halt HIV transmission, with the more common latex condoms, which do. *Sex Respect* attempted, as well, to roll back the theory that sex roles were the product of society rather than biology. "From the moment we are conceived," argued Mast on the first page of the curriculum guide, "our male-ness or female-ness is determined."[45] *Sex Respect* seemed in some ways the perfect vehicle for a conservative countercrusade against sexual liberalism. In the end, however, despite the Sex Respect curriculum's prochastity slogans, its scare tactics, and its strategic omissions, Mast's claim that *Sex Respect* could somehow return more than 11 million sexually active teens to chastity strained credulity.

The *Sex Respect* curriculum did not even fully fulfill William Bennett's desire for a sex education program that would not hide its values behind the skirts of "health." Despite Bennett's critique of the ways in which the imperatives of public health had replaced values in the curriculum, abstinence educators have not been conspicuously successful in stepping outside the framework of public health. On the contrary, *Sex Respect* returned time and again to the sexually active youth's high likelihood of contracting AIDS or herpes. Having eliminated the prophylactic alternatives, the *Sex Respect* curriculum counseled that the only defense against HIV was to remain a virgin until marriage, and then to marry only a virgin.[46] Thus, despite their desire to teach abstinence only because it is right morally, conservative educators harked back to the earliest sex hygienists, who could not resist pointing out that God had conveniently arranged life so that morality and hygiene were indistinguishable.

*Sex Respect*'s attempt to replace SIECUS and other sexuality education organizations did not go unchallenged. Supporters of mainstream sex education quickly published exposés of *Sex Respect*'s numerous conceptual failures and factual fallacies. And though Grady Webb-Wood called his sex education mostly "a good waste of 45 minutes," his parents and six other Jacksonville families found the *Teen-Aid* curriculum to be so inaccurate and biased that they joined in a lawsuit to prohibit the county from continuing to use the curriculum. Similarly, in 1991 a number of parents in East Troy joined with the American Civil Liberties Union of Wisconsin to argue in court that the school district's *Sex Respect* curriculum illegally discriminated on the basis of gender, marital status, sexual orientation, and religion. In Massachusetts and elsewhere, Planned Parenthood and state departments of health sponsored workshops for parents and activists to organize against the conservative movement in sex education. These instances of liberal activism against the schools provided an interesting counterpoint to the more familiar stories of conservative and religious activists banding together to defeat what they see as overly permissive programs.[47]

As a measure of their wider political significance, these developments in sex education were accompanied by vituperative public exchanges, bitter school board battles, and numerous lawsuits over various programs' infringements on parental rights, student rights, and laws against discrimination based on race, sex, or religion. Conservative Christian groups aroused particular controversy with their attempts in hundreds of localities to run candidates for the school board who were overtly or covertly antagonistic to sex education, and more liberal activists expended tremendous energy in opposing or exposing these machinations.

The controversies surrounding sex education since the 1960s have underscored the subject's centrality in a culture in which sexuality is simultaneously more public and more politicized. As the pendulum swings back and forth between sexual liberalism and social conservatism, the debate over sex education has seemed to become less a dispute over the curriculum than a ritual dance to signify a broader range of social and sexual attitudes.

By causing a wider dissemination of sex education programs, the "epidemics" of teenage pregnancy and AIDS multiplied the possible battlegrounds for the culture wars, but they did little to change the terms of the debate over sex in the schools. Sex educators have always shown, for example, a propensity for conflating moral issues with matters of health and illness, and sex educators and their opponents in the AIDS era continue to mix morality with medicine. In this approach, they reflect a general American tendency in the twentieth century to conceive of sexuality and adolescence primarily in terms of danger. Teenage pregnancy and the AIDS epidemic have buttressed a peculiarly American disposition to view adolescent sexuality as a hazard, and intensified the impulse for educators to regulate adolescent desire.

Thus, like the social hygienists at the dawn of the twentieth century, contemporary Americans have wielded the educational system as an instrument for sexual and social reform. Moving beyond their predecessors, many Americans have come to accept this instrumentalist model of sex education as somehow natural and inevitable. But despite the prominence of sex education as a possible solution to the problems of a sexually liberated society, despite its resonance with broader beliefs in American culture, opponents and supporters still run into one central problem: sex education does not work this way.

# CHAPTER EIGHT

# The Myth of Reform

School and out of school are two totally different things.

Thirteen-year-old student,
Lawrence, Kansas (1999)

Sex education in the decades after the 1960s became a potent symbol of contention in the "culture wars" over the moral direction of the United States, for it involves both sexuality and family authority, and the debates necessarily become debates over control of the coming generation.[1] Too often, however, commentators and activists have taken this political cleavage to be the central issue in sex education, and have failed to look beyond the immediate past for a clearer perspective. Sex education at the turn of the twenty-first century is organically connected to the sex education of the previous century.

Even as they have reckoned with the novel crises of teenage pregnancy and AIDS in the aftermath of the sexual revolution, sex educators have navigated by familiar stars. The dominance of danger and disease in thinking about adolescent sexuality, a deep faith in the instrumentalist model of sex education, and a conviction that adolescence is somehow a thing apart from adult society—these are the unchanging boundaries of the universe within which sex education continues to be conceived. Despite the political controversy, it is an exceedingly narrow cosmos. Although teenage pregnancy and AIDS have in some ways reinforced the boundaries of sex education, they have also begun to underscore the inadequacy of our inherited conceptions of education, sexuality, and adolescence.

Liberals and conservatives in the 1990s generated their own mythology to explain why adolescent sexual behavior had become such a problem since the 1960s. Both pointed to sex education for at least part of their explanation, but in doing so they risked misunderstanding both sex education and adolescence. Many conservatives argued, for example, that the sexual revolution coincided with the universal dissemination of sex education, and implied that young people since the 1960s simply acted on the amoral suggestions they received in health class or sex education. "We need to know," asserted Thomas Sowell, a conservative editorialist, in 1994, "that teenage pregnancy and venereal disease were both declining steadily for more than a decade before such programs moved massively into the public schools—and then both rose sharply thereafter."[2] At the center of this critique lay the argument that sexual knowledge *does* induce sexual experimentation. And while some conservatives grudgingly conceded that connections between sex education and what they perceived as a national sexual crisis were more correlative or coincidental than causal, the dominant image remained of a sex education course that encouraged students to engage in sexual behavior.

More liberal sex educators rejoined that soaring rates of teenage pregnancy and sexually transmitted disease were partly consequences of the *absence* of comprehensive sexuality education, as supporters have labeled their program. The sexual revolution of the 1960s began well before sex education became common in the schools—indeed, the reinvigoration of sex education in that decade came as a response to sexual changes already under way—and from the 1970s onward, fewer than 10 percent of high school students have ever received anything like comprehensive, value-neutral sexuality education.[3] Defenders argued that a wider dissemination of sexuality education might have dampened the explosion in teenage sexual behavior before it started.

Superficially opposed to each other, the conservative mythology and the liberal mythology were really flip sides of the same coin. Both conservatives and liberals paid obeisance to the practical power of education and knowledge; both operated within the instrumentalist interpretation of public education. But even as the issues of unwed teenage pregnancy and AIDS led supporters of sex education to cling more tightly to the instrumentalist model, these crises also underscored the practical and conceptual weaknesses of this timeworn approach.

An understanding of sex education's practical ineffectiveness has been a long time coming. At the beginning of the twentieth century, social hygienists had turned toward sex education in the schools because they felt it held the greatest promise for changing Americans' sexual behavior. Not only did the public schools touch far more Americans than any other institution, they also touched them at a critical age. Steeped in the progressive faith in human malleability, social reformers were attracted to the opportunity to affect young people before they grew rigid in the bad habits of adulthood. From the beginning, supporters looked to sex education not to spread intellectual enlightenment but to foster an improvement in behavior.

In an age less concerned with statistical sampling and longitudinal studies, the early reformers did not bother particularly to measure their programs' impact. Common sense told them that if they taught about the dangers of sexual immorality with enough care and vigor, students would heed their warnings. Unfortunately, researchers since then have found virtually no evidence that sex education causes students to change their behavior in one direction or another. Various studies from the 1950s onward have determined that students who complete a sex education course invariably know more sexual facts than students who have not, and some recent studies have claimed that some students after a sex education class evince the intention, at least, to alter elements of their behavior to comport more with the curriculum's values.[4] But none of the dozens of studies by sociologists, psychologists, and educators has discovered that sex education has a significant effect in either direction on adolescent rates of intercourse, use of contraception, and rates of unwanted pregnancies and births.[5] Contrary to conservative charges, the sex education courses have not seemed to make adolescents more likely to engage in sexual behavior, but, critical for those hoping to use sex education as a tool for social reform, they also have not seemed to make adolescents less likely to have sex, or more likely to have "responsible" sex with contraceptives.

Even courses that relied mainly on religious instruction seemed not to prevent young people from becoming sexually active before marriage. While such programs might delay a virgin teen's first coitus by a few months, according to one investigation, "Youths who receive such instruction become sexually active at the same rate as their non-religious peers, and they then experience a greater inability to effectively use contraception." No wonder that the director of one abstinence education program in her 1996 testimony before Congress fell back on an older mode of evaluation. Lisa Hosler of Susquehanna Valley (Pennsylvania) Pregnancy Services based her belief that her group's presentation was "effective in decreasing teenage pregnancy" on such data as "the popularity of the presentation with students and school districts, the students' attentiveness during the presentation, and the number of students who take our literature and 'I'm Worth Waiting For' pins."[6] As with more mainstream sexuality education, the alternative to this "common sense" interpretation of effectiveness is simply an admission of failure. A value-laden *Sex Respect* curriculum seems to be as ineffective as a value-neutral program in changing adolescent behavior.

The reasons for sex education's "failure" to institute social reform range from concrete problems with the teaching itself to fundamental misconceptions about teenage sexual behavior. At a superficial level, sex education's supporters have a right to complain that students simply do not receive enough sex education. Students spend an average of only six and a half hours per year on sex education between seventh grade and high school graduation.[7] It is difficult to imagine that teachers could create significant changes in student behavior in such a short time.

And yet, more hours spent in the classroom would not necessarily produce greater results. The instrumentalist model depends largely on students' learning a clear behavioral lesson that counteracts or modifies the "improper" information they learn outside the school. But classrooms are porous: they cannot be sealed off from the outside world but tend, rather, to reflect larger patterns of social meaning. In a detailed ethnographic study of one representative high school sex education course in the early 1990s, a researcher found that the teacher, her students, the school environment, and the local community all collaborated to forge divergent "meanings" out of the sex education curriculum. The school health education teacher, "Mrs. Warren," for example, felt pressured by time constraints and her own per-

sonal and professional situation to avoid controversial subjects and to reduce the sexuality curriculum to an impersonal but easily digested series of
physiological "facts" for an examination.[8] In narrowing her curriculum,
Mrs. Warren was also likely responding directly to her students' needs: as
most educators recognize, the dominant question running through the
mind of a student sitting in class is not, "How does this information relate to
the rest of my daily experience?" but "Do we have to know this for the test?"
Mrs. Warren was one of the better sex education teachers, according to the
researcher, but she nevertheless allowed a more manageable fact-based curriculum to supplant sex education's reformist mission. Memorizing the location and function of the vas deferens did not convey any obvious behavioral lessons.

Despite the dominance of discrete, teachable facts, sexual values were
not absent from Mrs. Warren's classroom. But the multiplicity of sexual
values and sexual meanings generated even in that single classroom made a
shambles of the instrumentalist model. Contrary to conservative charges
against liberal social engineering, Mrs. Warren, like most frontline sex education teachers, held traditional social views about heterosexuality, premarital intercourse, and gender relations, and her position on these issues
filtered into the classroom. But her students did not automatically accept
her views or the values represented in the curriculum itself. Instead, notes
the investigator, students reinterpreted the curriculum's "facts" about sexuality "through their cultural experiences (which differed by gender, race,
and class) to reach different understandings about appropriate sexual behavior."[9] In this process, teacher and students created an open system of
meaning, sometimes in agreement with dominant morality, sometimes in
opposition to it. What was true of Mrs. Warren's classroom could be multiplied thousands of times, for every sex educator and his or her students ne-
gotiate the meaning of their curriculum under separate circumstances and
within unique social environments. Such diversity should give pause to educators interested in using the school for reformist purposes.

As students' reinterpretations of sex education suggest, sex educators
rely too heavily on young people's ability and desire to act on what they
learn in school. Were educators to succeed in presenting a single, unambiguous message about sexuality, their project might nevertheless founder on

the unwillingness or inability of large numbers of young people to respond to this message. Contrary to the traditional sex education view that young people can respond rationally to scientific sex information, individual sexual behavior is actually deeply enmeshed with the social context. In the most comprehensive survey of carnal activity ever conducted in the United States, Alfred Kinsey found at midcentury that American sexual patterns differed according to gender, class status, race, educational attainment, religion, decade of birth, age at puberty, and geographical location.[10] Kinsey found sexual patterns to be so bound up with social variables that the *future* class status of his male subjects had significantly affected their adolescent sexual patterns, regardless of their parents' class status. No one has successfully explained how three or six or twenty hours of sexuality education in a year is meant to displace these deep and often puzzling determinants of behavior.

Facts alone seldom alter sexual behavior. Nothing is more obvious to educated adults in the AIDS era than the absolute necessity of either abstaining from risky behavior or protecting oneself from the consequences of this behavior. Sex education programs in the schools and publicity campaigns in general have made clear both the dangers of contracting HIV and the ways in which to protect oneself. Yet every year millions of Americans continue to engage in behaviors that place them at risk, and adolescents consistently take even more risks. Why?

The disconnection between sexual information and sexual behavior suggests that a student's response to education is itself socially determined. The critical question is not whether students understand the mechanics of the condom but whether their vision of their own life is such that preventing pregnancy or avoiding disease is important enough for the condom to seem relevant. The willingness to respond to education, notes Roderick Wallace, an epidemiologist researching the spread of AIDS, does not exist "in a social vacuum" but is "strongly determined" and "finely patterned by political, socio-economic and sociogeographic contexts."[11]

The sex educator's expectation that students will respond rationally to classroom knowledge is a peculiarly middle-class ideal. The educational reformers' middle- and upper-class backgrounds determine their ways of approaching social problems, for reformers have long expected that adolescents would heed these educational messages with the same alacrity with which the reformers themselves once had, or would have, responded. Their faith in education is generally justified, however only insofar as the students share their social background. Because young people of higher socioeconomic status are more oriented toward the future than their less advantaged peers, they may be more likely to change their behavior in response to new knowledge. Thus, high school students who consider themselves bound for college respond more readily to the information they receive from sex educators or other sources that abstinence or safe sex will protect them against pregnancy or sexually transmitted diseases, for they perceive that their current actions will have important consequences for the future. To students who lack this future orientation, who find the question of where they will be in five or ten years a matter of fatalism or indifference, an education based on future consequences has little meaning. If receptivity to sex education is socially conditioned, then an educational program by itself will have little tangible effect on those students most at risk for the ills associated with adolescent sexual behavior.

The "epidemic" of unwed teenage pregnancy is perhaps the best example of the ways in which a middle-class bias has distorted our image of adolescent sexual behavior and led to misplaced hopes for sex education. Many of the liberal crusaders against unwed teenage pregnancy have agreed with Senator Edward Kennedy, one of the leaders of the movement, who argued in 1978 that teenage pregnancy was "the leading cause of high school dropouts among girls," and that the birth of a child plunged these teenage mothers into "a cycle of dependency on social welfare."[12] Adolescent pregnancy, in this view, causes young mothers and their children to fall into poverty. Middle-class activists have therefore concluded that these pregnancies are accidents, the products of ignorance, for who would "choose" voluntarily to fall into or stay in poverty? If these teenage mothers had only been taught how pregnancy occurs, and how to prevent it, sex educators have argued, then they would not have made these "mistakes."

This interpretation of teenage pregnancy rests on a number of mistaken assumptions that are common to sex education in general. Perhaps the central problem is that no epidemic actually existed. The teenage birthrate in the 1970s had increased only marginally over that of the previous decade;

the figures appeared shocking primarily because far fewer of the young mothers were marrying. At the same time, the overall American birthrate was declining, so births to unwed teenagers made up a significantly greater proportion of American fertility. Nevertheless, teenage women were not reproducing at a greater rate than their counterparts from the 1950s. If an epidemic existed, it was an epidemic of nonmarriage.

Further, the epidemic of teenage pregnancy was not so clearly a teenage problem. Contrary to the dominant image of "children having children," more than 60 percent of all teenage mothers were eighteen or nineteen years old—legal adults in almost every sense. More important, the popular focus on teenage moms left fathers out of the picture. Politicians and publicists not only heaped most of the blame for teenage pregnancy on young women, but they also ignored the role that adult men played in teenage pregnancy. As one close analysis of the birth record in the mid-1980s demonstrated, men over the age of twenty were responsible for impregnating about 70 percent of all teenage mothers and about 60 percent of all "school-age" mothers (conservatively defined as under nineteen years of age).[13] Similar percentages held true for sexually transmitted diseases among teenage women. Conversely, boys under the age of nineteen accounted for only about 15 percent of all teenage pregnancies. Given their high reported rates of sexual activity, these teenage boys were actually strikingly successful at averting unwanted pregnancies. "Thus," noted one investigator in 1992, "a man over the age of 25 is as likely to cause a 'teenage' pregnancy, birth, or STD case as a school-age boy."[14] In general, fathers and mothers who were both under age eighteen were responsible for fewer than 5 percent of all teenage pregnancies. The policymakers' continued belief that high school males and females together were creating a pregnancy epidemic handicapped their response to pregnancy among teenage women.

Nevertheless, from the 1970s on, teenage women did continue giving birth to more than half a million babies per year, but concerned observers misinterpreted the significance of this figure. Although Senator Kennedy argued with the best of intentions that teenage pregnancy caused and perpetuated poverty for young mothers, the converse is more true: as one recent researcher explains, "A high rate of youth poverty *precedes* a high rate of teen-age childbearing." From 1960 onward, the poverty rate among youth in any given year predicted more than 90 percent of the teen birth-rate nine years later, when more of those children became middle and late adolescents. Nor does pregnancy necessarily begin a downward socioeconomic spiral by leading adolescent mothers to drop out of junior high and high school; rather, a female student already at high risk of dropping out is much more likely to become pregnant. The majority of girls who give birth while still in school are in the bottom academic quartile of their class *before* they become pregnant.[15]

These young women, most of them already mired in poverty and an environment of diminished expectations, do not necessarily perceive motherhood as interrupting their career trajectory. To be sure, a significant percentage of the 300,000 to 400,000 teenage pregnancies that end in abortion each year must indeed have been accidental pregnancies, but that figure still leaves another approximately 600,000 annual births to teenagers. And though a 1995 survey concluded that the mothers considered nearly two-thirds of these births to be "either unwanted or unintended at conception," it is important to puzzle out the *level* of unwantedness or unintention.[16]

In fact, many teenage women either become pregnant intentionally in an attempt to establish a family for themselves, or they take fewer precautions against conception because they do not perceive the possibility of motherhood to be such a disastrous outcome. As Valerie Kee, a teenage mother from Baltimore, told Senator Kennedy at the 1978 hearings, "Most of my friends do have their babies. It seems like most of them are lost and that seems like the only thing—they feel needed, and I figure that is why they get pregnant, because they want to be needed."[17] If motherhood does not necessarily drop a poor teenager further into poverty, and if it can at the same time give her someone to love, then teenage pregnancy can be at some level a rational decision, not an accident.

More hours of sex education will not necessarily bring these at-risk young women to make life decisions as if they were college-bound, middle-class students. This is not to argue that teenagers who "make the decision" to become pregnant or to let themselves risk pregnancy are fully free moral agents, for they make their choices within a severely constrained context, but they are making choices nonetheless. They make these choices, however, at a level that is too deep to be reached by a form of sex education that tries to protect them from "accidental" pregnancies.

If we still consider unwed teenage pregnancy to be a problem, solutions must therefore also go deeper. Epidemiologists and social scientists suggest that significant, planned reductions in the rates of unwed teen pregnancy and STDs will come only with intensive social, political, and economic efforts to reduce what Roderick Wallace calls "social disintegration." As one researcher argues, a society that continues to tolerate "high rates of impoverishment" will likely continue to "generate large numbers of girls seeking escape from harsh childhoods by early family establishment, primarily with adult men."[18] In turning toward sex education to lower unwed teenage pregnancy rates, sex educators have seldom taken the issues of choice and social context into account.

Although the diversity of meanings in American classrooms, the complexity of sexual behavior, and the influence of the social environment all handicap the sex educator's reformist mission, educators and the public at large have continued to cling to the instrumentalist model of sex education. Why? To some extent, the majority of supporters are still drawn in simply by the common-sense myth of effectiveness: if you teach it, they will learn. Professional sex educators also have more particular reasons for holding on to this ideal. These educators, most of them sincerely engaged in social reform, clearly believe in what they do. However, their training and their personal and professional predispositions have also locked many of them into the delusions of expertise—the belief that all social problems may be solved if reformers only approach them with sufficient resources, statistics, and goodwill. The idea of education as reform reinforces many of the sex educators' views of their own social role and the general role of experts in modern society.

As measured by funds disbursed, the instrumentalist model of sex education has significant appeal for public health officials, as well. Many public health officials see sex education in the schools as their most significant conduit to American youth—they have learned, in other words, to view the schools as important delivery systems for youth social services. Treating the schools as an arm of the public health system, however, creates tension with the more traditional vision of the schools, for the public health ethos is consciously nonmoral while many Americans continue to believe that the public schools must play a role in passing on particular moral and intellectual values. Public health officials have few alternatives. In recent years as in the past, most at-risk youths seldom visit physicians, and adolescents who do see a doctor under managed care are hustled into and out of the office. Physicians cannot play a significant role in counseling adolescents on their sexual development. In contrast, the public schools continue to enroll very close to the entire adolescent population. As the Progressives first suggested, youth reformers look to the schools because that's where the youths are.

Parents have given educators other reasons for taking over the responsibility for teaching about sexuality. Although most young people, when asked, claim they would prefer to obtain information about sex from their parents, according to one report in the early 1990s, "fewer than 20 percent of the parents were a major source of information regarding sexuality education." A study of parent-teen communication in 1998 found that between 30 and 40 percent of high school students had had "one good talk" with their parents—almost always their mother—about STDs and whether teen sex was "okay," and these figures were substantially higher than in previous studies.[19] As public health officials and perhaps parents themselves have realized, the schools really must be the primary delivery system for responsible sexual knowledge.

Sex education's role in shaping adolescent behavior has seemed all the more important in recent decades as society's other agents of social control have declined in influence. When the movement for sex education in the schools began in the first decade of the twentieth century, reformers conceived of sex education as only one element in their broader strategy for reforming youthful behavior. Reformers intended sex education to help students develop internal discipline, but they also surrounded adolescents with a variety of external regulations and regulators. Progressive Era reformers created the juvenile court system, for example, as a way of offering guidance and enforcing community standards on young people who seemed not to be responding to parental authority—their crimes could range from theft and assault to mere "incorrigibility" and "promiscuity," especially for girls. The police and these courts over the next half century were to increasingly adjudicate the new category of "status offenses," such as underage smoking, drinking, and, especially, female sexual activity. Reformers at the dawn of the twentieth century also passed laws for compulsory education out of the same desire to guide youthful behavior. Educators intended to foster morality among minors through not only the content of the curriculum but also the school's physical layout and the educators' constant surveillance of students. The sex educators' allies were numerous.

To its supporters, this system of moral regulation seemed part of a seamless fabric of adult authority. Both compulsory education and the juvenile court system occasionally interfered with parental prerogatives, but more often these systems reinforced the parents' power, or extended it outside the family circle. In matters of discipline and behavior, public schools could act in loco parentis because educators claimed to have a fair idea of what the *parentes* desired. Chaperones and dress codes, for example, helped the public schools police adolescent sexuality in a way that seemed consistent with what the students' parents also wanted. Likewise, the juvenile court in its early years often responded directly to parents' pleas for help with their "incorrigible" children.[20]

By the 1970s, if not before, much of this system for regulating adolescent sexuality was in tatters. After arrests for status offenses reached a high point in the 1950s, most police departments began devoting far fewer resources to stopping such minor vices, even as the number of youths engaged in status offenses such as premarital intercourse increased spectacularly. Although the double standard of sexual behavior surely persists at the end of the twentieth century, it is now nearly impossible to imagine the police hauling a young woman into court merely because she was sexually active—for example, not a single female stood before the Los Angeles County Juvenile Court during the 1980s solely for sexual delinquency.[21]

Colleges and secondary schools have likewise given up much of their authority in loco parentis, particularly in policing their students' sexual behavior—or rather, the schools continue to act in loco parentis, but the parental leads they follow have changed significantly over the past several decades. By the 1960s, parental supervision and control over adolescent sexual behavior had already declined significantly, largely as a consequence of adolescent sexual activity's having moved from "front porch to back seat," as one historian has put it.[22] Since the 1960s, the average parent has seemed to exert even less control over youthful sexual activity. Society also seems to expect less of parental supervision—in a series of cases beginning in the 1970s, the Supreme Court has occasionally suggested that sexually active minors need not obtain parental permission for contraceptives or for abortions, and in 1999 a well-publicized lawsuit in which one set of parents sued another for allowing their son to impregnate the first couple's teenage daughter was nearly laughed out of a Nebraska courthouse.[23]

While adults have lost much of their physical and legal control over adolescent sexual behavior, they have not entirely given up their fear of youthful sexuality and its consequences. As society's ability to regulate adolescent sexual behavior through external coercion declines, the adolescent's internal regulation becomes increasingly important. Adults therefore place even more of their hopes on a sex education that will teach adolescents to police themselves. Sex education holds out the promise that self-control can replace social control.

Perhaps the strongest arguments in favor of the instrumentalist model are some tantalizing hints in the 1990s that some special forms of sex education might even make a small impact on adolescent behavior. Douglas Kirby, a director of research for the educational firm ETR Associates and the most prominent researcher involved in evaluating sex education's effects, cautiously endorses a handful of educational programs narrowly tailored to encourage abstinence or contraceptive use by teaching social skills, such as how to recognize and resist pressures for sex, and by demonstrating socially desirable behavior and offering the skills to emulate this behavior. Based on "social learning theory," or the idea that students can best learn certain lessons by observing others employing the lessons and then by acting them out with peers, such programs have slightly reduced unprotected sexual behavior among youths who had not had intercourse before the course, "either by delaying the onset of intercourse or by increasing contraceptive use." Kirby also discerns some decreases in adolescent pregnancies, if not sexual behavior, in schools that have combined similarly intensive educational and peer programs to prevent pregnancy or STDs with reproductive health services, such as school-based clinics that dispense contraceptives. All such programs, however, still suffer from unclear or ambiguous evaluations.[24]

And yet, sex education's basic failure to reform behavior does not mean that sex education itself is, or must always be, a failure—even in instrumentalist terms. Even if any particular course on sex education has less effect on behavior than a student's general social environment, the sex education course nevertheless becomes part of the social environment and influences at some vague level the student's views of sexuality. More broadly, the public dispute over sex education also makes up part of this social environment, and the public debate itself plays an educational role. This debate has raged within very narrow boundaries, but who knows what American sexual ideals and behavior would look like if no movement for sex education existed to raise certain issues publicly?

Sex education's general social role notwithstanding, the inadequacy of an instrumentalist approach should compel sex educators to stop "selling" their programs as solutions to teenage pregnancy, sexually transmitted diseases, and other real or imagined crises of adolescent sexual behavior. Already sex educators have grown more cautious in their claims for effectiveness, but they have not been particularly eager to press this caution on commentators in the popular media, who continue to invoke sex education as a central weapon in the fight against AIDS and the "epidemic" of teenage pregnancy. Greater prudence in making claims for sex or sexuality education could lessen the disappointment that follows when a new curriculum has little impact on students' sexual behavior.

Giving up the reform rationale for sex education should also force supporters to reconsider the subject's relevance and meaning in a very different historical context. Americans' ways of thinking about sex education have signified not an inevitable progression toward objective truth but a series of historically contingent responses to social change. Like the growth rings on a tree, each new development in the history of sex education has left its mark, has become a permanent part of the structure. We take the shape of sex education almost for granted today, but cut away at the tree and you see concentric circles of historically specific elements, such as the politicized character of sex education, the centrality of public education, the dominance of instrumentalist thinking, and sex education's antierotic bias. At the core of sex education lies G. Stanley Hall's founding insight that adolescence is a separate stage of life defined by sexual awakening and deferred gratification.

This core idea has given shape to all the subsequent stages of sex education, but the time has come to reexamine its validity. Contrary to Hall's expectations, the repeated sexual "crises" of this century have made it abundantly clear that adolescent sexual behavior is not a thing apart from adult sexual behavior. Sex educators first seriously reckoned with this problem in the 1920s, when many marriage authorities began to laud the potential of a sexually fulfilling "companionate marriage" for adults. Much to the educators' distress, youthful "flappers" and their boyfriends seemed to conclude that they deserved the same personal fulfillment, even though they were not married. The sex educators' task, then, seemed to be one of buttressing the wall that was supposed to separate youthful behavior from adult sexual ideals, while still preparing youths for their roles as adults. The educators of the 1920s were not conspicuously successful, and future generations of sex educators learned little from their failure.

Since the 1970s, educators and public health officials have treated the "epidemic" of unwed teen pregnancy as if sex and pregnancy out of wedlock were problems peculiar to teenagers. In fact, the explosion in rates of sexual activity among teenagers and teenage out-of-wedlock pregnancies and births from the 1960s forward merely mimicked many of the same trends among older Americans. Correlations between teenage and adult sexual behavior are more than a matter of an amorphous sexual revolution trickling down into the high schools and junior highs. Rather, teenage pregnancy rates particularly follow the rates among adults from similar races, ethnicities, and socioeconomic backgrounds. One investigator has argued that each year's birthrate among teenage mothers "can be predicted to within 95 percent of its true total from two 'nonteenage' factors: the corresponding rates of adult births and of youth poverty," the latter of which also follows closely the poverty rates among adults of the same racial and ethnic groups. Further, the adult world intrudes quite literally on adolescent sexual behavior. Not only are 70 percent of pregnant teenagers sexually involved with adult men, but also a majority of pregnant teenagers have consistently reported that they were sexually abused by adult male family members or friends during childhood.[25] No magic wall separates teens' behavior from the patterns of their elders.

A belief in this imaginary wall continues to distort adults' understanding of adolescent behavior. Sexuality is only one area of confusion among many. Although hardly comparable to teenage sex, a wave of shooting sprees by high school students in the late 1990s, for example, inspired much searching inquiry into the peculiarities of adolescence, especially such problems as depression, anomie, and parental neglect. The teenage male's predilection for violent video games seemed to underscore the unique rage that motivated the adolescent killers. But to explain the series of tragedies at Littleton, Colorado; Jonesboro, Arkansas; and West Paducah, Kentucky, at the end of the twentieth century as expressions of adolescent maladjustment also diverts attention away from America's broader culture of violence, especially among adult men.[26] Adolescent behavior is a mirror, only slightly distorted, of adult values and behavior.

Indeed, we might ask whether "adolescence" is still a useful category, for the characteristics of adolescence have changed significantly since G. Stanley Hall first popularized the concept at the turn of the twentieth century. The probationary period between sexual awakening and "legitimate" sexual activity within marriage has grown significantly. Even as the average age at puberty has dropped, the increased demand for educational credentials has forced young people to extend their period of dependency on their parents into their early twenties, on average. Following the baby-boom era, the average age at first marriage for Americans reached historic highs—the median age for women in the 1990s was almost twenty-five.[27]

At the same time as these markers for adolescence have widened, the lived experience of adolescence seems to have been changing. Although young people at the turn of the century generally spend far more time than their nineteenth-century forebears did in a peer society, rather than in intergenerational groups, they behave in many ways more like adults. Adolescents are well aware of the change, even if adults have been slow to catch on: "Kids today are more mature than our parents were at that age," maintained Bree Beasley, a fourteen-year-old in Lawrence, Kansas. "There's a lot more going on with young people than their parents really think—drugs, sex, drinking. Junior high kids are doing now what college kids used to do." Beasley's friends agreed that parents, teachers, and other adults tend to miss the reality of contemporary adolescence. "They're not ready for their little girls and boys to grow up," argued Hilda Audaidottir, while Beasley noted, "I think parents think, yeah, they're too young to do it."[28]

Adolescents have achieved greater freedom to engage in certain "adult" activities—including sexual activity. By twelfth grade, according to statistics gathered in 1998 by the U.S. Department of Health and Human Welfare, approximately two-thirds of all students have had sexual intercourse.[29] In a striking departure from earlier eras, young women in the 1990s were nearly as likely as young men to have engaged in coitus before high school graduation. The widespread dissemination of birth control has eroded much of the economic justification for the probationary period, and changing social attitudes toward premarital sex in general have lessened the condemnation that sexually active teenage women used to meet. Deferred sexual gratification no longer seems integral to the definition of adolescence.

Nor has marriage become such an obvious goal for adolescents since the 1970s. Divorce rates jumped 90 percent between 1960 and 1980, and the number of men and women who had been divorced rose by almost 200 percent. By the end of the 1980s, nearly a quarter of adult African Americans and 10 percent of Caucasians had been divorced. Perhaps in recognition of such odds, a great many Americans have chosen not to marry at all. But they have not thereby surrendered their right to sexual activity. In some cases, cohabitation has replaced marriage; in others, avowedly single men and women have simply continued trading in the free market of flesh.[30] We might consider the implications of such social developments for sex education without reverting automatically to our inherited bias toward perceiving adolescent sexuality only as a danger.

Reformers founded the movement for sex education largely to aid youths in remaining chaste until the time of their monogamous, heterosexual marriage. Much of this impulse remains in sex education at the turn of the twenty-first century, buried deep beneath the accretions of "positive sexuality" and "nondirective sex education," but the adolescent's position in society has changed significantly. Sex educators and others interested in the sexual and social behavior of the young must learn to take these changes into account.

A better understanding of instrumentalism and the contemporary position of adolescence might prompt the contestants over sex education in the schools to become more forthright about their reasons for supporting or opposing certain kinds of teaching. While examining their own assumptions more consciously, they could expand the debate over sex education beyond the borders of social reform and public health and into a dialogue about which community values the schools should pass on to the next generation.

A handful of novel proposals at the end of the century further suggests the wide range of possibilities not taken up by the practitioners of sex education. Some educators have proposed that the schools take on the task of educating youth for "emotional intimacy," to help young people overcome the inarticulateness and self-delusions that these educators believe can impede deeper human connections. As one fourteen-year-old Kansas girl complained about her sex education, "They just tell us to prepare ourselves emotionally, but they don't tell us what it means to be emotionally prepared."[31] Sexuality education could become a component of the humanities, with history, social studies, and literature courses all consciously exploring the diversity of desire in different ages and places. This sort of sex education would have no reformist goal beyond fostering a deeper understanding of an important facet of human existence.

Finally, a revised sexuality education might struggle against the educational system's deadening of eros and imagination. "In a better world," notes Allan Bloom, more in his role as classical scholar than conservative polemicist, "sexual education would be concerned with the development of taste . . . The progress of civilization is intimately connected with the elaboration of erotic sensibility and a real examination of the delicate interplay of human attractions."[32] These alternative conceptions bear little relation to Dr. Prince Morrow's vision of sex education as an adjunct of the crusade against venereal disease and prostitution, but they could play some small role in freeing the public discussion about adolescent sexuality from its inherited boundaries.

# Notes / Index

# Notes

### 1 THE INVENTION OF THE SEXUAL ADOLESCENT

1. G. Stanley Hall, *Life and Confessions of a Psychologist* (New York: D. Appleton and Co., 1923), p. 589.
2. Ibid., pp. 131–132.
3. Ibid.
4. Ibid.
5. Ibid.
6. Michel Foucault, *The History of Sexuality,* vol. 1: *An Introduction,* trans. Robert Hurley (New York: Vintage Books, 1990); Ronald G. Walters, *Primers for Prudery: Sexual Advice to Victorian America* (Englewood Cliffs, N.J.: Prentice-Hall, 1974), p. 10. See John D'Emilio and Estelle B. Freedman, *Intimate Matters: A History of Sexuality in America* (New York: Harper and Row, 1988); Peter Gay, *The Bourgeois Experience: Victoria to Freud,* vol. 1: *Education of the Senses* (New York: Oxford University Press, 1984); and Carl Degler, "What Ought to Be and What Was: Women's Sexuality in the Nineteenth Century," in Michael Gordon, ed., *The American Family in Social-Historical Perspective* (New York: St. Martin's Press, 1978), pp. 403–425.
7. John Todd, *The Student's Manual: Designed, by Specific Directions, to Aid in Forming and Strengthening the Intellectual and Moral Character and Habits of the Student* (Northampton, Mass.: J. H. Butler, 1837).
8. "Ideology seeking to be established" is a phrase Degler applies to William Acton's view of women as "passionless" in Degler, "What Ought to Be and What Was," p. 406.
9. George H. Napheys, *The Transmission of Life: Counsels on the Nature and Hygiene of the Masculine Function* (Philadelphia: H. C. Watts Co., 1877), pp. 263–264.
10. John Todd, *The Young Man: Hints Addressed to the Young Men of the United States* (Northampton, Mass.: J. H. Butler, 1845), p. 368.
11. For a moderate view, see Napheys, *Transmission of Life,* pp. 47–48; also Orson S. Fowler, *Amativeness: Embracing the Evils and Remedies of Excessive and Perverted Sexuality, Including Warning and Advice to the Married and Single* (New York: 1889), in Charles Rosenberg and Carroll Smith-Rosenberg, eds., *Sex and Science:*

*Phrenological Reflections on Sex and Marriage in Nineteenth Century America* (New York: Arno Press, 1974), pp. 53–55; Sylvester Graham, *A Lecture to Young Men* (1834; repr. New York: Arno Press, 1974).

12. Peter Cominos, "Late-Victorian Sexual Respectability and the Social System," *International Review of Social History* 8, nos. 1 and 2 (1963): 18–48 and 216–250.

13. E. H. Hare, "Masturbatory Insanity: The History of an Idea," *Journal of Medical Science* 108 (Jan. 1962): 1–25.

14. Graham, *A Lecture to Young Men*, p. 44.

15. Fowler, *Amativeness*, p. 14.

16. Samuel A. A. D. Tissot, *Onanism* (orig. English trans., 1766; repr., New York: Garland Publishing, 1985); see also Eliza B. Duffey, *The Relations of the Sexes* (1876; repr., New York: Arno Press, 1974), p. 179.

17. W. O. Frick, Pasadena, California, communication with the author, 13 Oct. 1995.

18. Cominos, "Late-Victorian Sexual Respectability," 32–33.

19. Napheys, *Transmission of Life*, p. 83, 90–92.

20. Gail Pat Parsons, "Equal Treatment for All: American Medical Remedies for Male Sexual Problems: 1850–1900," *Journal of the History of Medicine and Allied Sciences* 32 (Jan. 1977): 55–71.

21. Max Weber, *The Protestant Ethic and the Spirit of Capitalism*, trans. Talcott Parsons (New York: Charles Scribner, 1958); also Stephen Nissenbaum, *Sex, Diet, and Debility in Jacksonian America: Sylvester Graham and Health Reform* (Westport, Conn.: Greenwood Press, 1980).

22. Graham, *Lecture to Young Men*, p. 7.

23. Paul E. Johnson, *A Shopkeeper's Millennium: Society and Revivals in Rochester, New York, 1815–1837* (New York: Hill and Wang, 1978).

24. Linda Gordon, *Woman's Body, Woman's Right: A Social History of Birth Control in America* (New York: Grossman Publishers, 1976), pp. 105–106.

25. William Leach, *True Love and Perfect Union: The Feminist Reform of Sex and Society*, 2nd ed., (Middletown, Conn.: Wesleyan University Press, 1989), p. 91.

26. Nancy F. Cott, "Passionlessness: An Interpretation of Victorian Sexual Ideology, 1790–1850," in Nancy F. Cott and Elizabeth H. Pleck, eds., *A Heritage of Her Own* (New York: Simon and Schuster, 1979), pp. 162–181.

27. Joseph Kett, *Rites of Passage: Adolescence in America 1790 to the Present* (New York: Basic Books, 1977), pp. 30–31; also John Demos, *Past, Present, and Personal: The Family and the Life Course in American History* (New York: Oxford University Press, 1986), pp. 99–100.

28. R. P. Neuman, "Masturbation, Madness, and the Modern Concepts of Childhood and Adolescence," *Journal of Social History* 8 (Spring 1975): 1–27.

29. See Anthony Comstock, *Traps for the Young* (1883), new ed., ed. Robert Bremner (Cambridge, Mass.: Belknap Press of Harvard University Press, 1967).

30. On the infrastructure supporting this rapid social change, see, for example, George R. Taylor, *The Transportation Revolution, 1815–1860* (New York: Rinehart, 1951); also Nissenbaum, *Sex, Diet, and Debility in Jacksonian America,* preface.

31. Todd, *The Young Man,* pp. 118–120, 142.

32. Ibid., 354.

33. Peter Gay, "Victorian Sexuality: Old Texts and New Insights," *American Scholar* 49 (Summer 1980): 374–375.

34. See Karen Lystra, *Searching the Heart: Women, Men, and Romantic Love in Nineteenth-Century America* (New York: Oxford University Press, 1989).

35. G. Stanley Hall, *Adolescence: Its Psychology and Its Relations to Physiology, Anthropology, Sociology, Sex, Crime, Religion and Education,* 2 vols. (1904; new ed., New York: D. Appleton and Co., 1908). Neuman cautions against confusing the universal biology of puberty with the socially determined period of adolescence, in "Masturbation," 23.

36. U.S. Department of Commerce, Bureau of the Census, *Historical Statistics of the United States: Colonial Times to 1970,* Part 1 (White Plains, N.Y.: Kraus International Publications, 1989), p. 369.

37. Neuman, "Masturbation," 6–7.

38. *Historical Statistics of the United States,* p. 19.

39. Dorothy Ross, *G. Stanley Hall: The Psychologist as Prophet* (Chicago: University of Chicago Press, 1972), p. 338n.

40. Sanford Bell, "A Preliminary Study of the Emotion of Love between the Sexes," *American Journal of Psychology* 13 (July 1902): 327–328.

41. Hall, *Adolescence,* 2: 453.

42. William James, *Principles of Psychology,* 1: 22–23; quoted in Nathan G. Hale, Jr., *Freud and the Americans: The Beginnings of Psychoanalysis in the United States, 1876–1917* (New York: Oxford University Press, 1971), p. 110.

43. Herbert Spencer, *The Principles of Sociology,* 3rd ed. (1885; repr., New York: D. Appleton and Co., 1925), 1: 621–622.

44. Hall, *Adolescence,* 1: xiii; George W. Stocking, Jr., *Race, Culture, and Evolution: Essays in the History of Anthropology* (Chicago: University of Chicago Press, 1982), pp. 110–132.

45. Hall, *Adolescence,* 1: x.

46. Bell, "Emotion of Love," 327.

47. Ibid.

48. George M. Beard, *American Nervousness: Its Causes and Consequences* (New York: G. P. Putnam's Sons, 1881), p. 26; George M. Beard, *Sexual Neurasthenia: Its Hygiene, Causes, Symptoms and Treatment,* ed. A. D. Rockwell (5th ed., New York: E. B. Treat and Co., 1902); see also Barbara Sicherman, "The Uses of a Diagnosis: Doctors, Patients, and Neurasthenia," *Journal of the History of Medicine* 32 (Jan. 1977): 33–55.

49. Bell, "Emotion of Love," 328; Hall, *Adolescence*, 1: 285–286.

50. Bell, "Emotion of Love," 327–328; Hall, *Adolescence*, 1: 453. For a less sanguine evaluation of civilized repression before Freud, see Charles W. Page, "The Adverse Consequences of Repression," *American Journal of Insanity* 49 (Jan. 1893): 372–390.

51. Hall, *Adolescence*, 1: 322.

52. Stocking, *Race, Culture, and Evolution*, p. 242.

53. Hall, *Adolescence*, 1: 324.

54. On racial thought, see John S. Haller, *Outcasts from Evolution: Scientific Attitudes of Racial Inferiority, 1859–1900* (Chicago: University of Illinois Press, 1971).

55. See Demos, *Past, Present, and Personal*, pp. 104–105.

56. U.S. Bureau of the Census, *Eleventh Census, 1890, Population*, 1: clxxix–clxxxvi.

57. *Historical Statistics of the United States*, pp. 11–12.

58. G. Stanley Hall, "The Moral and Religious Training of Children and Adolescents," *Pedagogical Seminary* 1 (1891): 196.

59. Hall, *Adolescence*, 1: 321.

60. Ross, *G. Stanley Hall*, pp. 330–332.

## 2   REGULATING ADOLESCENT APPETITES

1. See "American Society of Sanitary and Moral Prophylaxis Regular Meeting Minutes," 8 Feb. 1905, Folder 2: 7, American Social Hygiene Association Papers, Social Welfare History Archives, University of Minnesota (hereafter ASHA Papers).

2. Prince A. Morrow, *Social Diseases and Marriage* (New York and Philadelphia: Lea Brothers and Co., 1904).

3. Prince A. Morrow quoted in Charles R. Henderson, *Education with Reference to Sex*, Eighth Yearbook of the National Society for the Scientific Study of Education, Parts 1 and 2 (Chicago: University of Chicago Press, 1909), p. 73; and Prince Morrow, "Sanitary and Moral Prophylaxis," *Boston Medical and Surgical Journal* 154 (14 June 1906): 677.

4. Interview with Edward L. Keyes, Jr., 12 Nov. 1946, Folder 1: 1, ASHA Papers.

5. "Conspiracy of silence" was a phrase first used by the English journalist and reformer William T. Stead, according to Walter Clarke, *Taboo: The Story of the Pioneers of Social Hygiene* (Washington, D.C.: Public Affairs Press, 1961), pp. 25–27.

6. For the conspicuous exception to this pattern, see David Pivar, *Purity Crusade: Sexual Morality and Social Control, 1868–1900* (Westport, Conn.: Greenwood Press, 1973), pp. 52–56.

7. Allan M. Brandt, *No Magic Bullet: A Social History of Venereal Disease in the United States since 1880* (New York: Oxford University Press, 1987), pp. 71, 74.

8. Morrow, *Social Diseases and Marriage*, pp. 26–27.

9. Helen C. Putnam, "Education for Parenthood," *Religious Education* 6 (June 1911): 161.

10. Prince A. Morrow, *The Teaching of Sex Hygiene* (repr., New York: American Federation for Sex Hygiene, 1912), p. 7, Folder 1: 8, ASHA Papers.

11. Ibid.

12. Morrow, *Social Diseases and Marriage,* pp. 347–348.

13. John Higham, *Strangers in the Land: Patterns of American Nativism, 1860–1925* (New Brunswick, N.J.: Rutgers University Press, 1955).

14. G. Stanley Hall, "The Needs and Methods of Educating Young People in the Hygiene of Sex," *Pedagogical Review* 15 (Mar. 1908): 82.

15. This and following quotations are from George E. Dawson, "The Child's Rights: The Right of the Child to be Well-Born," *Religious Education* 6 (June 1911): 167.

16. John Franklin Bobbitt, "Practical Eugenics," *Pedagogical Seminary* 16 (Sept. 1909): 385–394.

17. Dawson, "The Child's Rights."

18. On fears of degeneration and more general racial concern leading to the eugenics movement, see Mark H. Haller, *Eugenics: Hereditarian Attitudes in American Thought* (New Brunswick, N.J.: Rutgers University Press, 1963), pp. 21–57.

19. On antiprostitution sentiments and the desire for a common moral order, see Pivar, *Purity Crusade,* pp. 256–260. A useful look at historians' involvement with prostitution is offered in Timothy J. Gilfoyle, "Prostitutes in History: From Parables of Pornography to Metaphors of Modernity," *American Historical Review* 104 (Feb. 1999): 117–141.

20. Letter from Herbert W. Gates quoted in Henderson, *Education with Reference to Sex,* p. 9; see also Kathy Peiss, *Cheap Amusements: Working Women and Leisure in Turn-of-the-Century New York* (Philadelphia: Temple University Press, 1986), pp. 185–188.

21. Eugène Brieux, *Damaged Goods* (*Les Avariès*), trans. John Pollock, in Eugène Brieux, *Three Plays by Brieux* (New York: Brentano's, 1912), pp. 185–254.

22. Morrow, *Social Diseases and Marriage,* p. 23. On concerns that "lower-class" entertainments in New York at this time were enticing "respectable" people, see Lewis Erenberg, *Steppin' Out: New York Nightlife and the Transformation of American Culture, 1890–1930* (Westport, Conn.: Greenwood Press, 1981), pp. 60–91.

23. Aaron M. Powell, ed., *The National Purity Congress: Its Papers, Addresses, Portraits* (New York: American Purity Alliance, 1896; repr., New York: Arno Press, 1976). Geneology in "Steps in the Development of the A.S.H.A.," unpublished document, ca. 1922, Folder 1: 1, ASHA Papers.

24. The following discussion relies on Pivar, *Purity Crusade,* but see also William Leach, *True Love and Perfect Union: The Feminist Reform of Sex and Society,* 2nd ed. (Middletown, Conn.: Wesleyan University Press, 1989), pp. 85–86; Anna Garlin Spencer,

"Milestones in Social Hygiene," unpublished document, Folder 1: 1, ASHA Papers; and Frances Willard, "The White-Cross Movement in Education," *National Education Association Journal of Proceedings and Addresses* (the title varied; hereafter, *NEA Journal of Addresses and Proceedings*), 28 (1890): 161.

25. Morrow, *Social Diseases and Marriage*, p. 332.

26. Henderson, *Education with Reference to Sex*, p. 10.

27. Delcevare King to Philip R. Mather, 9 Dec. 1958, Folder 1: 1, ASHA Papers; King to Prince A. Morrow, 23 May 1910, Folder 1: 4, ibid; Morrow to King, 24 May 1910, Folder 1: 4, ibid.

28. Anna Garlin Spencer, "Pioneers," *Journal of Social Hygiene* 16 (Mar. 1930): 157.

29. On the merger, see *Vigilance* 27 (Dec. 1913): 1; and "Minutes of the Executive Committee of the American Federation for Sex Hygiene," 19 July 1913, Folder 2: 2, ASHA Papers; "Minutes of the American Vigilance Association," 21 Nov. 1912 and 20 Dec. 1912, Folder 2: 5, ASHA Papers.

30. G. Stanley Hall, "Education and the Social Hygiene Movement," *Transactions of the American Society for Sanitary and Moral Prophylaxis* 5 (Oct. 1914): 213. George A. Coe, *Education in Religion and Morals* (Chicago: Revel Publishers, 1904); see also Robert T. Handy, *A Christian America: Protestant Hopes and Historical Realities* (New York: Oxford University Press, 1971).

31. James L. McConaughy, "Moral Education," *Journal of Education* 79 (12 Feb. 1914): 171.

32. Frances M. Greene, "Sex Hygiene," *NEA Journal of Addresses and Proceedings* 49 (1911): 918–920; Emanuel Sternheim, "The Sex Problem in Education," *Educational Review* 50 (Oct. 1915): 276; also Clara Schmitt, "The Teaching of the Facts of Sex in the Public School," *Pedagogical Seminary* 17 (June 1910): 234.

33. Helen C. Putnam, "Sex Instruction in Schools," in Henderson, *Education with Reference to Sex*, p. 77; see also Charles H. Keene and Mabel M. Wright, "Shall Sex Hygiene Be Taught in the Public Schools?" in *NEA Journal of Addresses and Proceedings* 52 (1914): 700.

34. Greene, "Sex Hygiene," 918–920.

35. Ralph E. Blount, "The Responsibility of the Teacher with Regard to the Teaching of Sex Hygiene," *NEA Journal of Addresses and Proceedings* 52 (1914): 470.

36. "Minutes of Meeting of the Executive Committee, American Federation for Sex Hygiene," 4 Mar. 1912, Folder L1: 1, ASHA Papers.

37. M. J. Exner, "Progress in Sex Education," *Journal of Social Hygiene* 15 (Oct. 1929): 396; Clarke, *Taboo*, p. 82. The fainting anecdote comes from Clarke.

38. The examples of this reasoning are numerous: see, for example, Calvin S. White, "Some Practical Problems of Social Hygiene," [Chicago] *City Club Bulletin* 7 (10 July 1914): 233. On sexual ignorance, see Morrow, "Sanitary and Moral Prophylaxis," 674–675.

39. Morrow, *Social Diseases*, p. 35.

40. Ibid., pp. 358–359.

41. See "Minutes of Meeting of the Executive Committee," American Federation for Sex Hygiene, 4 Mar. 1912, Folder L1: 1, ASHA Papers.

42. Bernard S. Talmey, reply to Richard Cabot, "Are Sanitary Prophylaxis and Moral Prophylaxis Natural Allies?" *Journal of the Society for Sanitary and Moral Prophylaxis* 5 (Jan. 1914): 41–42.

43. John N. Hurtz, "The Moral Factors in the Reduction of Venereal Diseases," ibid. 6 (July 1915): 95.

44. Helen C. Putnam, "Instruction in the Physiology and Hygiene of Sex: Its Practicability as Demonstrated in Several Public Schools," *Boston Medical and Surgical Journal* 156 (31 Jan. 1907): 133.

45. U.S. Department of Commerce, Bureau of the Census, *Historical Statistics of the United States: Colonial Times to 1970*, Part 1 (White Plains, N.Y.: Kraus International Publications, 1989), p. 368; Charles Rugh, "Reorganization of the Curriculum," *Religious Education* 7 (Feb. 1913): 638–639.

46. Lawrence Cremin, *The Transformation of the School: Progressivism in American Education, 1876–1957* (New York: Alfred A. Knopf, 1962), pp. 66–126.

47. Herbert M. Kliebard, *The Struggle for the American Curriculum 1893–1958* (Boston: Routledge and Kegan Paul, 1986), pp. 1–29. Also see National Education Association Committee of Ten, *Report of the Committee of Ten on Secondary School Studies* (1892; New York: American Book Company, 1894), pp. 40, 56–57; for background, see Herbert Spencer, *Education: Intellectual, Moral, and Physical* (1860; New York: D. Appleton and Co., 1895), p. 31.

48. James R. Cook, "The Evolution of Sex Education in the Public Schools of the United States, 1900–1970," Ph.D. diss., College of Education, Southern Illinois University, 1972, p. 27.

49. Quoted in "Sex Education in the Schools," *Vigilance* 27 (Jan. 1914): 5.

50. Clifford Barnes, "Moral Training thru the Agency of the Public School," *NEA Journal of Addresses and Proceedings* 45 (1907): 373.

51. See "How Shall We Teach? The Parent and the Problem," *Social Hygiene* 1 (June 1915): 423–438; William F. Snow, "Schools and the Social Hygiene Movement," *Proceedings of the Eighth Congress of the American School Hygiene Association* 5 (American School Hygiene Association, 1916): 133–140.

52. Putnam, "Sex Instruction in Schools," p. 77.

53. Morrow, *Social Diseases and Marriage*, pp. 338–339.

54. Maurice A. Bigelow, *Sex Education: A Series of Lectures concerning Knowledge of Sex in Its Relation to Human Life* (1916; New York: MacMillan, 1918), p. 233.

55. ASHA's program embodied both "positive environmentalism" and "negative environmentalism," as outlined in Paul Boyer, *Urban Masses and Moral Order in America, 1820–1920* (Cambridge, Mass.: Harvard University Press, 1992), pp. 175–232.

56. Prince A. Morrow, "Eugenics and Venereal Diseases," reprinted from *The Dietetic and Hygienic Gazette* (Jan. 1911): 18–19, Folder 1: 8, ASHA Papers.

57. Anthony Comstock, "The Work of the New York Society for the Prevention of Vice, and Its Bearings on the Morals of the Young," *Pedagogical Seminary* 16 (Sept. 1909): 404.

58. Ibid.

59. Putnam, "Instruction in the Physiology and Hygiene of Sex," 133. For sporadic nineteenth-century attempts at sex education, see "The National Woman's Christian Temperance Union and Social Vice," *The American Bulletin* 8 (Nov. 1885): 2, Folder L1: 2, ASHA Papers; Amelie Rives, "Innocence versus Ignorance," *North American Review* 155 (Sept. 1892): 287–292; and Leach, *True Love and Perfect Union,* pp. 48, 56–62.

60. Winfield Hall, "The Teaching of Social Hygiene, and the Bearing of Such Teaching on the Moral Training of the Child," *Religious Education* 3 (Oct. 1908): 129.

61. G. Stanley Hall, *Adolescence: Its Psychology and Its Relations to Physiology, Anthropology, Sociology, Sex, Crime, Religion and Education,* 2 vols. (1904; New York: D. Appleton and Co., 1908); G. Stanley Hall, "Sex Hygiene in Infantile and Pre-Pubertal Life," in Thomas A. Storey, ed., *Fourth International Congress on School Hygiene, Buffalo, New York, U.S.A., Aug. 25–30, 1913, Transactions* (Buffalo: American School Hygiene Association, 1914), 4: 10–15.

62. Max J. Exner, "The Sex Factor in Social Life," unpublished manuscript, p. 1 (4 Oct. 1929), Folder 171: 15, ASHA Papers.

63. Ibid., p. 10. See also Thomas W. Galloway, *Sex and Social Health: A Manual for the Study of Social Hygiene* (New York: American Social Hygiene Association, 1924), p. 85.

64. Exner, "Sex Factor in Social Life," p. 10. See also Maurice A. Bigelow, "The Established Points in Social Hygiene Education, 1905–1924," *Journal of Social Hygiene* 10 (Jan. 1924): 5.

65. Bigelow, "Established Points, 1905–1924," 5.

66. Ibid.

67. Max J. Exner, *What Is Social Hygiene?* (New York: American Social Hygiene Association, 1930), p. 4, Folder 172: 7, ASHA Papers.

68. See, for example, Maurice A. Bigelow, "The Physical Basis of Character Education," *Journal of Social Hygiene* 16 (Dec. 1930): 515–518.

69. Thomas W. Galloway, "The Bearing of Sex-Education upon Character," *NEA Journal of Addresses and Proceedings* 60 (1922): 416–421.

70. Thomas W. Galloway, "Sex Hygiene," *Journal of Education* 78 (24 July 1913): 95.

71. Clara Schmitt, "The Teaching of the Facts of Sex in the Public Schools," *Pedagogical Seminary* 17 (June 1910): 232.

72. Quotations from M. J. Exner, "Sex Education by the Young Men's Christian Associations in Universities and Colleges," *Social Hygiene* 1 (Sept. 1915): 575.

73. Ibid.

74. Thomas Galloway, "Sex Instruction," *NEA Journal of Addresses and Proceedings* 51 (1913): 643.

75. Ibid.

76. Ibid., 644.

77. Exner, "Sex Education by the Young Men's Christian Associations," 575–576.

78. Schmitt, "Teaching of the Facts of Sex," 231.

79. Joseph Kett, *Rites of Passage: Adolescence in America 1790 to the Present* (New York: Basic Books, 1977), pp. 215–216.

80. Hall, *Adolescence*, 1: 465. Henry F. May, *The End of American Innocence: A Study of the First Years of Our Own Time, 1912–1917* (New York: Alfred A. Knopf, 1959; repr., New York: Oxford University Press, 1971); see also John C. Burnham, "The Progressive Era Revolution in American Attitudes toward Sex," *Journal of American History* 59 (Mar. 1973): 885–908.

81. Henry S. Curtis, "Education in Matters of Sex," *Pedagogical Seminary* 28 (Mar. 1921): 41.

82. Henderson, *Education with Reference to Sex*, p. 35.

83. Bigelow, *Sex Education*, p. 68.

84. Ibid., p. 72.

85. Miriam C. Gould, "The Psychological Influence upon the Adolescent Girl of the Knowledge of Prostitution and Venereal Disease," *Social Hygiene* 2 (Apr. 1916): 197–198.

86. Dawson, "The Child's Rights," 170–171.

87. For an opposing interpretation, see Christina Simmons, "Modern Sexuality and the Myth of Victorian Repression," in Kathy Peiss and Christina Simmons, eds., *Passion and Power: Sexuality in History* (Philadelphia: Temple University Press, 1989), pp. 157–177.

88. This and the following quotations come from Bigelow, *Sex Education*, pp. 68–70, 75–77.

89. Mabel S. Ulrich, *The Girl's Part*, ASHA pamphlet (New York: ca. 1917–1919), unpaginated, Folder 170: 9, ASHA Papers.

90. Morrow, "Eugenics and Venereal Diseases," 20.

91. Ibid.

92. Schmitt, "Teaching of the Facts of Sex," 234–235.

93. R. E. Blount, "Several Aspects of the Teaching of Sex Physiology and Hygiene," in Sophronisba P. Breckinridge, ed., *The Child in the City: A Series of Papers Presented at the Conferences Held during the Chicago Child Welfare Exhibit* (Chicago: Department of Social Investigation, Chicago School of Civics and Philanthropy, 1912), p. 138.

94. Prince A. Morrow, *The Teaching of Sex Hygiene* (New York: American Federation for Sex Hygiene, ca. 1913), p. 10, Folder 1: 8, ASHA Papers.

95. *Report of the Special Committee on the Matter and Methods of Sex Education,* (New York: American Federation for Sex Hygiene, 1913), p. 3.

96. As Exner complained in "Sex Education by the Young Men's Christian Associations," 574.

97. John L. Heffron, "The Moral Value of the Teaching of the Physiology and Hygiene of Sex in the Public Schools," *Religious Education* 4, no. 6 (Feb. 1910): 543.

98. Fletcher B. Dresslar, *The Fifteenth International Congress on Hygiene and Demography,* U.S. Bureau of Education Bulletin No. 18 (Washington, D.C.: Government Printing Office, 1913), p. 35.

99. A more complete account of the "Chicago experiment" and its significance is given in Jeffrey P. Moran, "'Modernism Gone Mad': Sex Education Comes to Chicago, 1913," *Journal of American History* 83 (Sept. 1996): 481–513.

100. See Vice Commission of Chicago, *The Social Evil in Chicago* (Chicago: Vice Commission of the City of Chicago, 1911), pp. 3–4; for the women's experiences, see Joanne J. Meyerowitz, *Women Adrift: Independent Wage Earners in Chicago, 1880–1930* (Chicago: University of Chicago Press, 1988), pp. 1–42.

101. John T. McManis, *Ella Flagg Young and a Half-Century of the Chicago Public Schools* (Chicago: 1916), p. 28.

102. Thomas W. Gutowski, "The High School as an Adolescent-Raising Institution: An Inner History of Chicago Public Secondary Education, 1856–1940," Ph.D. diss., University of Chicago, 1978, p. 124; Walter Sumner, reply to Richard C. Cabot, "Are Sanitary Prophylaxis and Moral Prophylaxis Natural Allies?" *Transactions of the American Society for Sanitary and Moral Prophylaxis* 5 (Jan. 1914): 33–34; *Chicago Daily Tribune,* 26 June 1913, p. 8

103. "Sex Education in the Schools," *Vigilance* 27, no. 1 (Jan. 1914): 5.

104. The content of these talks is outlined in the debate between Keene and Wright, "Shall Sex Hygiene Be Taught in the Public Schools?" 698; *Chicago Daily Tribune,* 26 June 1913, p. 8.

105. Keene and Wright, "Shall Sex Hygiene Be Taught in the Public Schools?" 697–701.

106. Ibid., 698–700; see also *Milwaukee Journal,* 29 Oct. 1913, cited in "Sex Education," *Vigilance* 27 (Dec. 1913): 25–26; these estimates may have been inflated, for Young herself claimed that only 1.06 percent of the students brought requests from their parents that they be excused, in *Proceedings of the Chicago Board of Education,* 31 Dec. 1913, p. 601.

107. "Sex Hygiene," *Journal of Education* 79 (5 Mar. 1914): 268; *Chicago Daily Tribune,* 11 Dec. 1913, p. 2; *Chicago Record-Herald,* 25 July 1913, p. 1; 26 July 1913, p. 2; and 28 July 1913, p. 3.

108. *Chicago Citizen,* 5 July 1913, p. 4.

109. *Chicago Daily Tribune,* 11 Dec. 1913, pp. 1–2; 13 Dec. 1913, p. 1; and 14 Dec. 1913, p. 2; *Proceedings of the Chicago Board of Education,* 31 Dec. 1913, pp. 596–597. *Chi-*

*cago New World,* 22 Nov. 1913, p. 4; see also Grace C. Strachan, "Wanted: A Twentieth-Century Ideal," *NEA Journal of Addresses and Proceedings* 52 (1914): 317.

110. Thomas M. Balliet, "Sex Hygiene and Sex Morality as the Aim of Sex Education," *NEA Journal of Addresses and Proceedings* 53 (1915): 152.

111. Ibid., 151.

112. Exner, "Sex Education by the Young Men's Christian Association," 574.

113. Here and below, see Gould, "Psychological Influence upon the Adolescent Girl," 195–196, 203.

114. Wallace H. Maw calls this one of the most important international meetings for sex education, in "Fifty Years of Sex Education in the Public Schools of the United States (1900–1950): A History of Ideas," Ph. D. diss., Graduate Faculty of the Teachers' College of the University of Cincinnati, 1953, p. 64; see Fletcher B. Dresslar, *The Fifteenth International Congress on Hygiene and Demography,* U.S Bureau of Education Bulletin No. 18 (Washington, D.C.: Government Printing Office, 1913).

115. See "Minutes of the Executive Committee, American Federation for Sex Hygiene," 12 Apr. 1912, Folder L1: 1, ASHA Papers; see as well the actual text, *Report of the Special Committee on the Matter and Methods of Sex Education* (New York: American Federation for Sex Hygiene, 1913).

116. Max Exner called Bigelow's book the "authoritative interpretation" for the sex education movement, in *Social Hygiene* 2 (Oct. 1916): 596–597.

117. C. W. Hargitt, "Place and Function of Biology in Secondary Education," *Education* 15 (1905): 480.

118. Otto B. Christy, "The Development of the Teaching of General Biology in the Secondary Schools," *Journal of the Tennessee Academy of Science* 12 (July 1936): 280.

119. Ibid., 182 and 317–329; see also Francis E. Lloyd and Maurice A. Bigelow, *The Teaching of Biology in the Secondary School* (New York: Longmans, Green, and Co., 1909).

120. The discussion below is taken from the *Report of the Special Committee on the Matter and Methods of Sex Education,* pp. 4–9.

121. Examples are multitudinous, but see Schmitt, "Teaching of the Facts of Sex," 231.

122. *Vigorous Manhood* (New York: ASHA, ca. 1914), p. 3, Folder 170: 14, ASHA Papers; U.S. Public Health Service, *Keeping Fit* (Washington, D.C.: U.S. Public Health Service, 1920), p. 6; and "Keeping Fit" poster series, Folder 171: 8, ASHA Papers.

123. Many educators and eugenicists recommended studying these families, among them James E. Peabody, "Some Experiments in Sex Education," *Educational Review* 48 (Nov. 1914): 391; and Bigelow, *Sex Education,* pp. 103–105. The studies have been republished in Nicole Hahn Rafter, ed., *White Trash: The Eugenic Family Studies, 1877–1919* (Boston: Northeastern University Press, 1988).

124. *Report of the Special Committee,* as noted in Dresslar, *Congress on Hygiene and Demography,* p. 35.

125. See Putnam, "Instruction in the Physiology and Hygiene of Sex," 136.

126. G. Stanley Hall, "The Needs and Methods of Educating Young People in the Hygiene of Sex," *Pedagogical Review* 15 (Mar. 1908): 89.

127. Bigelow, *Sex Education,* pp. 121–123; Bryan Strong, "Ideas of the Early Sex Education Movement in America, 1890–1920," *History of Education Quarterly* 12 (Summer 1972): 149.

128. See Bigelow's discussion of his own textbooks, *Applied Biology* and *Introduction to Biology,* which otherwise emphasized the "reproduction of organisms" more than other high schools books, in *Sex Education,* p. 110. The American Federation for Sex Hygiene (later, ASHA) special committee had counseled avoiding "detailed descriptions of external human anatomy" in *Report of the Special Committee,* pp. 3–4.

129. *Report of the Special Committee,* p. 2.

130. The metaphor comes from Thomas W. Galloway, "Sex Instruction," *NEA Journal of Addresses and Proceedings* 51 (1913): 645.

131. Strong, "Ideas of the Early Sex Education Movement," 141–147; H. E. Vittum, "Some Aspects of the Vice Problem," [Chicago] *City Club Bulletin* 25 (June 1914): 229; C. W. Eliot, "The Pioneer Qualities of Dr. Morrow," *Social Diseases* 4 (July 1913): 135.

132. Nancy F. Cott, "Passionlessness: An Interpretation of Victorian Sexual Ideology, 1790–1850," in Nancy F. Cott and Elizabeth H. Pleck, eds., *A Heritage of Her Own* (New York: Simon and Schuster, 1979), pp. 162–181.

133. Here and below, Bigelow, *Sex Education,* p. 177.

134. Max J. Exner, "Friend or Enemy?" *Social Hygiene* 2, no. 4 (Oct. 1916): 482.

135. Here and below, Bigelow, *Sex Education,* p. 58.

136. Mary Odem, *Delinquent Daughters: Protecting and Policing Adolescent Female Sexuality in the United States, 1885–1920* (Chapel Hill: University of North Carolina Press, 1995), pp. 108–111.

137. "Sexually unresponsive" comes from Strong, "Ideas of the Early Sex Education Movement," 141; for differences in "fundamental facts" for boys and girls, see Walter Hollis Eddy, *Reproduction and Sex Hygiene: A Text and a Method* (New York: ASHA, 1916), pp. 77–79, Folder 171: 1, ASHA Papers.

138. Ralph Blount, "Responsibility of the Teacher," 472–473.

139. U.S. Bureau of Education, *Report of the Commissioner of Education, 1914,* vol. 1 (Washington, D.C.: Government Printing Office, 1915), p. 60.

140. Richard J. Tierney, "Character and the Sex Problem," in *Buffalo Congress on School Hygiene August 25–30, 1913,* U.S. Bureau of Education Bulletin No. 48 (Washington, D.C.: Government Printing Office, 1913), p. 62.

141. Fannie Casseday Duncan, "Teaching Sex Hygiene," reprinted from *New York World* in *Journal of Education* 79 (12 Feb. 1914): 187.

142. Tierney, "Character and the Sex Problem," 62.

143. Benjamin Malzberg, "The Child's Mind à la Freud," *Social Hygiene* 6 (Jan. 1920): 110.

144. Tierney, "Character and the Sex Problem," 62.

145. Duncan, "Teaching Sex Hygiene," 187.

146. Agnes Repplier in the *Atlantic Monthly* (Mar. 1914), reprinted in Bigelow, *Sex Education*, p. 203.

147. Tierney, "Character and the Sex Problem," p. 62.

148. Repplier in Bigelow, *Sex Education*, p. 204.

149. Ibid.

150. *Boston Post*, quoted in "Sex Education in the Schools," *Vigilance*, 4.

151. Keene and Wright, "Shall Sex Hygiene Be Taught in the Public Schools?" 697; see also "Bars Out Sex Hygiene," *New York Times*, 26 Oct. 1913, sec. 2, p. 12.

152. *Chicago Citizen*, 20 July 1912, p. 4; 5 July 1913, p. 4; 17 May 1913, p. 4.

153. *Chicago New World*, 26 July 1913, p. 4.

154. Felix M. Kirsch, *Training in Chastity: A Problem in Catholic Character Education* (New York: Benziger Brothers, 1930), p. xiii.

155. Bigelow, *Sex Education*, pp. 61, 192.

156. Bigelow, "Educational Attack," 171.

157. Bigelow, *Sex Education*, pp. 64–65, derived his argument for "all satisfying monogamic affection," or mutuality, in part from Swedish feminist Ellen Key.

### 3   THE REVOLT OF YOUTH

1. The following is based on the most complete discussion of social hygiene and the war: Allan M. Brandt, *No Magic Bullet: A Social History of Venereal Disease in the United States since 1880*, expanded ed. (New York: Oxford University Press, 1987), pp. 52–121.

2. H. E. Kleinschmidt, "Educational Prophylaxis of Venereal Diseases," *Social Hygiene* 5 (Jan. 1919): 29, quoted in Brandt, *No Magic Bullet*, p. 65.

3. Brandt, *No Magic Bullet*, p. 62.

4. Prince A. Morrow, quoted in Walter Hollis Eddy, *Reproduction and Sex Hygiene* (New York: American Social Hygiene Association, 1916), p. 73, in Folder 171: 1, ASHA Papers.

5. For an influential racialized interpretation of the army tests, see Carl C. Brigham, *A Study of American Intelligence* (Princeton, N.J.: Princeton University Press, 1923), pp. 54–56.

6. Brandt, *No Magic Bullet*, pp. 105–106.

7. Ibid., pp. 110–116.

8. Henrietta S. Additon, "Work among Delinquent Women and Girls," *Annals of the American Academy of Political and Social Science* 79 (Sept. 1918): 152.

9. Ibid., 155; figures taken from Neil A. Wynn, *From Progressivism to Prosperity: World War I and American Society* (New York: Holmes and Meier, 1986), pp. 113–114.

10. Here and below, Additon, "Work among Delinquent Women and Girls," 154–155.

11. Brandt, *No Magic Bullet*, p. 115; *The Problem of Sex Education in the Schools* (Washington, D.C.: United States Public Health Service, ca. 1918), p. 3.

12. "Sex Education Needed among Adolescents," *Social Hygiene Bulletin* 6 (Oct. 1919): 7.

13. Norman F. Coleman, "Social Hygiene in Relation to National Defense," *NEA Journal of Addresses and Proceedings* (1917): 88–91; Norman F. Coleman, "Sex Education and the War," ibid. (1918): 195–196.

14. H. H. Moore, "Four Million Dollars for the Fight against Venereal Diseases," *Social Hygiene* 5 (Jan. 1919): 15; Michael Imber, "The First World War, Sex Education, and the American Social Hygiene Association's Campaign against Venereal Disease," *Journal of Educational Administration and History* 16 (Jan. 1984): 47–56.

15. Imber, "First World War," 50–51; "Federal Appropriation for Social Hygiene," *Social Hygiene Bulletin* 5 (July 1918): 2.

16. Thomas A. Storey, "A Summary of the Work of the United States Interdepartmental Social Hygiene Board, 1919–1920," *Social Hygiene* 7 (Jan. 1921): 76; Henry S. Curtis, "Education in Matters of Sex," *Pedagogical Seminary* 28 (Mar. 1921): 40–51.

17. Thomas A. Storey, "The Influence of the Government on Hygiene," *Pedagogical Seminary* 29 (Dec. 1922): 406.

18. The following discussion comes from Henry M. Grant, "Education in Sex and Heredity: A Practical Program," *Journal of Social Hygiene* 8 (Jan. 1922): 5–21.

19. Brandt discusses the film in greater detail in *No Magic Bullet*, pp. 68–70.

20. Imber, "First World War," 51 and 52; James R. Cook, "The Evolution of Sex Education in the Public Schools of the United States, 1900–1970," Ph.D. diss., College of Education of Southern Illinois University, 1972, pp. 83–84.

21. "Teachers Are Alert," *Social Hygiene Bulletin* 6 (Sept. 1919): 6.

22. "Is the Younger Generation in Peril?" *Literary Digest* 69 (14 May 1921): 61; Mr. Grundy [pseud.], "'Polite Society,'" *Atlantic Monthly* 125 (May 1920): 607; Florence Guy Woolston, "Girls, and Then Some," *New Republic* 30 (15 Mar. 1922): 79.

23. Paula Fass, *The Damned and the Beautiful: American Youth in the 1920's* (New York: Oxford University Press, 1977), pp. 125–126, 227–228, 244.

24. "The Case against the Younger Generation," *Literary Digest* 73 (17 June 1922): 38.

25. This quotation and the following examples are from "Is the Younger Generation in Peril?" pp. 9–12, 61.

26. Alfred C. Kinsey, Wardell B. Pomeroy, and Clyde E. Martin, *Sexual Behavior in the*

*Human Male* (Philadelphia: W. B. Saunders Co., 1948), p. 411; Alfred C. Kinsey, Wardell B. Pomeroy, Clyde E. Martin, and Paul H. Gebhard, *Sexual Behavior in the Human Female* (Philadelphia: W. B. Saunders Co., 1953), pp. 243–244.

27. Woolston, "Girls, and Then Some," p. 79. Dorothy Parker quotation: *The Macmillan Dictionary of Quotations* (New York: Macmillan, 1987), p. 411.

28. Frederick Lewis Allen, *Only Yesterday: An Informal History of the Nineteen-Twenties* (New York: Harper and Brothers, 1931), pp. 88–122; "The Case against the Younger Generation," 38.

29. This and following examples are from "Is the Younger Generation in Peril?" 9–12, 58, 61.

30. Maurice A. Bigelow, *Sex Education: A Series of Lectures concerning Knowledge of Sex in Its Relation to Human Life* (New York: Macmillan, 1918), pp. 129–130.

31. Paul Boyer, *Purity in Print: The Vice-Society Movement and Book Censorship in America* (New York: Charles Scribner's Sons, 1968), pp. 44–46.

32. On MacFadden, see Robert Ernst, *Weakness Is a Crime: The Life of Bernarr Mac-Fadden* (Syracuse, N.Y.: Syracuse University Press, 1991).

33. Bigelow, *Sex Education,* pp. 129–130; see also Brandt, *No Magic Bullet,* pp. 123–129.

34. Lucy S. Curtiss, "Sex Instruction through English Literature," *Social Hygiene* 6 (Apr. 1920): 268.

35. Kathy Peiss, *Cheap Amusements: Working Women and Leisure in Turn-of-the-Century New York* (Philadelphia: Temple University Press, 1986); Joanne J. Meyerowitz, *Women Adrift: Independent Wage Earners in Chicago, 1880–1930* (Chicago: University of Chicago Press, 1988).

36. "The Case against the Younger Generation," 38.

37. Charlotte Perkins Gilman in Freda Kirchwey, ed., *Our Changing Morality: A Symposium* (New York: Albert and Charles Boni, 1930; repr., New York: Arno Press, 1972), p. 58.

38. U.S. Public Health Service, *Keeping Fit* (Washington: U.S. Public Health Service, 1920), p. 7.

39. For a contrary interpretation, see Christina Simmons, "Modern Sexuality and the Myth of Victorian Repression," in Kathy Peiss and Christina Simmons, eds., *Passion and Power: Sexuality in History* (Philadelphia: Temple University Press, 1989), pp. 157–177.

40. Beatrice M. Hinkle, "Women and the New Morality," in Kirchwey, ed., *Our Changing Morality,* p. 235.

41. Ibid., pp. 235, 237.

42. Katherine Fullerton Gerould, "Reflections of a Grundy Cousin," *Atlantic Monthly* 125 (Aug. 1920): 158.

43. "Is the Younger Generation in Peril?" 61.

44. Gerould, "Reflections of a Grundy Cousin," 159.

45. See, for example, "Notes and Comment," *Social Hygiene* 6 (Oct. 1920): 600.

46. One finds hints of this in Allen, *Only Yesterday,* pp. 81–82; Leslie Fishbein, "Freud and the Radicals: The Sexual Revolution Comes to Greenwich Village," *The Canadian Review of American Studies* 12 (Fall 1981): 173–189.

47. Margaret Mead, *Coming of Age in Samoa: A Psychological Study of Primitive Youth for Western Civilization* (New York: W. Morrow and Co., 1928); David Levering Lewis, *When Harlem Was in Vogue,* new ed. (New York: Penguin Books, 1997).

48. "Is the Younger Generation in Peril?" 61.

49. Ezra Pound, "Hugh Selwyn Mauberly" (1920), *Norton Anthology of Poetry,* 3rd ed. (New York: W. W. Norton and Co., 1983), p. 578.

50. V. F. Calverton and Samuel D. Schmalhausen, eds., *Sex in Civilization* (Garden City, N.Y.: Garden City Publishing, 1929), p. 12.

51. Thomas Parran, Jr., "Social Hygiene and Public Health," *Journal of Social Hygiene* 13 (Jan. 1927): 25.

52. Pearl R. Wasson, "Fundamental Ethical Problems of Today," *NEA Journal of Addresses and Proceedings* (1921): 417.

53. Hinkle, "Women and the New Morality," p. 248.

54. Gerould, "Reflections of a Grundy Cousin," 157.

55. "Is the Younger Generation in Peril?" 10.

56. Ibid., 10–11.

57. This definition differs from the popular understanding that came from Ben B. Lindsey of "companionate marriage" as a trial marriage.

58. William L. O'Neill, *Divorce in the Progressive Era* (New Haven, Conn.: Yale University Press, 1967), pp. viii, 6–7; Elaine Tyler May, *Great Expectations: Marriage and Divorce in Post-Victorian America* (Chicago: University of Chicago Press, 1980).

59. Fass, *The Damned and the Beautiful,* p. 262.

60. See Barbara Sicherman, "The Uses of a Diagnosis: Doctors, Patients, and Neurasthenia," *Journal of the History of Medicine* 32 (Jan. 1977): 33–54.

61. Fass, *The Damned and the Beautiful,* pp. 118–130, 370. See also Robert S. Lynd and Hellen Merrell Lynd, *Middletown: A Study in American Culture* (New York: Harcourt Brace Jovanovich, 1929), pp. 131–152; and Roberta Lyn Wollons, "Educating Mothers: Sidonie Matsner Gruenberg and the Child Study Association, 1881–1929," Ed.D. diss., University of Chicago, 1983.

62. Warren Susman, *Culture as History: The Transformation of American Society in the Twentieth Century* (New York: Pantheon Books, 1984), pp. 271–285.

63. Fass, *The Damned and the Beautiful,* pp. 309–310; Beth Bailey, *From Front Porch to Back Seat: Courtship in Twentieth-Century America* (Baltimore: Johns Hopkins University Press, 1988), pp. 20–26, 77–96.

64. Marion L. Weil, New York, New York, letter to the author, 14 Oct. 1995.

65. Mary Ware Dennett, *The Sex Side of Life: An Explanation for Young People* (pub-

lished by the author, 1928), p. iii; Dennett and Sanger are discussed in James Reed, *The Birth Control Movement and American Society: From Private Vice to Public Virtue*, rev. ed. (Princeton: Princeton University Press, 1984), pp. 98–105.

66. Dennett, *Sex Side of Life*, pp. 6–7; for more on the Dennett case, see Constance M. Chen, *"The Sex Side of Life": Mary Ware Dennett's Pioneering Battle for Birth Control and Sex Education* (New York: New Press, 1996).

67. Dennett, *Sex Side of Life*, pp. iii–iv.

68. On ASHA's opposition to birth control, see Louis I. Dublin, "Birth Control," *Social Hygiene* 6 (Jan. 1920): 5–16; Karl Schwitalla, "Aims and Achievements of Social Hygiene," *Journal of Social Hygiene* 15 (Jan. 1929): 4.

69. Thomas D. Eliot, "Some Future Issues in the Sex Problem," *International Journal of Ethics* (Apr. 1920), cited in "Notes and Comment," *Social Hygiene* 6 (Oct. 1920): 599–600.

70. Maurice A. Bigelow, "The Established Points in Social Hygiene Education, 1905–1924," *Journal of Social Hygiene* 10 (Jan. 1924): 9.

71. Eliot, "Some Future Issues in the Sex Problem," 600.

72. Ibid., 600–601.

73. Ibid., 600.

74. Here and below, M. J. Exner, *The Question of Petting* (1926; rev. ed., New York: American Social Hygiene Association, 1952), unpaginated, in Folder 173: 2, ASHA Papers.

75. Hornell Hart, letter to the editor, *Journal of Social Hygiene* 17, no. 5 (May 1931): 305.

76. On family sociology and the "helping professions" in general, see Christopher Lasch, *Haven in a Heartless World: The Family Besieged* (New York: Basic Books, 1977).

77. Excerpted in "And What of the Family?" *Journal of Social Hygiene* 14 (Feb. 1928): 95.

78. Ibid., 96. See also Michael Gordon, "From an Unfortunate Necessity to a Cult of Mutual Orgasm: Sex in American Marital Education Literature, 1830–1940," in James M. Henslin and Edward Sagarin, eds., *The Sociology of Sex*, rev. ed. (New York: Schocken Books, 1978), pp. 59–83.

79. "And What of the Family?" 95.

80. Here and below, Roy E. Dickerson, "Prepare Them for Marriage," *Parents' Magazine* 12 (Dec. 1937): 24–25.

81. Eleanor Rowland Wembridge, "Social Backgrounds in Sex Education," *Journal of Social Hygiene* 9 (Feb. 1923): 71, 72.

82. Dickerson, "Prepare Them for Marriage," 25.

83. Ibid., 40.

84. Gerould, "Reflections of a Grundy Cousin," 162.

85. Sigmund Freud, "'Civilized' Sexual Morality and Modern Nervous Illness," in James Strachey, ed. and trans., *The Standard Edition of the Complete Psychological Works of Sigmund Freud* (London: Hogarth Press, 1953), 9: 217.

86. Benjamin C. Gruenberg, *The Teacher and Sex Education* (New York: American Social Hygiene Association, 1924), p. 15, in Folder 171: 11, ASHA Papers.

87. Bigelow, "Established Points in Social Hygiene Education," 6.

88. Hart, letter to *Journal of Social Hygiene* 17 (May 1931): 305.

89. "Sex Education Opposed as Unscientific," *School Science and Mathematics* 41, no. 355 (Feb. 1941): 114.

### 4  PUTTING SEX IN THE SCHOOLS

1. Maurice A. Bigelow, "Health Education concerning Venereal Diseases," *Journal of Social Hygiene* 26 (Oct. 1940): 314.

2. Ibid.

3. Maurice A. Bigelow, "Sex Education in America Today," *Journal of Social Hygiene* 24 (Dec. 1938): 532.

4. Maurice A. Bigelow, "The Past and Future of the Educational Program of the American Social Hygiene Association," *Journal of Social Hygiene* 21 (Jan. 1935): 13.

5. Max Exner, "Sex Education by the Young Men's Christian Associations in Universities and Colleges," *Social Hygiene* 1 (Sept. 1915): 573.

6. Maurice A. Bigelow, "The Established Points in Social Hygiene Education, 1905–1924," *Journal of Social Hygiene* 10 (Jan. 1924): 9; Paul Strong Achilles, *The Effectiveness of Certain Social Hygiene Literature* (New York: American Social Hygiene Association, 1923), p. 93.

7. "Students Want Social Hygiene Instruction," *Journal of Social Hygiene* 11 (Nov. 1925): 559; *Barnard Bulletin* 26 (11 Apr. 1922), quoted in Achilles, *Effectiveness of Certain Social Hygiene Literature*, p. 46n.

8. Alice Barker-Ellsworth, "Sex Education in Junior High School," *Journal of Social Hygiene* 16 (Feb. 1930): 107; "Health Education in High Schools," ibid. 11 (Nov. 1925): 496–497.

9. Maurice A. Bigelow, *Sex Education: A Series of Lectures concerning Knowledge of Sex in Its Relation to Human Life* (New York: Macmillan, 1918), p. 27.

10. Here and below, Benjamin C. Gruenberg, *High Schools and Sex Education* (Washington, D.C.: Government Printing Office, 1922), pp. 50–52, 64–79.

11. Louise B. Thompson, "Opportunities for Sex Education in English Classes," *Social Hygiene* 6 (July 1920): 393–397.

12. Lucy S. Curtiss, "Sex Instruction through English Literature," *Social Hygiene* 6 (Apr. 1920): 268.

13. Thompson, "Opportunities for Sex Education in English Classes," 399.

14. National Education Association, *Report of the Commission on the Reorganization of Secondary Education,* U. S. Bureau of Education Bulletin No. 35 (Washington, D.C.: Government Printing Office, 1918), reprinted in Melvin Lazerson, ed., *American Education in the Twentieth Century: A Documentary History* (New York: Teachers College Press, 1987), pp. 79–87.

15. See "Biology in High Schools," *Social Hygiene* 6 (June 1920): 435–438; Gruenberg, *High Schools and Sex Education,* pp. 25–45.

16. Here and below, NEA Department of Superintendence, *Character Education* (Washington, D.C.: Department of Superintendence of the National Education Association, 1932), pp. 189–197.

17. Ibid., p. 194.

18. Thomas M. Balliet, *Introduction of Sex Education into Public Schools* (New York: American Social Hygiene Association, 1927), p. 1, in Folder 172: 3, ASHA Papers.

19. Vivian Hadley Harris, "The Status of Sex Education in Public Educational Institutions," *Social Hygiene* 7 (Apr. 1921): 169–171; the response rate to Harris's questionaire was 65 percent, or 228 of the country's approximately 350 normal schools.

20. Ibid., 171.

21. Newell W. Edson, *Status of Sex Education in High Schools,* U.S. Bureau of Education Bulletin No. 14 (Washington, D.C.: Government Printing Office, 1922); and Lida J. Usilton and Newell W. Edson, *Status of Sex Education in the Senior High Schools of the United States in 1927,* U.S. Public Health Service, Division of Venereal Diseases, Venereal Disease Bulletin No. 87 (Washington, D.C.: Government Printing Office, 1928).

22. Usilton and Edson, *Status of Sex Education, 1927,* p. 3. The number of schools reporting some sex education remained consistent because the total number of high schools in the country increased from 12,025 in 1920 to 16,937 in 1927.

23. Edson, *Status of Sex Education* [1920], 4; Usilton and Edson, *Status of Sex Education, 1927,* pp. 3–5; unfortunately, the investigators did not trace longitudinally whether this assertion held for specific schools replying to both studies.

24. Percentages substantially similar to Edson and Usilton's percentages (reported below) appeared in Harry H. Moore, "The Attitudes of High School Teachers toward Sex Education," *Educational Review* 70 (Sept. 1925): 90–94.

25. Usilton and Edson, *Status of Sex Education, 1927,* pp. 8–9.

26. Ibid., pp. 8, 9.

27. Ibid., p. 8.

28. Ibid., p. 6; that is, about 57 percent of these large schools offered some sex education, as compared with the average for all schools of 45 percent, and sex education was integrated in 37.5 percent of large schools, against 29 percent of total schools. Unfortunately, Edson and Usilton do not provide figures for the number of students reached in each kind of school.

29. Usilton and Edson, *Status of Sex Education, 1927*, p. 14.

30. Max J. Exner, "Progress in Sex Education," *Journal of Social Hygiene* 15 (Oct. 1929): 397.

31. Benjamin C. Gruenberg, "Sex Education in Secondary Schools: 1938," *Journal of Social Hygiene*, 24 (Dec. 1938): 534.

32. Usilton and Edson, *Status of Sex Education, 1927*, pp. 2–3.

33. Brandt, *No Magic Bullet*, pp. 123–126.

34. Usilton and Edson, *Status of Sex Education, 1927*, pp. 2–3.

35. Ibid.; see also Harris, "Status of Sex Education," pp. 174–177, 180.

36. Michael Imber, "Analysis of a Curriculum Reform Movement: The American Social Hygiene Association's Campaign for Sex Education 1900–1930," Ph.D. diss., Stanford University, 1980, esp. pp. 111–118.

37. For a representative emphasis on secrecy in sex education, see Balliet, *Introduction of Sex Education into Public Schools*, p. 3.

38. Curtis, "Education in Matters of Sex," 44–45.

39. Imber, "Analysis of a Curriculum Reform Movement," p. 118.

40. Edson, *Status of Sex Education* [1920], p. 4.

41. Usilton and Edson, *Status of Sex Education, 1927*, p. 8.

42. Aimee Zillmer, "Parents on the Spot," *Journal of Social Hygiene* 23 (Oct. 1937): 427.

43. Here and below, E. K. Wickman, *Children's Behavior and Teachers' Attitudes* (New York: The Commonwealth Fund, 1928), reported in Department of Superintendence, *Character Education*, pp. 172–174.

44. Reported in Mabel Craig Stillman, "Practical Talks for Parents and Teachers," *Pedagogical Seminary* 29 (Mar. 1922): 24.

45. Benjamin Gruenberg, *The Teacher and Sex Education* (New York: American Social Hygiene Association, 1924), p. 26, in Folder 171: 11, ASHA Papers.

46. Charles H. Judd, *Problems of Education in the United States* (New York: McGraw-Hill Book Co., 1933), p. 69.

47. "Kansas Educational Campaign Under Way," *Social Hygiene Bulletin* 8 (June 1921): 12; J. S. Mitchener, "The North Carolina Venereal Disease Program," *Journal of Social Hygiene* 9 (May 1923): 288–292; W. C. Blasingame, "The Alabama Venereal Disease Control Program," ibid. 9 (June 1923): 343–347.

48. W. C. Blasingame, "A State Program of Social Hygiene Educational Matters," *Journal of Social Hygiene* 14 (Jan. 1928): 8.

49. Ibid., 10.

50. Hugh S. Cumming, "Guarding the Nation's Health," *Journal of Social Hygiene* 12 (Jan. 1926): 29.

51. Ibid.

52. Army venereal disease statistics for black soldiers were notoriously unreliable: see Brandt, *No Magic Bullet*, p. 116. See also Christina Simmons, "African Americans

and Sexual Victorianism in the Social Hygiene Movement, 1910–40," *Journal of the History of Sexuality* 4 (July 1993): 51–75.

53. "Negro Educational Institutions Support Program," *Social Hygiene Bulletin* 8 (Jan. 1921): 12, in ASHA Papers.

54. See Simmons, "African Americans," 60–63.

55. Exner, "Progress," 405–406; See also Franklin O. Nichols, "Social Hygiene and the Negro," *Journal of Social Hygiene* 15 (Oct. 1929): 408–413; "Association Notes," ibid. 13 (Dec. 1927): 563–564; and Franklin O. Nichols, "Social Hygiene in Racial Problems: The Negro," ibid. 18 (Nov. 1932): 447–451.

56. Reported in Louis I. Dublin, "The Future of the Social Hygiene Movement in America," *Journal of Social Hygiene* 22 (Feb. 1936): 64.

57. On Parran, see Brandt, *No Magic Bullet*, pp. 122–160, esp. pp. 136–137.

58. Arthur W. Towne, "Should Social Hygiene Associations Engage in Both Syphilis Control and Sex Education?" *Journal of Social Hygiene* 25 (Dec. 1939): 420–421.

59. State laws noted in "Record of a Record Year," *Journal of Social Hygiene* 24 (Jan. 1938): 83.

60. Zillmer, "Parents on the Spot," 425–427.

61. "Record of a Record Year," 74.

62. Maurice A. Bigelow, "Sex Education in America Today," *Journal of Social Hygiene* 24 (Dec. 1938): 527–532, quotation on 532; Maurice A. Bigelow, "Health Education concerning Venereal Diseases," *Journal of Social Hygiene* 26 (Oct. 1940): 314.

63. Bigelow, "Health Education concerning Venereal Diseases," 314.

64. Brandt, *No Magic Bullet*, pp. 155–160.

65. NEA Department of Superintendence, *Character Education*, p. 193.

## 5  DOMESTICATING SEX

1. Maurice A. Bigelow, "Social Hygiene and Youth in Defense Communities, *Journal of Social Hygiene,* 28 (Nov. 1942): 437.

2. Joel T. Boone, "The Sexual Aspects of Military Personnel," *Journal of Social Hygiene,* 27 (March 1941): 116.

3. Leo A. Shifrin, "Venereal Diseases: A Navy Problem," *New York State Journal of Medicine* 43 (1 Oct. 1943): 1829.

4. William Bisher, "Venereal Disease Control as Applied to the Army," *New York State Journal of Medicine* 43 (1 Oct. 1943): 1833.

5. Shifrin, "Venereal Diseases," 1829.

6. Granville W. Larrimore and Thomas H. Sternberg, "Does Health Education Prevent Venereal Disease?" reprinted from *American Journal of Public Health* 35 (Aug. 1945 : 800; Paul L. Getzoff, "Factors Affecting the Response to Venereal Disease Education," *Journal of Social Hygiene* 32 (Jan. 1946): 23.

7. Shifrin, "Venereal Diseases," p. 1832; Allan M. Brandt, *No Magic Bullet: A Social History of Venereal Disease in the United States since 1880*, expanded ed. (New York: Oxford University Press, 1987), pp. 164, 170.

8. Richard A. Koch and Ray Lyman Wilbur, "Promiscuity as a Factor in the Spread of Venereal Disease," *Journal of Social Hygiene* 30 (Dec. 1944): 518–519.

9. For the initial conflation of prostitutes and "promiscuous" women (and men), see Bascom Johnson, "Prostitution and Quackery in Relation to Syphilis Control," *Journal of Social Hygiene* 26 (Jan. 1940): 7.

10. Evelyn Millis Duvall, "Growing Edges in Family Life Education," *Marriage and Family Living* 6 (May 1944): 21; American Social Hygiene Association, *Young America Needs You!* (New York: 1944), unpaginated pamphlet, Folder 175: 6, ASHA Papers.

11. Here and below, American Association of School Administrators, *Education for Family Life*, Nineteenth Yearbook (Washington, D.C.: American Association of School Administrators, 1941), pp. 35–36.

12. The following discussion derives largely from Brandt, *No Magic Bullet*, pp. 159, 170–171.

13. Charles Walter Clarke, "Penicillin: Help or Hindrance in Venereal Disease Control?" *Journal of Social Hygiene* 31 (Dec. 1945): 600–604.

14. Brandt, *No Magic Bullet*, pp. 7–50.

15. "The Status of Venereal Disease Control," *American Journal of Public Health* 40 (July 1950): 865.

16. William F. Snow and H. H. Hazen, "Report of the Section on Education and Community Action," *Journal of Social Hygiene* 31 (Jan. 1945): 52–53; also see "Report of Social Hygiene Education Conference, U.S. Office of Education" (Washington, D.C., 1945), Folder 82: 6, ASHA Papers. Out of such activities came ASHA's guiding report, Jacob A. Goldberg, ed., *Education for Personal and Family Living as Applied to the Social Hygiene Field* (New York: American Social Hygiene Association, 1948), Folder 82: 7, ASHA Papers.

17. Duvall, "Growing Edges in Family Life Education," 22.

18. Beth Bailey, "Scientific Truth . . . and Love: The Marriage Education Movement in the United States," *Journal of Social History* 20 (Summer 1987): 714.

19. William H. Chafe, *The American Woman: Her Changing Social, Economic, and Political Roles, 1920–1970* (New York: Oxford University Press, 1972), p. 89.

20. Paul Popenoe, "A College Education for Marriage," *Journal of Social Hygiene* 25 (Apr. 1939): 168.

21. Here and below, J. Laurence Meader, "Education and the Family," *Journal of Social Hygiene* 24 (Dec. 1938): 548–551.

22. Figures derived from Henry A. Bowman, "Marriage Education in the Colleges," *Journal of Social Hygiene* 35 (Dec. 1949): 407–409; on Kinsey's marriage course, see James H. Jones, *Alfred C. Kinsey: A Public/Private Life* (New York: W. W. Norton and Co., 1997), pp. 322–336.

23. Elizabeth S. Force, *Teaching Family Life Education: The Toms River Program* (New York: Teachers College, Columbia University, 1962), pp. 1, 7, Folder 96: 7, ASHA Papers.

24. "Promotion of Mental Health in the Primary and Secondary Schools," Report No. 18 (Jan. 1951), p. 6, in Folder 96: 7, ASHA Papers.

25. Ibid.; Force, *Teaching Family Life Education*, p. 3.

26. Force, *Teaching Family Life Education*, pp. 6, 15–16.

27. Elizabeth S. Force, "Toms River Looks Back: 1951–1941," Folder 96: 7, ASHA Papers.

28. Elizabeth S. Force, "High School Education for Family Living," *Annals of the American Academy of Political and Social Science* (Nov. 1950): 158, Folder 96: 7, ASHA Papers.

29. Here and below, Force, *Teaching Family Life Education*, pp. 12–24.

30. Goldberg, ed., *Education for Personal and Family Living*, pp. 3–4.

31. *Education for Human Relations and Family Life on the Secondary School Level*, rev. 2nd ed. (New York: American Social Hygiene Association, 1947), p. 7.

32. James T. Patterson, *Grand Expectations: The United States, 1945–1974* (New York: Oxford University Press, 1996), pp. 76–81.

33. Kingsley Davis, "The American Family: What It Is—and Isn't," *New York Times Magazine*, 30 Sept. 1951, p. 18.

34. Elaine Tyler May, *Homeward Bound: American Families in the Cold War Era* (New York: Basic Books, 1988), p. 11.

35. O. Spurgeon English and Constance J. Foster, "How Good a Family Man Is Your Husband?" *Parents' Magazine* 27 (Sept. 1952): 76–77.

36. May, *Homeward Bound*, pp. 137, 140–146.

37. Robert M. Goldenson, "Why Boys and Girls Go Wrong or Right," *Parents' Magazine* 26 (May 1951): 84.

38. Ellis F. White and Edgar C. Cumings, "Regional Projects in Education for Personal and Family Living," internal memorandum, n.d. (*ca.* 1957), pp. 1–2, Folder 85: 6, ASHA Papers.

39. "The Kids Grow Worse," *Newsweek*, 6 Dec. 1954, p. 26. For background on juvenile delinquency in the United States, see James A. Gilbert, *A Cycle of Outrage: America's Reaction to the Juvenile Delinquent in the 1950s* (New York: Oxford University Press, 1986).

40. "Senseless," *Time*, 30 Aug. 1954, p. 15; "The Kids Grow Worse," p. 26.

41. Alfred C. Kinsey, Wardell B. Pomeroy, and Clyde E. Martin, *Sexual Behavior in the Human Male* (Philadelphia: W. B. Saunders Co., 1948), hereafter Kinsey, *Male*; Alfred C. Kinsey, Wardell B. Pomeroy, Clyde E. Martin, and Paul H. Gebhard, *Sexual Behavior in the Human Female* (Philadelphia: W. B. Saunders Co., 1953), hereafter Kinsey, *Female*. See Regina Markell Morantz, "The Scientist as Sex Crusader: Alfred C. Kinsey and American Culture," *American Quarterly* 29 (Winter 1977): 563–589;

further information on responses to the "Kinsey Reports" is available in the clippings file at the Kinsey Institute for Sexual Relations, Indiana University, Bloomington.

42. Bruce Bliven, "Hullabaloo on K-Day," *New Republic* 129, 9 Nov. 1953, pp. 17–18.

43. Kinsey, *Male*, p. 347.

44. Ibid., p. 411.

45. Kinsey, *Female*, p. 243.

46. Ibid., pp. 243–244. Kinsey was actually silent on the postwar adolescent generation—those born in the 1930s and afterward.

47. *Preinduction Health Manual* (New York: American Social Hygiene Association, 1951–1953); also R. B. Oldfather to Esther E. Sweeney, 30 Apr. 1952, Folder 82: 12, ASHA papers.

48. "Support Our Stronghold . . . the Family," *Journal of Social Hygiene* 37 (Feb. 1951): 49–50.

49. Bernice Milburn Moore, "Free Families Build Free Persons," *Journal of Home Economics* 43 (Oct. 1951): 613.

50. Sheldon and Eleanor Glueck, *Unraveling Juvenile Delinquency* (New York: The Commonwealth Fund, 1951), quoted in Goldenson, "Why Boys and Girls Go Wrong or Right," 84.

51. Quotation in reference to the origins of ASHA's work in family life education, in *The Story of the Rocky Mountain Project* (Chicago: National Congress of Parents and Teachers, 1964), p. 3, Folder 89: 3, ASHA Papers.

52. This quotation and the preceding extract are from C. Van Hyning and Elizabeth Force, "Family Life Education: A Cause for Action," unpublished report, p. 12, Folder 89: 6, ASHA Papers.

53. Quoted in Goldenson, "Why Boys and Girls Go Wrong or Right," 84.

54. Van Hyning and Force, "Family Life Education," p. 10.

55. Quoted in Dorothy Barclay, "Training for Happy Family Living," *New York Times Magazine*, 6 Jan. 1952, p. 34.

56. U.S. Bureau of Education, *Life Adjustment Education for Every Youth*, Bulletin No. 22 (Washington, D.C., 1951), reprinted in Sol Cohen, ed., *Education in the United States: A Documentary History*, vol. 4 (New York: Random House, 1974), p. 2629.

57. Ray H. Everett to Esther E. Sweeney, 18 Oct. 1953, Folder 83: 6, ASHA Papers.

58. On the Bagley Project, see files at ASHA Papers.

59. Quoted in Barclay, "Training for Happy Family Living," p. 34.

60. Irwin Harrris, Phoenix, Arizona, personal communication with author, 28 Sept. 1995; Barbara Benziger, New York, New York, personal communication with author, 7 Oct. 1995.

61. Conrad Van Hyning, interoffice memorandum, 27 Aug. 1954, Folder 84: 1, ASHA Papers.

62. See Elizabeth McQuaid to Conrad Van Hyning, 31 Aug. 1954; Eleanor Shenehan to

Conrad Van Hyning, 7 Sept. 1954; and Esther Sweeney to Conrad Van Hyning, 3 Sept. 1954, all in Folder 84: 1, ASHA Papers.

63. R. S. Cartwright, "Marriage and Family Living," *National Education Association Journal* 45 (Feb. 1956): 92–93.

64. Ibid.

65. Anna O. Stephens, "Dating 'Do's and Dont's' [*sic*] for Girls," Folder 175: 12, ASHA Papers.

66. Cartwright, "Marriage and Family Living," 93.

67. Una Funk, "A Realistic Family-Life Program," *National Education Association Journal,* 44 (March 1955): 163–164.

68. Cartwright, "Marriage and Family Living," 93.

69. "Minutes of the Meeting of the Education Advisory Committee," 9–10 Jan. 1956, Folder 86: 1, ASHA Papers; on conflation of family life education and sex education as an obstacle, see "Connecticut Conference on Family Life Education: Report of the Proceedings," 9 July 1957, Folder 85: 2, ASHA Papers.

70. Elizabeth McQuaid to Conrad Van Hyning, 31 Aug. 1954, Folder 84: 1, ASHA Papers.

71. Cartwright, "Marriage and Family Living," 93.

72. Moore, "Free Families Build Free Persons," 614.

73. Judson T. Landis, "The Challenge of Marriage and Family Life Education," *Marriage and Family Living* 19 (Aug. 1957): 249.

74. Lawrence K. Frank, "Preparation for Marriage in the High School Program," *Living* (later *Marriage and Family Living*) 1 (Jan. 1939): 10.

75. See Paul H. Landis, "Training Teachers for Family Life Education in High Schools," *Marriage and Family Living* 10 (Fall 1948); earlier, see Paul Popenoe, "A College Education for Marriage," *Journal of Social Hygiene* 25 (Apr. 1939): 168–173.

76. Lawrence K. Frank in "Proceedings of the Annual Conference of Social Hygiene Executives," 30–31 Mar. 1948, in-house report, p. 137, Folder 128: 8, ASHA Papers.

77. Erik H. Erikson, *Childhood and Society* (New York: W. W. Norton and Co., 1950; see also Margaret Mead, *Male and Female: A Study of the Sexes in a Changing World* (New York: William Morrow and Co., 1949); on the connection between sex-role acquisition and promiscuity, see T. Lefoy Richman, "Is There a Morals Revolt Among Youth?" *The PTA Magazine* (Nov. 1959), ASHA reprint, Folder 176: 13, ASHA Papers.

78. Howard M. Slutes, "A Report of the American Social Health Association Study Committee" (July 1960), appendix, pp. 7–8, Folder 125: 5, ASHA Papers; on working-class delinquents and middle-class ideals, see Albert K. Cohen, *Delinquent Boys: The Culture of the Gang* (Glencoe, Ill.: Free Press, 1955), pp. 73–119

79. *Rebel without a Cause,* 1955, directed by Nicholas Ray.

80. Nolan C. Kearney, "Sex Education in Public Schools," in Edgar C. Cumings, ed., *A Symposium on Sex Education* (New York: American Social Hygiene Association, 1957), pp. 12–13.

81. Quoted in Grace Palladino, *Teenagers: An American History* (New York: Basic Books, 1996), p. 167.

82. English and Foster, "How Good a Family Man Is Your Husband?" 81.

83. Cartwright, "Marriage and Family Living," 93.

84. "Report on Family Life Education Programs (1953–1961)," Jan. 1962, Folder 84: 14, ASHA Papers.

85. Robert K. Merton, *Social Theory and Social Structure,* rev. and enlarged ed. (New York: Free Press, 1957), pp. 225–386; see also Lawrence K. Frank, "The Psycho-cultural Approach in Sex Research," in Jerome Himelhoch and S. F. Fava, eds., *Sexual Behavior in American Society* (New York: Norton Books, 1955), pp. 3–11.

86. John F. Cuber, "Can We Evaluate Marriage Education?" *Marriage and Family Living* 11 (Summer 1949): 94–95; also "Faith, Works, and Social Hygiene Progress," *Journal of Social Hygiene* 34 (Jan. 1948): 1–3.

87. Duvall, "Growing Edges in Family Life Education," 22–23.

88. "There is no yardstick for results," noted Elizabeth Force in *Teaching Family Life Education,* p. 9.

89. Francis J. Brown quoted in "Birth Rate Rise among Educated Credited to New College Courses," *Flint (Michigan) Journal,* 26 Dec. 1954, Folder 83: 10, ASHA Papers.

90. Panos D. Bardis, "Influence of Family Life Education on Sex Knowledge," *Marriage and Family Living* 25 (Feb. 1963): 85–88; also Duncan V. Gillies and Carlo L. Lastrucci, "Validation of the Effectiveness of a College Marriage Course," *Marriage and Family Living* 16 (Feb. 1954): 55–58.

91. John F. Cuber and Mark Ray, "Reflections on Sex Education in the High School," *Marriage and Family Living* 8 (Winter 1946): 15.

92. See "Minutes of the Meeting of the Education Advisory Committee," 20–21 June 1957, p. 9, Folder 86: 1, ASHA Papers; and Edgar C. Cumings, memorandum to members of the Education Advisory Committee, 10 May 1961, p. 3, Folder 86: 7, ASHA Papers.

93. "Minutes of the Education Advisory Committee of the ASHA," 14–15 May 1959, p. 14, Folder 86: 7, ASHA Papers.

94. "Minutes of the Meeting of the Education Advisory Committee," 18–19 May 1961, p. 4, Folder 86: 1, ASHA Papers.

95. Frances R. Harper and Robert A. Harper, "Are Educators Afraid of Sex?" *Marriage and Family Living* 19 (Aug. 1957): 240.

96. Edward Z. Dager, Glenn A. Harper, and Robert N. Whitehurst, "Family Life Education in Public High Schools: A Survey Report on Indiana," *Marriage and Family Living* 24 (Nov. 1962): 365–366. Disagreements over certification of sex instructors continued well through the next decade, as noted in Derek L. Burleson, "Who Is a Sex Educator—the Certification Dilemma?" *SIECUS Report* 2 (July 1974): 1, 14.

97. Edgar C. Cumings, "Family Life Education in School and College: Work and Philosophy of the American Social Hygiene Association," ms., Folder 85: 3, ASHA Papers.

98. J. H. Black to Walter Clarke, 6 June 1948, Folder 82: 7, ASHA Papers.

99. See "Minutes of the Meeting of the Education Advisory Committee," 9–10 Jan. 1956, Folder 86: 1, ASHA Papers.

100. Harper and Harper, "Are Educators Afraid of Sex?" 240.

101. Kenneth E. Oberholtzer and Myrtle F. Sugarman, "Denver Educates for Home and Family Living," *Journal of Social Hygiene* 37 (Feb. 1951): 55.

102. I. L. Kandel, "Adjustment to Life," *School and Society* 65 (24 May 1947): 372.

103. Ibid.

104. Oberholtzer and Sugarman, "Denver Educates for Home and Family Living," 54.

105. Gerald R. Leslie, "Personal Values, Professional Ideologies, and Family Specialties," *Marriage and Family Living* 21 (Feb. 1959): 5–6; also see Edgar C. Cumings to Donald Adams Clarke, 3 Mar. 1959, Folder 84: 9, ASHA Papers.

106. Leslie, "Personal Values," 6.

107. James H. S. Bossard, "What Are We Educating for in Marriage?" *Journal of Social Hygiene* 35 (June 1949): 247–248; also see William L. Kolb, "Family Sociology, Marriage Education, and the Romantic Complex," *Social Forces* 29 (Oct. 1950): 65–72.

108. Richard Hofstadter, *Anti-Intellectualism in American Life* (New York: Alfred A. Knopf, 1963), p. 356.

109. Slutes, "Report of the ASHA Study Committee."

110. American Association of School Administrators, *Education for Family Life*, pp. 102–103.

111. Robert Rutherford, "Report on a Questionnaire and a Discussion concerning Family Life Education in Bangor, Maine," unpublished report, Sept. 1959, Folder 85: 4, ASHA Papers.

112. Herbert S. Conrad to Walter Clarke, 10 May 1948, Folder 82: 7, ASHA Papers.

### 6 FIGHTING THE SEXUAL REVOLUTION

1. James T. Patterson, *Grand Expectations: The United States, 1945–1974* (New York: Oxford University Press, 1996), pp. 358–360.

2. Lester A. Kirkendall, "Now Is the Time to Prepare! The Need for Social Hygiene Education in a Long Range Program," *Journal of Social Hygiene* 28 (Nov. 1942): 458–463.

3. Lester A. Kirkendall, "Physical Educators and High School Sex Education," *Journal of Health and Physical Education* 15 (Mar. 1944): 115, 156–158.

4. Lester A. Kirkendall, "Sound Attitudes toward Sex," *Journal of Social Hygiene* 37 (June 1951): 244–245.

5. Lester A. Kirkendall, *Sex Education as Human Relations* (New York: Inor Publishing Co., 1950), p. 104.

6. Kirkendall, "Sound Attitudes toward Sex," 244.

7. Lester A. Kirkendall, "Values and Premarital Intercourse: Implications for Parent Education," *Marriage and Family Living* 22 (Nov. 1960): 320, 317.

8. Ibid., 321; for reactions to Kirkendall's 1960 article, see the symposium on premarital sexual behavior in *Marriage and Family Living* 24 (Aug. 1962): 254–278.

9. "The Morals Revolution on the U.S. Campus," *Newsweek*, 6 Apr. 1964, pp. 52–53.

10. "Morals: The Second Sexual Revolution," *Time*, 24 Jan. 1964, p. 57.

11. "Morals Revolution," pp. 52–53.

12. Eleanore B. Luckey, "Family Life Ed and/or Sex Ed?" *Journal of Marriage and the Family* 29 (May 1967): 377–378.

13. Edgar C. Cumings to Conrad Van Hyning, 9 July 1962, in Folder 85: 9, ASHA Papers.

14. Lester Kirkendall to Wallace C. Fulton, 31 Mar. 1963, in Folder 94: 8, ASHA Papers.

15. Mary Steichen Calderone to Betty Gillespie, 27 June 1963, in Folder 12: 205, Mary Steichen Calderone Papers, Schlesinger Library, Harvard University (hereafter, Calderone Papers).

16. Wallace C. Fulton memorandum, 3 June 1963, in Folder 94: 8, ASHA Papers; Mary S. Calderone, "Sexual Health and Family Planning," *American Journal of Public Health* 58 (Feb. 1968): 228; membership in "Proposal for a Sex Information and Education Council of the U.S. (SIECUS)," in Folder 94: 8, ASHA Papers.

17. Arguments recalled in Lester Kirkendall to David H. Olsen, 8 Dec. 1969, in Folder 96: 3, ASHA Papers.

18. Lester Kirkendall to Wallace C. Fulton, 31 Mar. 1963, in Folder 94: 8, ASHA Papers.

19. Calderone quoted in John Kobler, "Sex Invades the Schoolhouse," *Saturday Evening Post* 241 (29 June 1968): 64.

20. Mary S. Calderone, "Sexual Energy: What To Do?" *Western Journal of Surgery, Obstetrics and Gynecology* 71 (Nov.–Dec. 1963): 276, in Folder 13: 223, Calderone Papers; Lester A. Kirkendall, *Sex Education*, SIECUS Study Guide No. 1 (New York: SIECUS, 1965), p. 14.

21. See, for example, Isadore Rubin, "Transition in Sex Values: Implications for the Education of Adolescents," *Journal of Marriage and the Family* 27 (May 1965): 187; and John L. Thomas, "Sexuality and the Total Personality," *SIECUS Newsletter* 1 (Fall 1965): 1.

22. Biographical information on Calderone taken from profiles in the *Milwaukee Journal*, 14 Dec. 1969, p. 6; John G. Rogers, "Dr. Mary Calderone, Sex Educator," *Parade Magazine*, 18 June 1967, pp. 12–14; and "Mary Steichen Calderone," *Current Biography* 28, no. 10 (Nov. 1967): 5–8; all three articles in Folder 1: 1, Calderone Papers.

23. Mary S. Calderone, "A Doctor Talks to Vassar College Freshmen about Love and

Sex," *Western Journal of Surgery, Obstetrics and Gynecology* 72 (Mar.–Apr. 1964): 112, in Folder 13: 224, Calderone Papers.

24. Faye Flam, "M. Calderone: Doctor and Sex Educator," *Philadelphia Online Inquirer,* 26 Oct. 1998.

25. Mary S. Calderone, "Mother's Health: Key to Family Health," *Journal of the American Medical Women's Association* 15 (Sept. 1960): 851, in Folder 13: 222, Calderone Papers.

26. Mary S. Calderone, "Public Health Aspects of Family Planning," *Applied Therapeutics* 6 (Apr. 1964): 2, in Folder 13: 223, Calderone Papers. Mary S. Calderone, ed., *Abortion in the United States: Report of a Conference Sponsored by the Planned Parenthood Federation of America* (New York: Harper-Hoeber Books, 1958), p. 183.

27. Mary Steichen Calderone, "Mental Health Programs in Schools," *Journal of School Health* (June 1955), in Folder 13: 222, Calderone Papers.

28. Calderone, "Doctor Talks to Vassar College Freshmen," 114–117.

29. Ibid., 116 and 117.

30. Lester A. Kirkendall and Deryck Calderwood, "Changing Sex Mores and Moral Instruction," *Phi Delta Kappan* 46 (Oct. 1964): 68.

31. See also a contrasting analysis in James Hottois and Neal A. Milner, *The Sex Education Controversy* (Lexington, Mass.: Lexington Books, 1975), pp. 35–38.

32. U.S. Bureau of the Census, *Historical Statistics of the United States, Colonial Times to 1970* (White Plains, N.Y.: Kraus International Publications, 1989), p. 19.

33. John D'Emilio and Estelle B. Freedman, *Intimate Matters: A History of Sexuality in America* (New York: Harper and Row, 1988), p. 334.

34. Anonymous, "Facts about Sexual Freedom," *PTA Magazine* 62 (Apr. 1968): 2–3.

35. Kobler, "Sex Invades the Schoolhouse," 27.

36. Ibid.

37. *Vaccination* was the term employed by a Citizens' School Advisory Committee of the City of Baltimore, reprinted as "Recommendations on Family Life Education" in G. Pat Powers and Wade Baskin, eds., *Sex Education: Issues and Directives* (New York: Philosophical Library, 1969), pp. 325–328.

38. Hottois and Milner, *Sex Education Controversy,* p. 12; Gallup poll from 23 June 1968 discussed in "Public Favors Sex Education Courses in Schools, But Stricter Laws on Pornography," *SIECUS Newsletter* 5 (Oct. 1969): 4.

39. "On Teaching Children about Sex," *Time,* 9 June 1967, p. 37; Richard K. Kerckhoff, "Family Life Education in America," in Harold T. Christensen, ed., *Handbook of Marriage and the Family* (Chicago: Rand McNally and Co., 1964), 902.

40. Mary Steichen Calderone, "Sexual Behavior: Whose Responsibility?" *Phi Delta Kappan* 46 (Oct. 1964): 69–70, in Folder 13: 223, Calderone Papers; and Calderone, "Sexual Health," 227–228.

41. Kobler, "Sex Invades the Schoolhouse," 24.

42. Harold Howe, commissioner of education in the U.S. Department of Health, Education, and Welfare, issued a "Policy on Family Life Education and Sex Education" on 20 Aug. 1966, pledging financial and curricular support for experiments in the subject in colleges, schools, and communities.

43. William Braden, "Evanston Plan Stops at the City Limits," *Chicago Sun-Times,* Oct. (n.d.) 1965, in Family Life Education Curriculum Supplement Box 13: Illinois-Chicago, ASHA Papers.

44. Kobler, "Sex Invades the Schoolhouse," 26.

45. Office of Sacramento County Superintendent of Schools, "Planning for Curriculum Development in Family Life and Sex Education," Feb. 1968, in Family Life/Sex Education Materials, National Council on Family Relations Papers, Social Welfare History Archives, University of Minnesota.

46. "Report of Family Life Education Project: 1965–67," developed by Oakland Unified School District and the Alameda County Health Department, in Family Life Education Curriculum Supplement Box 12: Oakland, ASHA Papers.

47. Sacramento County Superintendent, "Planning for Curriculum Development in Family Life and Sex Education," p. 12.

48. Mary Breasted, *Oh! Sex Education!* (New York: Praeger Publishers, 1970), p. 15.

49. Paul Cook, "Superintendent Pens Defense of Sex Education," newspaper clipping, 11 Apr. 1969, in Folder 95: 11, ASHA Papers.

50. See Larry Cuban, *How Teachers Taught: Constancy and Change in American Classrooms, 1890–1980* (New York: Longman, 1984), pp. 147–201.

51. Esther D. Schulz and Sally R. Williams, *Family Life and Sex Education: Curriculum and Instruction* (New York: Harcourt, Brace and World, 1968), p. 92.

52. Ibid., pp. 4–5, 92.

53. Ibid., pp. 134, 136, 185.

54. Ibid., pp. 101–102, 111–112, 169.

55. Ibid., pp. 109, 154–155.

56. Ibid., pp. 108–109, 223–225.

57. Ibid., pp. 145–152, 218; Breasted, *Oh! Sex Education!* pp. 109–10.

58. Schulz and Williams, *Family Life and Sex Education,* p. 135.

59. Ibid., pp. 151–152.

60. Ibid., p. 218.

61. William Martin, *With God on Our Side: The Rise of the Religious Right in America* (New York: Broadway Books, 1996), p. 104.

62. Breasted, *Oh! Sex Education!* pp. 26–27, 80; Martin, *With God on Our Side,* p. 106.

63. Breasted, *Oh! Sex Education!* p. 74.

64. Mary S. Calderone, "Special Report: SIECUS in 1969," *Journal of Marriage and the Family* 31 (Nov. 1969).

65. Breasted, *Oh! Sex Education!* pp. 75–76, 203.

66. Gordon V. Drake, *Is the Schoolhouse the Proper Place to Teach Raw Sex?* (Tulsa, Ok.: Christian Crusade Publications, 1968), pp. 21–24, 17–18.

67. Robinson, "Sex Education," p. 77; Luther G. Baker, Jr., unpublished ms., 1969, in Folder 96: 4, ASHA Papers.

68. Information on Gordon Drake derived from Breasted, *Oh! Sex Education!* pp. 199–204; quotation from Mary S. Calderone, "Sex Education and the American Democratic Process," *SIECUS Newsletter* 4 (Apr. 1969): 2.

69. Drake, *Is the Schoolhouse the Proper Place to Teach Raw Sex?* pp. 5–11.

70. The best sources for Christian Crusade thought are the house periodicals *Christian Crusade*, a monthly, and *Weekly Crusader;* also see Billy James Hargis, *The Far Left* (Tulsa, Ok.: Christian Crusade, 1964).

71. Breasted, *Oh! Sex Education!* p. 206.

72. Drake, *Is the Schoolhouse the Proper Place to Teach Raw Sex?* p. 31.

73. Ibid., pp. 31, 20.

74. Chronology and meeting reported in Breasted, *Oh! Sex Education!* pp. 35–36, 73–79.

75. Paul W. Cook, published letter to Mary S. Calderone, *SIECUS Newsletter* 5 (Oct. 1969): 5.

76. Ibid.; "Sex Education Suffers Setback," *San Jose Mercury,* 30 Mar. 1970, Folder 96: 3, ASHA Papers.

77. Joanne Zazzaro, "Sex Education: A Controversy Becomes a Crisis," *Education Digest* 35 (Nov. 1969): 10–11.

78. Breasted, *Oh! Sex Education!* pp. 211–212.

79. "Board Steers Away from Sex Education," newspaper clipping, no source given, ca. 1969, in Folder 96: 4, ASHA Papers; Douglas Robinson, "Sex Education Battles Splitting Many Communities across U.S.," *New York Times,* 14 Sept. 1969, p. 1.

80. Ron Moskowitz, "Teaching Morality—Navy Style," *San Francisco Chronicle,* 9 May 1969; and Ron Moskowitz, "Board OKs Morality Guidelines," *San Francisco Chronicle,* 10 May 1969, both in Folder 96: 1, ASHA Papers.

81. Moskowitz, "Board OKs Morality Guidelines."

82. Breasted, *Oh! Sex Education!* p. 11.

83. Zazzaro, "Sex Education," 10–11; Robinson, "Sex Education Battles," 77; Breasted, *Oh! Sex Education!* pp. 10–11.

84. Quoted in Janet S. Brown to Elizabeth S. Force, ASHA office memorandum, 25 Mar. 1969, in Folder 95: 11, ASHA Papers.

85. Jerome Himmelstein, *To the Right: The Transformation of American Conservativism* (Berkeley: University of California Press, 1990), p. 104; William B. Hixson, Jr., *Search for the American Right Wing: An Analysis of the Social Science Record, 1955–1987* (Princeton, N.J.: Princeton University Press, 1992), pp. 245–247.

86. Breasted, *Oh! Sex Education!* pp. 193–194.

87. Letter from William E. Glover of the Hollywood, California, Homosexual Information Center to Nat Lehrman, senior editor of *Playboy*, 16 Mar. 1970, in Folder 14: 231, Calderone Papers.

88. Gloria Lenz, *Raping Our Children: The Sex Education Scandal* (New Rochelle, N.Y.: Arlington House, 1972), p. 35.

89. The framework for the following is partly derived from D'Emilio and Freedman, *Intimate Matters*.

90. Kristin Luker, "Sex, Social Hygiene, and the State: The Double-Edged Sword of Social Reform," *Theory and Society* 27 (1998): 602, 605–606.

91. Martin, *With God on Our Side*, p. 118.

92. Richard M. Cohen, "Teaching Sex in School," *New Republic*, 28 June 1969, p. 12.

93. Alice Weiner of Belmont, California, quoted in *Los Angeles Times* [n.d.], Folder 95: 10, ASHA Papers.

94. Cook, "Superintendent Pens Defense."

95. See Hottois and Milner, *Sex Education Controversy*, pp. 3–5; the most complete statement of sex education's value neutrality comes from Derek L. Burleson, "Values and Valuing in Sex Education," *SIECUS Newsletter* 7 (Feb. 1972): 1–2.

96. "Message from Dr. Billy James Hargis, President, Christian Crusade," 27 June 1968, radio broadcast transcript of Gordon Drake's remarks, Folder 95: 10, ASHA Papers.

### 7   THE TRIUMPH OF SEXUAL LIBERALISM?

1. Janet S. Brown to Elizabeth S. Force, memorandum on the Interagency Conference on Current Opposition to Family Life and Sex Education, 25 Mar. 1969, Folder 95: 11, ASHA Papers.

2. "SIECUS Position Statements," *SIECUS Report* 2 (May 1974): 2–3; also "SIECUS—Where Next?" ibid., 1, 3.

3. Phyllis A. Katz, "Sex Roles: A Journal of Research," *Sex Roles* 1 (1975): 1.

4. For examples, see N. Frazier and Myra Sadker, *Sexism in School and Society* (New York: Harper and Row, 1973); and David Sadker, *Being a Man: A Unit of Instructional Activities on Male Role Stereotyping* (Washington, D.C.: Women's Program Staff, U. S. Office of Education, Department of Health, Education, and Welfare, 1977); Nancy Frazier, "We Must Liberate Our Children from Sexism," *PTA Magazine* 68 (Oct. 1973): 29; James Lincoln Collier, "Are Men Really Men Anymore? An Interview with Lester A. Kirkendall," *Readers Digest* 101 (Aug. 1972): 156.

5. Susan Shurberg Klein, "Sex Equity and Sexuality in Education: Breaking the Barriers," in Susan Shurberg Klein, ed., *Sex Equity and Sexuality in Education* (Albany: State University of New York Press, 1992), pp. 12–13; Michelle Fine, "Sexuality, Schooling, and Adolescent Females: The Missing Discourse of Desire," *Harvard Ed-*

*ucational Review* 58, no. 1 (Feb. 1988): 29–53; also Mariamne H. Whatley, "Goals for Sex-Equitable Sexuality Education," in Klein, ed., *Sex Equity and Sexuality Education,* pp. 83–95.

6. John D'Emilio and Estelle B. Freedman, *Intimate Matters: A History of Sexuality in America* (New York: Harper and Row, 1988), pp. 318–321.

7. Thomas Sowell, "Power Plays," *Forbes,* 19 Dec. 1994, p. 233.

8. D'Emilio and Freedman, *Intimate Matters,* p. 330; Demographic and Behavior Sciences Branch, "Report to National Advisory Child Health and Human Development Council," 17 Sept. 1990, p. 35.

9. D'Emilio and Freedman, *Intimate Matters,* p. 334.

10. Kristin Luker, *Dubious Conceptions: The Politics of Teenage Motherhood* (Cambridge, Mass.: Harvard University Press, 1996), p. 89; D'Emilio and Freedman, *Intimate Matters,* p. 333.

11. G. Peter Suta, Sunburst, Montana, interview with author, July 1989.

12. U.S. Department of Health and Human Services, *Trends in the Well-Being of America's Children and Youth* (1998): 325; Demographic and Behavior Sciences Branch, "Report to National Advisory Child Health and Human Development Council," p. 55; D'Emilio and Freedman, *Intimate Matters,* pp. 334–335.

13. Luker, *Dubious Conceptions,* pp. 197–199; *Trends in the Well-Being of America's Children and Youth,* 353.

14. Senate Committee on Labor and Human Resources, *Adolescent Family Life,* 97th Congress, 1st sess., 1981, S. Report No. 97–161, p. 2; Wendy H. Baldwin, "Adolescent Pregnancy and Childbearing: Growing Concerns for Americans," *Population Bulletin* 31 (May 1977): 7–8.

15. Joseph A. Califano, Jr., testimony before Senate Committee on Human Resources, *Adolescent Health, Services, and Pregnancy Prevention and Care Act of 1978,* 95th Congress, 2nd sess., 14 June and 12 July 1978 (Washington, D.C.: Government Printing Office, 1978), p. 18.

16. Adolescent Health Services and Prevention and Care Act of 1978 (Public Law 95-626), esp. Title VI.

17. Senate Committee on Labor and Human Resources, *Adolescent Family Life,* 97th Cong., 1st sess., 1981, S. Report No. 97-161, p. 4.

18. Jacqueline Kasun, "Family Planning Expenditures in California," (1982), printed in House Select Committee on Children, Youth, and Families, *Teen Parents and Their Children: Issues and Programs,* 98th Cong, 1st sess., 20 July 1983 (Washington, D.C.: Government Printing Office, 1983), p. 133; James H. Ford, "Teenage Pregnancy, Contraception and Abortion: An Analysis of Changing Trends," talk delivered in Phoenix, Arizona, Nov. 1981, reprinted in ibid., p. 128; Diane Ravitch, "Implicit Values: The New Sex Education," *The New Leader,* 13 Dec. 1982, p. 19, reprinted in ibid., p. 200.

19. Information about AFLA and the "squeal rule" excerpted from Rachel N. Pine and Lori F. Fischler, "The United States of America," in Sandra Coliver, ed., *The Right to Know: Human Rights and Access to Reproductive Health Information* (Philadelphia: Article 19 and University of Pennsylvania Press, 1995), secs. 2.3.1–2.3.2.

20. D'Emilio and Freedman, *Intimate Matters*, p. 349.

21. James H. Price et al., "High School Students' Perceptions and Misperceptions of AIDS," *Journal of School Health* 55, no. 3 (Mar. 1985): 107–109.

22. U.S. Public Health Service, *Information/Education Plan to Prevent and Control AIDS in the United States* (1987), cited in Barbara A. Rienzo and Steve M. Dorman, "Ten Consequences of the AIDS Crisis for the Health Education Profession," *Journal of School Health* 58, no. 8 (Oct. 1988): 335.

23. "How Should We Teach Our Children about Sex?" *Time,* 24 May 1993, p. 61; House Select Committee on Children, Youth, and Families, *A Decade of Denial: Teens and AIDS in America,* 102nd Cong., 2nd sess., May 1992 (Washington, D.C.: Government Printing Office, 1992), p. 22.

24. *Trends in the Well-Being of America's Children and Youth,* 198.

25. House Select Committee on Children, Youth, and Families, *A Generation in Jeopardy: Children and AIDS,* 100th Cong., 1st sess., Dec. 1987 (Washington, D.C.: Government Printing Office, 1988), pp. 27–29.

26. Ibid., p. 135.

27. Ibid., pp. 135–136, 40.

28. *A Generation in Jeopardy,* p. 135; *A Decade of Denial,* pp. 247, 249, 259–260; funding had its limits: see *Boston Globe,* 15 Oct. 1987, p. 3; also Centers for Disease Control, "Guidelines for Effective School Health Education to Prevent the Spread of AIDS," *Journal of School Health* 58, no. 4 (Apr. 1988): 142–148.

29. D. deMauro, "Sexuality Education 1990: A Review of State Sexuality and AIDS Education Curricula," *SIECUS Reports* 18 (1989–1990): 1–9.

30. Donald E. Greydanus, Helen D. Pratt, and Linda L. Dannison, "Sexuality Education Programs for Youth: Current State of Affairs and Strategies for the Future," *Journal of Sex Education and Therapy* 21 (Winter 1995): 239; "Sex in America," *Gallup Poll Monthly* 56, no. 1 (1991): 71, noted in Kathleen J. Welshimer and Shirley E. Harris, "A Survey of Rural Parents' Attitudes toward Sexuality Education," *Journal of School Health* 64, no. 9 (Nov. 1994): 347–348.

31. Sarah Glazer, "Sex Education: How Well Does It Work?" *Editorial Research Reports* 1, no. 23 (23 June 1989): 341; Wilson defined "healthy sexuality" as the idea that humans "are sexual people, and it's normal, natural and healthy to feel sexual desire, and that's wonderful." Susan Wilson, taped interview with author, 26 Jan. 1996, Cambridge, Massachusetts, in author's possession.

32. Barbara Dafoe Whitehead, "The Failure of Sex Education," *Atlantic Monthly* 274 (Oct. 1994): 55–80; Susan N. Wilson, "Critique of 'The Failure of Sex Education,'

*Atlantic Monthly,* Oct., 1994," unpublished manuscript, available from Network for Family Life Education, Rutgers University.

33. Susan Wilson, interview with author.

34. "Teens: The Rising Risk of AIDS," *Time,* 2 Sept. 1991, p. 60.

35. Gary Remafedi, "The Impact of Training on School Professionals' Knowledge, Beliefs, and Behaviors regarding HIV/AIDS and Adolescent Homosexuality," *Journal of School Health* 63 (Mar. 1993): 153.

36. Sharon Thompson, "Putting a Big Thing into a Little Hole: Teenage Girls' Accounts of Sexual Initiation," *Journal of Sex Research* 27 (Aug. 1990): 341–361; D. Worth, "Sexual Decision-Making and AIDS: Why Condom Promotion among Vulnerable Women Is Likely to Fail," *Studies in Family Planning* 20 (Nov.–Dec. 1989): 297–307; Karen J. Pittmen et al., "Making Sexuality Education and Prevention Programs Relevant for African-American Youth," *Journal of School Health* 62 (Sept. 1992): 339–344; Janie Victoria Ward and Jill McLean Taylor, "Sexuality Education for Immigrant and Minority Students: Developing a Culturally Appropriate Curriculum," in James T. Sears, ed., *Sexuality and the Curriculum: The Politics and Practices of Sexuality Education* (New York: Teachers College Press, 1992), pp. 183–202, esp. pp. 192–194.

37. William J. Bennett, "Why Johnny Can't Abstain," *National Review,* 3 July 1987, pp. 38, 36.

38. Robert L. Simonds, "A Plea for the Children," *Educational Leadership* 51 (Dec. 1993–Jan. 1994): 12.

39. Simonds, "Plea for the Children," 13; see also Janice M. Irvine, "Birds, Bees, and Bigots," *Women's Review of Books* 11 (July 1994): 23.

40. Bennett, "Why Johny Can't Abstain," 37; also Thomas Lickona, "Where Sex Education Went Wrong," *Educational Leadership* 51 (Nov. 1993): 85.

41. Nancy Wartik, "A Florida Suit Challenges an Abstinence-Only Sex Ed Course," *Ms. Magazine* 4 (July–Aug. 1993): 90.

42. "A Battle over Teaching Sex Ed," *Newsweek,* 17 June 1991, p. 69.

43. Patricia Goodson and Elizabeth Edmundson, "The Problematic Promotion of Abstinence: An Overview of *Sex Respect,*" *Journal of School Health* 64 (May 1994): 205; "Making the Case for Abstinence," *Time,* 24 May 1993, pp. 64–65.

44. Reported in Bonnie Trudell and Mariamne Whatley, "Sex Respect: A Problematic Public School Sexuality Curriculum," *Journal of Sex Education and Therapy* 17 (1991): 125–140; see p. 127.

45. Colleen Kelly Mast, *Sex Respect: The Option of True Sexual Freedom,* student workbook, rev. ed. (Bradley, Ill.: Respect Incorporated, 1990), pp. 39, 1; Colleen Kelly Mast, *Sex Respect: The Option of True Sexual Freedom,* teacher manual, rev. ed. (Bradley, Ill.: Respect Incorporated, 1990), p. 12; Goodson and Edmundson, "The Problematic Promotion of Abstinence," 209; Simonds, "Plea for the Children," 13.

46. Mast, *Sex Respect* student workbook, pp. 54–55.

47. Wartik, "Florida Suit"; "Battle over Teaching Sex Ed," *Newsweek,* 17 June 1991, p. 69; *Boston Sunday Globe,* 5 Dec. 1993, sec. 2, p. 41; Tony Hiss, "The End of the Rainbow: Annals of Education," *New Yorker* 69 (12 Apr. 1993): 43.

## 8  THE MYTH OF REFORM

1. James Davison Hunter, *Culture Wars: The Struggle to Define America* (New York: Basic Books, 1991).

2. Thomas Sowell, "Power Plays," *Forbes,* 19 Dec. 1994, p. 233.

3. Donald E. Greydanus, Helen D. Pratt, and Linda L. Dannison, "Sexuality Education Programs for Youth: Current State of Affairs and Strategies for the Future," *Journal of Sex Education and Therapy* 21 (Winter 1995): 241.

4. Lucinda L. Thomas et al., "High School Students' Long-Term Retention of Sex Education Information," *Journal of School Health* 55 (Sept. 1985): 274–278; and Eli Saltz et al., "Attacking the Personal Fable: Role-Play and Its Effect on Teen Attitudes toward Sexual Abstinence," *Youth and Society* 26 (Dec. 1994): 223–242.

5. Douglas Kirby, "Sexuality Education: A More Realistic View of Its Effects," *Journal of School Health* 55 (Dec. 1985): 421–424; also Cecelia Dine Jacobs and Eve M. Wolf, "School Sexuality Education and Adolescent Risk-Taking Behavior," ibid. 65 (Mar. 1995): 91–95.

6. Greydanus, Pratt, and Dannison, "Sexuality Education Programs for Youth," 244–255; Lisa Hosler, prepared statement for the Senate Subcommittee of the Committee on Appropriations, *Abstinence Education,* 104th Cong., 2nd sess., 11 July–29 July 1996 (Senate Hearing 104–801) (Washington, D.C.: U.S. Government Printing Office, 1997), p. 150

7. Greydanus, Pratt, and Dannison, "Sexuality Education Programs for Youth," 241.

8. Bonnie Nelson Trudell, *Doing Sex Education: Gender Politics and Schooling* (New York: Routledge, 1993), pp. 122, 167–169, and 172–173. Similarly, a survey found a group of sixth-grade teachers to be most comfortable teaching about self-esteem, sexually transmitted diseases, and communication skills, and least comfortable with birth control and "the emotional, social, and physical aspects of various student sexual behaviors," although leaders in sexuality education find these latter subjects to be critical topics; see Phyllis Levenson Gingiss and Richard Hamilton, "Teacher Perspectives after Implementing a Human Sexuality Education Program," *Journal of School Health* 59 (Dec. 1989): 427–431.

9. Trudell, *Doing Sex Education,* p. 172.

10. Alfred C. Kinsey, Wardell B. Pomeroy, and Clyde E. Martin, *Sexual Behavior in the Human Male* (Philadelphia: W. B. Saunders Co., 1948), esp. pp. 419–436; Alfred C.

Kinsey, Wardell B. Pomeroy, Clyde E. Martin, and Paul H. Gebhard, *Sexual Behavior in the Human Female* (Philadelphia: W. B. Saunders Co., 1953).

11. Roderick Wallace, "Social Disintegration and the Spread of AIDS: Thresholds for Propagation along 'Sociogeographic' Networks," *Social Science and Medicine* 33 (Nov. 1991): 1161.

12. Edward M. Kennedy, opening statement, Senate Committee on Human Resources, *Adolescent Health, Services, and Pregnancy Prevention and Care Act of 1978*, 95th Cong., 2nd sess., 14 June and 12 July 1978, Senate Document 2910 (Washington, D.C.: Government Printing Office, 1978), p. 42.

13. Mike Males, "Adult Liaison in the 'Epidemic' of 'Teenage' Birth, Pregnancy, and Venereal Disease," *Journal of Sex Research* 29 (Nov. 1992): 532–533.

14. Ibid.

15. Kristin Luker, *Dubious Conceptions: The Politics of Teenage Pregnancy* (Cambridge, Mass.: Harvard University Press, 1996), pp. 195–199; Mike Males, "School-Age Pregnancy: Why Hasn't Prevention Worked?" *Journal of School Health* 63 (Dec. 1993): 431; Mike Males, "Adult Partners and Adult Contexts of 'Teenage Sex,'" *Education and Urban Society* 30 (Feb. 1998): 193–194.

16. U.S. Department of Health and Human Services, *Trends in the Well-Being of America's Children and Youth* (1998): 340n.

17. Senate Committee on Human Resources, *Adolescent Health, Services, and Pregnancy Prevention and Care Act of 1978*, p. 136.

18. Males, "School-Age Pregnancy," 432.

19. Greydanus, Pratt, and Dannison, "Sexuality Education Programs for Youth," 242; Marcela Raffaelli et al., "Parent-Teen Communication about Sexual Topics," *Journal of Family Issues* 19 (May 1998): 315–334.

20. Mary Odem, *Delinquent Daughters: Protecting and Policing Adolescent Female Sexuality in the United States, 1885–1920* (Chapel Hill: University of North Carolina Press, 1995), pp. 157–158.

21. Steven Schlossman and Robert B. Cairns, "Problem Girls: Observations on Past and Present," in Glen H. Elder, Jr., John Modell, and Ross D. Parke, eds., *Children in Time and Place: Developmental and Historical Insights* (New York: Cambridge University Press, 1993), pp. 116, 124.

22. Beth L. Bailey, *From Front Porch to Back Seat: Courtship in Twentieth-Century America* (Baltimore: Johns Hopkins University Press, 1988).

23. *Boston Globe*, 26 Feb. 1999, p. A10.

24. Douglas Kirby, "School-Based Programs to Reduce Sexual Risk-Taking Behaviors," *Journal of Social Health* 62 (Sept. 1992): 282–285; Greydanus, Pratt, and Dannison, 245–248; Jonathan Crane, "The Epidemic Theory of Ghettos and Neighborhood Effects on Dropping Out and Teenage Childbearing," *American Journal of Sociology* 96 (Mar. 1991): 1251–1252.

25. Males, "Adult Partners and Adult Contexts of 'Teenage Sex,'" 194–197 and 199–200.

26. See, for example, Eric Pooley, "Portrait of a Deadly Bond," *Time*, 10 May 1999, pp. 26–32; also Lance Morrow, "The Boys and the Bees," ibid., 31 May 1999, p. 110.

27. Cheryl Russell, "The Rorschach Test," *American Demographics* 19 (Jan. 1997): 10.

28. Bree Beasley and Hilda Audaidottir, interview with the author, 26 May 1999.

29. *Trends in the Well-Being of America's Children and Youth*, p. 326.

30. John D'Emilio and Estelle B. Freedman, *Intimate Matters: A History of Sexuality in America* (New York: Harper and Row, 1988), pp. 331–332.

31. Michael F. Shaughness and Paul Shakesby, "Adolescent Sexual and Emotional Intimacy," *Adolescence* 27 (Summer 1992): 475–480; Nell Bernstein, "Learning to Love," *Mother Jones* 20 (Jan.–Feb. 1995): pp. 44–54; and Fine, "Sexuality, Schooling, and Adolescent Females," 29–53; Erin Harrison, Lawrence, Kansas, interview with author, 26 May 1999.

32. Allan Bloom, *Love and Friendship* (New York: Simon and Schuster, 1993), pp. 24–25.

# Index

Lightning Source UK Ltd.
Milton Keynes UK
UKOW06f1231180917
309402UK00002B/445/P